THE BOOK of Yogurt

By

SONIA UVEZIAN

Introduction by
DAVID KAISERMAN

ecco

An Imprint of HarperCollinsPublishers

Printed in the United States of America. No part of this book may be used or reproduced in any manner whatsoever without written permission except in the case of brief quotations embodied in critical articles and reviews. For information address HarperCollins Publishers Inc., 10 East 53rd Street, New York, NY 10022.

HarperCollins books may be purchased for educational, business, or sales promotional use. For information please write: Special Markets Department, HarperCollins Publishers Inc., 10 East 53rd Street, New York, NY 10022.

LIBRARY OF CONGRESS CATALOGING-IN-PUBLICATION DATA

Uvezian, Sonia
    The book of yogurt : an international collection of recipes / by Sonia Uvezian ; introduction by David Kaiserman. – 1st ed.
        p.   cm.
    Includes index.
    ISBN 0-88001-651-5
    1. Cookery (Yogurt) 2. Cookery, International. 3. Yogurt.
I. Title.
TX759.5.&63U94   1999
641.6'71476—dc21   98-27771
                                                                    CIP

The text of this book is set in Granjon

20 19 18 17 16 15 14

FIRST ECCO EDITION 1999

Contents

PREFACE

Ever since I can remember I have had a culinary affair with yogurt. Thanks to my Lebanese-Armenian heritage, it has been a mainstay of my diet all my life. There seems to be no end to dishes made with yogurt in the repertoire of Middle Eastern cookery, where it is used in the preparation of a wondrous array of edibles, from hors d'oeuvre and soups to desserts and beverages.

A culture of yogurt was always being developed in our large, fragrant kitchen. It was not until one day when I was five years old, however, that I became intrigued by the ever-present blanket-wrapped earthenware bowl in which the yogurt (unknown to me) was fermenting. I was certain that the night before I had seen some milk being poured into that bowl. Yet the following morning what was spooned out of it was not milk but a custardlike substance that, upon my closer inspection, turned out to be none other than the yogurt I avidly consumed regularly. My amazement could hardly have been less than that of the unsuspecting desert nomad of long ago who filled his goatskin bag with milk and opened it hours later to discover yogurt instead. To my great delight I was allowed to participate in the preparation of the next batch of yogurt and, after it was ready, to make *jajik*, a cucumber and yogurt salad that was one of my favorites. *Jajik* is the first dish of any consequence that I can recollect doing. So I suppose my cooking career began with yogurt!

This collection had its start some years ago with a recipe for that very same cucumber and yogurt salad. I was a teenager in New York City then, having recently arrived from Beirut, Lebanon. One dreary March day, longing for the Lebanese sun and blue Mediterranean, I made my way through rain and slush to the corner supermarket. When I looked at the greenish objects that passed for tomatoes, not to mention the pallid loaves of spongy dough called bread, imprisoned in their plastic bags, I was overcome with nostalgia for the colorful Middle Eastern market stalls spilling over with luscious vegetables and fruits fresh from the fields and for the incomparable aroma of freshly baked bread that wafted daily from our country kitchen. Then suddenly, as I was reaching for an item in the dairy case, a most familiar word stared me in the face. Was I dreaming? I looked again and saw not one but a whole row of containers that read YOGURT! I can still remember my joy at discovering this link with my distant homeland, and the little containers eventually came to embody all that for which I was homesick. As I walked back through the crowded yet lonely streets to my apartment, I felt a sense of expectancy and the promise of a happy time ahead recreating some of the foods of my childhood that had meant so much in Lebanon and had come to mean even more in America. The first dish I tried with my newly purchased yogurt was, naturally, *jajik*.

As might be expected, the initial source for this collection was my Middle Eastern background, and I have included a number of these early memories in the form of unforgettable recipes. After I left Lebanon I discovered many other fascinating ways to cook with yogurt: ethnic recipes from various countries, traditional and classic ones from around the world that I adapted to the use of yogurt, and, finally, some recipes that I improvised myself. Thus the present volume has grown to encompass a range of dishes that not only pays tribute to the versatility of yogurt but is international in scope.

INTRODUCTION

By David Kaiserman

My initial encounter with yogurt as a ten-year-old was negative enough for me to dismiss it at once and rush back to my favorite all-American dairy products, milk and ice cream. In time my palate grew more adventurous and I came to know and appreciate many different cuisines from around the world, but one of the greatest culinary triumphs of them all, Middle Eastern food, eluded me until I met my Armenian wife-to-be. As for yogurt, it simply never entered my mind to try it again.

One day I arrived to visit Sonia while she was taking a batch of newly made yogurt out of her refrigerator. With typical Middle Eastern hospitality she offered me some, remarking how fond she was of yogurt, which was a basic part of her diet. Basic? I swallowed hard. Regaining my composure, I casually (I hope) declined, saying that I had just eaten. About a week later Sonia invited me over for dinner, which turned out to be an eight-course spread of exotic Middle Eastern dishes that would have sent the Caliph of Baghdad into transports of ecstasy! I eagerly devoured every morsel, savoring the exquisite mingling of tastes and textures, while Sonia looked on with a knowing smile. At the conclusion of this magnificent repast I was astonished to learn that the one ingredient common to each of the dishes was yogurt!

This gastronomic revelation and the subsequent enjoyment of countless other dishes made with yogurt piqued my curiosity about this versatile food and led me to investigate its history, characteristics, and uses. I found myself confronted with a fascinating but confusing jumble of claims, myths, half-truths, possible truths, and established facts that make it difficult to write a definitive account of yogurt. It would be all too easy, on the one hand, to wax lyrically over what may be no more than folk tales or, on the other, to become submerged in a morass of technical and scientific data that neither I nor most readers would be able to comprehend satisfactorily. Therefore, I have limited myself in the following pages to information that appeared substantive, understandable, and reliable, largely avoiding what was peripheral or subject to dispute.

Yogurt is known by different names in different parts of the world. For example, our word for it is derived from the Turkish *yoghurt*. In Arabic-speaking countries it is called *laban*, in Iran, *mast*. In India it is most commonly known as *dahi*. The Greeks refer to it as both *yaourti* and *oxygala*, the Bulgarians and Yugoslavs as *kiselo mleko*. In the former U.S.S.R. it appears under various names: Russians call it *varenetz*, *prostokvasha*, or *riazhenka*; Ukrainians, *kisloye moloko*; Armenians, *madzoon* or *matsun*; Azerbaijanis, *gatig*; and Georgians, *matsoni*. In Sardinia it is known as *gioddu*, in Sicily, *mezzoradu*. The French call it *yaourt*, the Dutch, *yoghei*.

There also exist fermented milk products related to yogurt but differing in their preparation, among them the *busa* of Turkestan, *kefir* and *kumiss*, both from the Caucasus, southern Russia, and Central Asia, *urda* from the Carpathian Mountains, *kaelder milk* from Norway, and *skuta* from Chile. All of these have an alcoholic content, ranging from less than one percent in the case of *kaelder milk* to 7.1 percent in *busa*, and all are more liquid in consistency than yogurt. *Kefir* and *kumiss* are the most widely known. Slightly alcoholic and effervescent, they have been drunk by mountaineers and nomads since pre-Christian times. A discussion of these and other international cousins of yogurt is, however, beyond the scope of this book.

Although yogurt's popularity in America and Western Europe is only a fairly recent development, it is in fact one of the oldest foods known to man, having been a staple in southeastern Europe, the Middle East, Central Asia, and parts of the Far East for thousands of years. References to yogurt abound in the written records of ancient civilizations. It appeared on the banquet tables of Egyptian pharaohs and was a favorite of the Israelites. The Greeks knew yogurt and were aware of its healthful properties. The historian Herodotus, who lived during the fifth century B.C., mentioned yogurt, as did Galen, a famous physician of the second century A.D., who praised its soothing and purifying effect on the intestinal tract. Yogurt was also enjoyed by the Romans; the first-century scholar and naturalist Pliny the Elder was one of its enthusiastic proponents. In the medieval Arab world yogurt was greatly respected, and works on diatetics written by Islamic physicians extolled its therapeutic properties.

But yogurt undoubtedly existed long before people wrote about it. Most likely it was discovered by accident. It is generally considered to have originated in the Middle East in what is now Turkey or, perhaps, neighboring Iran. Several theories have been advanced as to how yogurt was first created. One widely held theory is that a desert nomad, setting out on a journey, put some milk instead of water into a goatskin bag, which he then slung over the back of his camel. The heat of the sun and the bacteria in the bag combined to curdle the milk and transform it into yogurt, much to the nomad's astonishment when, hours later, he opened the bag to quench his thirst. Understandably frustrated (and probably desperate), he took a chance and tasted the custardlike substance, finding it pleasantly tart and creamy. Later, still alive and not even sick from the experience, he shared his discovery with his fellow tribesmen.

Another theory places the original discovery of yogurt at an even earlier time than that of the nomad, somewhere around the dawning of the Neolithic Age (about 10,000 B.C.), when man first learned about milking. A clay pot filled with milk was left outside, perhaps inadvertently, for several hours, with the result that the milk turned into yogurt. The combination of the hot climate of the Middle East and the absence of sanitary conditions provided a fertile environment for the yogurt bacilli to exist naturally and to multiply.

Whatever the circumstances of its discovery, it was soon found that yogurt, in addition to having a pleasant taste and texture, was a superior way to preserve milk. Eventually the early herdsmen learned to boil and then inoculate fresh milk with a little of the previous batch of yogurt and to keep it warm, perhaps with animal skins, while it incubated, and it was not long before this food became a staple of their diet.

It is believed that the use of yogurt spread from the Middle East to more distant areas as civilization began to evolve, trade was established, and wars were fought, although yogurt, or relatives of it, could also have been discovered independently by other peoples who used animal milk in their diet. A Persian invasion served to introduce yogurt into India, where it quickly became popular. Mixed with honey it was considered a food of the gods by yogis, who as long ago as 500 B.C. developed strict rules for the consumption of food and drink. In the seventh century A.D. the Bulgars, Asiatic nomads, settled in the Balkans, bringing yogurt with them. The vast army of the Mongol conqueror Genghis Khan used yogurt to preserve meat and subsisted on it entirely when nothing else was available.

The introduction of yogurt into Western Europe is often said to have occurred early in the sixteenth century. The French king François I, debilitated by an intestinal malady, was restored to health by a healer from Constantinople who, arriving on foot with a herd of sheep and goats, prepared yogurt from goat's milk and prescribed it for the monarch. This is how the French supposedly came to call yogurt *le lait de la vie éternelle*, "the milk of eternal life." Actually, the white curd had existed in the monasteries of Western Europe long before the sixteenth century, but this may not have been known to the general populace.

Yogurt was first brought to the United States by Middle Easterners, among them a few Armenians who reached our shores in the latter part of the seventeenth century. The great wave of immigration that took place over two hundred years later included various ethnic groups from the Balkans as well as the Middle East, who were not about to give up their yogurt upon arriving in the New World. But they were not the only ones. One gentleman of German descent from Milwaukee told me that about fifty years ago, when he was a boy growing up in Wisconsin dairy country, the German farmers there made a custardlike product they called "sour milk," which turned out to be none other than yogurt.

Pockets of faithful devotees notwithstanding, yogurt was very little known in the West as recently as the 1920s and '30s. The groundwork for the commercial production of yogurt was begun by a distinguished Russian-born French bacteriologist, Dr. Ilya Metchnikoff (1845–1916), director of the Pasteur Institute in Paris and, in 1908, co-winner of the Nobel Prize for physiology and medicine for his work on the infection-fighting properties of white blood cells. Metchnikoff's research into the problem of premature aging in humans led him to study the lifestyle and diet of the Bulgarians, who at the turn of the century were among the world's most impoverished people but whose average life expectancy, according to a report then current, was eighty-seven years (compared to forty-eight in the United States). Moreover, Bulgaria far outranked the other nations of the globe in the number of centenarians in proportion to its population, including the United States, which lagged dismally behind. Although their diet was lacking in some foods considered essential for nutritional well-being, these hardy country folk consumed quantities of yogurt along with raw vegetables, nuts, and garlic.

Metchnikoff's observations of the Bulgarians caused him to conclude that yogurt was responsible for their robustness and longevity. In his laboratory he succeeded in isolating the two types of bacilli that are responsible for changing milk into yogurt, thus making it possible for yogurt to be produced commercially. After Metchnikoff's death, a Spanish businessman named Isaac Carasso acquired yogurt cultures both from Bulgaria and from the Pasteur Institute. He began his career as a yogurt entrepreneur modestly by marketing a yogurt culture through pharmacies in his native Barcelona. In 1925 he opened the first modern yogurt plant, calling his firm the Danone Company after his son Daniel, and in 1929 he expanded his operation into France.

While Carasso was successfully attracting Frenchmen and other Western Europeans to yogurt, it was beginning to gain a commercial toehold on our side of the Atlantic. In 1931 an Armenian family, the Columbosians, founded the first yogurt dairy in America in Andover, Massachusetts, calling their product Colombo. A year later a Greek family in New York City launched the Oxygala Yogurt Company, named after the Greek word for yogurt. Both are still in business today, Oxygala having changed its name to Lacto. Also in 1932 the Rosell Institute, which produces cultures used in the manufacture of cultured dairy products, including yogurt, was founded near Montreal, Quebec, Canada, on the grounds of a monastery established by a group of Spanish Trappist monks, who were such yogurt *aficionados* that they actually brought a cow with them to provide milk for daily yogurt making during the long journey from their homeland. In 1939 the Institute's best yogurt culture began to be distributed in the United States. Among those who obtained a franchise was a Chicagoan, Richard Tille, who used the culture both as a basis for his commercial product and in a mix that he marketed for making homemade yogurt. In 1942 he moved to Los Angeles and founded the Yami Yogurt Company, which to this day employs Rosell cultures.

With the advent of World War II, Isaac Carasso's son Daniel emigrated from France to

New York, where he was soon joined by old friends from Spain, Joseph Metzger and his son Juan. Together they bought an existing yogurt factory, commencing their own production on a limited scale and naming their company Dannon, an Americanization of Danone. After the war Daniel returned to France, subsequently building the world's largest yogurt plant near Versailles, outside Paris. Today the Danone Company is one of Western Europe's major producers of yogurt, and Europeans themselves have enthusiastically adopted the cultured milk for their own, particularly the French, who have embraced it with such a passion that they lead all nations in its consumption.

Meanwhile, with the Metzgers at the helm, Dannon in New York embarked on a campaign to persuade the public that yogurt was much more than a mysterious health food with quasi-miraculous powers. Since in those years health foods were looked upon with suspicion and aversion, Dannon's clever advertising played down that aspect of yogurt's image and stressed the fact that its clean, pleasantly tart taste could be universally enjoyed. Still, many Americans, being the products of a sugar-filled and sugar-coated culinary environment, found the taste of yogurt too sour. Taking an ingenious idea first conceived and marketed by the Radlicka Dairy in Prague, Czechoslovakia, thirteen years before, Dannon in 1946 introduced sundae-style fruit-flavored yogurt. At first strawberry was the only flavor. A few spoonfuls of preserves were placed at the bottom of a container with plain yogurt above, the two to be mixed together with a spoon just before eating. The idea caught on and other flavors followed, until today there are over twenty-five different kinds available, including vanilla, coffee, and chocolate. Ironically, long before Dannon did so, Knudsen, now the largest yogurt manufacturer in southern California, almost decided to introduce fruit-flavored yogurt into its marketing area after its founder, Tom Knudsen, tried Radlicka's product, called Yovo, on a trip to Europe and became interested in it. Ultimately they decided against it, since they had

had very little luck trying to sell yogurt. With Dannon's success in the East and the ensuing growth in the popularity of yogurt, however, they later enthusiastically followed suit.

Two other kinds of flavored yogurt were subsequently developed: one similar to sundae-style, sometimes found in western states, which contains flavored syrup on top as well as fruit preserves on the bottom; and Swiss-style, in which the ingredients are pre-stirred.

The sweetening of yogurt was the turning point in making it palatable to the American public, although manufacturers had also tried to increase its appeal by making it with low-fat milk (about 1.7 percent milk fat) to reduce the number of calories (in the Balkans and Middle East yogurt is made from whole milk and is therefore richer and creamier). Although the sweetening more than cancels out the benefits of the low-fat milk, flavored yogurt, which is by far the most popular form of yogurt, is consumed primarily as a snack or dessert and as such is lower in calories than junk food and rich pastries and sweets. And surely it is poetic justice that today, with the tremendous interest in nutrition and natural foods, yogurt is appreciated for the healthful qualities that years ago were often the object of ridicule. In the past two decades sales have jumped an incredible twenty-five hundred percent and, with the recent mass marketing of frozen yogurt, they continue to spiral upward. Americans are now lapping up more than half a billion pounds of yogurt annually. In addition to the well-known manufacturers such as Brown Cow, Colombo, Dannon, and Stonyfield Farm in the East and Alta Dena, Knudsen, Mountain High, and Yami in the West, many dairies are now producing their own yogurt. This wonderful food, so ancient and yet so modern, is now available in virtually every supermarket across the land, a link that spans the ages to before the earliest recorded history of mankind.

Throughout the centuries a remarkable number of beneficial characteristics have been attributed to yogurt. It has been reputed to prolong life, increase sexual potency, remedy baldness, calm frazzled nerves, and cure a long list of bodily illnesses ranging from skin diseases to gastrointestinal ailments. Modern medical science has shown that some of these claims are without foundation. Others are the subject of controversy, with different researchers turning up conflicting results. One such example is the belief that eating yogurt restores helpful lactobacilli to the intestine after antibiotics have destroyed not only the harmful bacteria there but the beneficial ones as well; another is that the yogurt bacilli can manufacture B vitamins while in the intestine.

The chief controversy surrounding yogurt's claim as a health food is due to its status as a "live" food containing the bacilli which originally acted to change milk into yogurt. It was Metchnikoff's contention that the putrefactive bacteria that congregate in the large intestine are responsible for many of man's diseases and shorten his life span. The regular consumption of yogurt, he believed, would enable beneficial lactobacilli in yogurt to overcome the malevolent microorganisms in the large intestine and purge the system of them. This has not, however, been medically proven. Furthermore, according to some experts, the strains used in modern commercial yogurt cannot become established in man, since the only kinds of lactobacilli that can inhabit human intestines are those that come from human beings. It is quite possible that Metchnikoff's Bulgarians ate yogurt that was not produced under the most sanitary conditions, and thus it contained their own lactobacilli. (Unfortunately, the professor himself would have made a poor Bulgarian. After consuming large amounts of yogurt daily for some twenty years, he died at the age of only seventy-one.)

Today we realize that the mountain folk of Bulgaria and the Caucasus (where a large number of centenarians also exist, including the oldest people in the world) live long and healthy lives for several important reasons and not just because they are yogurt lovers. Their diet is based on natural foods, they lead a simple, active existence in an unpolluted environment, and they have far fewer emotional and psychological tensions than we do in the industrial West. Their culture differs from ours in that the elderly are highly respected members of society who continue to perform useful tasks and are not made to feel unwanted.

Yogurt is, however, an excellent food indeed. Being made from milk, it possesses almost identical nutritional specifications, but exactly what it contains depends on a variety of circumstances. In America cow's milk is used to make commercial yogurt, but it can be skim, low-fat, or whole milk, making a difference not only in fat content and calories but in the amounts of some nutrients as well. In addition, if yogurt is made from the milk of other animals, or even from soybean milk, its nutritional properties can vary greatly. Even the animal's diet and environment can be a factor. And since, like milk, yogurt is deficient in some essential nutrients, it should be considered not as a complete food in itself but rather as a component of a well-balanced diet. Yogurt's value was recognized earlier in our century by the Indian statesman and spiritual leader Mahatma Gandhi, who sought to improve the deplorable conditions of malnutrition and starvation among the impoverished citizens of his native country. In his book, *Diet Reform*, he suggested ways in which the poor could better their standard of nourishment and health. Among the foods he strongly advocated was yogurt, and he devoted an entire essay to its virtues.

One of yogurt's most beneficial characteristics is its easy digestibility, making it desirable fare for people with sensitive stomachs, including the very young, the elderly, and the ill or convalescent. The yogurt cultures predigest the sugar and protein found in milk so that ninety percent of a serving can be assimilated by the body in one hour, compared to only thirty percent of an equivalent amount of milk. Thus glucose can be delivered quickly to the bloodstream to raise low blood-sugar levels. People who are deficient in the enzyme lactase, which digests lactose (milk sugar), can safely eat yogurt without discomfort unless their deficiency is truly extreme. Those who are allergic to milk, however, cannot eat yogurt either.

The high calcium content of yogurt, like milk, may benefit older people whose bone tissue has become thin, causing easy fractures, curving spines, and loose teeth. In addition, calcium is thought to be helpful in alleviating nervous tension. Research has also indicated that yogurt, though it is considered high in cholesterol in its whole milk form, contains an element that inhibits cholesterol production and actually reduces its level in the blood.

Despite the controversy surrounding many of the benefits allegedly derived from its bacterial content, yogurt is, without question, a healthful, nutritious, and easily digestible product with a pleasantly tangy taste. Its current popularity in the West is still largely confined to that of a diet-health food and flavored snack or dessert. The versatility yogurt enjoys in the Balkans, Middle East, Caucasus, and India, where it is a basic ingredient in a myriad of delectable dishes ranging from appetizers to beverages, is only beginning to be discovered here. In time Americans too may recognize it as the many-faceted culinary gem it actually is. This cookbook is a great place to begin.

THE BOOK OF YOGURT

Before You Begin

WHAT IS YOGURT?

Yogurt is milk coagulated and fermented by two types of benign bacteria. The coagulation is due to the action of *Lactobacillus bulgaricus*, while *Streptococcus thermophilus* ferments the milk sugar into lactic acid. This gentle acid curdles the protein in yogurt and acts as a preservative. Sometimes a third strain of bacteria, *Lactobacillus acidophilus*, is included in the yogurt culture.

Depending on its country or area of origin, yogurt is made from the milk of various animals and by various methods, resulting in different flavors and consistencies. For instance, yogurt made from water buffalo's milk is richer and sweeter than that made from cow's milk. Both mare's and goat's milk are much higher in butterfat than cow's milk, while camel's milk contains no butterfat at all. Ass's milk yields a fine curd and is particularly digestible.

Yogurt is made almost exclusively from cow's milk in the United States. In north-central Europe it is made from cow's and, to a lesser extent, from goat's milk. In Turkey and southeastern Europe sheep's and goat's milk are favored, although cow's and water buffalo's milk are also used. Yogurt is made from the milk of cows, goats, and water buffalo in the Middle East and Caucasian republics as well as farther east in India and Burma; milk from the water buffalo is most frequently employed in the latter countries and in Egypt. Mare's milk is used in Lapland, Central Asia, and Siberia.

COMMERCIAL YOGURT

Commercial yogurt is made in the United States from fresh, pasteurized, and homogenized cow's milk under carefully controlled temperatures and incubating conditions. The many brands available differ widely in taste and texture. Examination of their labels reveals that they may be made from milk containing varying amounts of butterfat, enriched with non-fat milk solids, and stabilized with gelatin. Aside from a difference in calories and a reduction in the amount of actual yogurt, this is not particularly serious, although from a dieter's point of view, the lower the calories the better. Fruit flavorings add to calories and displace some of the yogurt, which is also to be expected. Often, however, other additives are present, such as artificial colors and flavors, sweeteners, preservatives, emulsifiers, and more stabilizers. A product adulterated with these ingredients bears a rather tenuous relationship to real yogurt. Of the three kinds of flavored yogurt, sundae-style, western-style, and Swiss-style, the last-named, with the preserves stirred in, contains the most additives. Many people object to its gummier texture, lack of tartness, and artificial ingredients. Even unflavored yogurt is available Swiss-style (i.e., with all its ingredients pre-stirred); its taste and texture are far removed from regular yogurt. Also, some commercial yogurt is pasteurized after the culture has been added. This lengthens shelf life, but it also kills the bacteria, so if one of the reasons you eat yogurt is because you consider its bacterial action helpful to your stomach and intestines, such yogurt would be useless to you.

HOMEMADE YOGURT

Although it is reassuring to know that good commercial brands can be purchased, if yogurt is to be used as an important element in cookery, it is well worth learning how to make it at home.

Unlike the preparation of other dairy products such as butter, cheese, and ice cream, making yogurt is remarkably uncomplicated. It is also considerably cheaper, well under half the cost of store-bought yogurt. In addition, you have control over freshness, quality of ingredients, flavor, and calorie count. You do not have to add chemical preservatives to extend shelf life, emulsifiers or stabilizers to thicken and firm the consistency, artificial colors and flavors to give it eye and taste appeal, or sugar to sweeten it.

When making homemade yogurt it is possible to regulate the taste according to your personal preference. You can, for instance, achieve either a mild or tart yogurt by adjusting its incubation period. The longer you incubate the tangier the final result will be. And by adding your own flavorings—fruit, preserves, or whatever—you can limit the amounts to suit your taste or calorie requirement.

Finally, yogurt making is a creative activity that gives one a satisfaction not unlike that of bread baking or planting a seed and watching it sprout and flourish.

INGREDIENTS NEEDED TO MAKE YOGURT

Only two ingredients are needed to make yogurt: milk and a culture, or starter. The milk of cows, sheep, goats, horses, asses, camels, yaks, water buffalo, reindeer, and even soybean milk can be used as a yogurt medium. But, as stated above, in America yogurt is almost always made from cow's milk. You can use fresh whole, low-fat, or skim milk, canned or powdered milk reconstituted with water, or a combination of these. I myself prefer the taste of yogurt made from fresh milk and recommend that for best results you use the freshest milk you can buy to make yogurt. If raw milk is used, it must first be pasteurized to kill any bacteria that, in addition to being a serious health hazard, might prevent the culturing process from taking place.

One quart of milk will make one quart of yogurt. The flavor and consistency will differ with the type of milk used. Whole milk will produce a smooth, custardlike, and pleasantly tart yogurt, while low-fat and skim milk will yield thinner results. For a richer, thicker, and sweeter yogurt, use half-and-half instead of milk or add 1 cup heavy cream to the milk. The addition of non-fat dry milk powder (1/3 cup per quart milk) to milk will also provide a thicker and more nutritious yogurt.

THE STARTER

The starter or culture that you introduce into the milk may be either a small amount of homemade or commercial yogurt or a dried culture. If the former is used it should be live (not pasteurized), fresh, and unflavored. Dried culture, which costs quite a bit more, is obtainable from health food stores. It will keep for several months in a cool place and can be used as a starter when fresh yogurt is unavailable.

The taste of your yogurt will depend on your choice of starter, as well as the type of milk you select. An older, more acidic culture will produce a sour-tasting yogurt (and take longer to incubate), while a fresher, sweeter one will effect a milder outcome.

Once you have selected the type of milk and starter, you are ready to proceed with the actual preparation of yogurt.

HEATING AND COOLING THE MILK

In an enameled, stainless steel, or flameproof glass saucepan bring 1 quart milk just to a boil. This will kill the bacteria in the milk that would otherwise render the bacteria in the starter ineffective. While the milk is heating, stir frequently with a wooden spoon to prevent any skin from forming on the surface. The skin consists of valuable protein that is lost to the yogurt once it forms. Should any skin form, remove it with a wooden spoon.

Remove the saucepan from the heat and, stirring occasionally, allow the milk to cool to a temperature of 112°F on a candy thermometer. This is the ideal temperature for the yogurt bacilli to multiply (the bacteria will die if the temperature of the milk is over 120°F and will remain inactive if it is under 90°F). If you do not have a candy thermometer, you can test the temperature of the milk by dipping your little finger into it: When you can comfortably hold your finger in the milk up to a slow count of ten, the temperature is about right. Or sprinkle a few drops of milk on your wrist: it should feel lukewarm, not hot. Make certain that your thermometer, finger, or whatever you are using to test is meticulously clean in order to prevent recontamination of the milk.

ADDING THE STARTER

Working quickly, place 2 tablespoons fresh live yogurt, at room temperature, or 1 package dried culture in a small bowl. If using fresh yogurt, beat it with a fork until almost liquid. Add a few tablespoons of the lukewarm milk, one at a time, beating vigorously until well blended. Stir this into the remaining milk in the saucepan until thoroughly mixed. If using dried culture, add it to the lukewarm milk and mix well, making certain that it is thoroughly combined with the milk. If you wish to increase or decrease the amount of milk, adjust the amount of starter accordingly. Take care not to use too much starter; otherwise your yogurt will be excessively sour.

For a firmer-bodied yogurt, some people add a little gelatin to the milk. To prepare, soften 1 teaspoon unflavored gelatin in 1 tablespoon cold water. (For an even firmer, more jellylike product, you may double the amount of gelatin and water.) Stir over low heat until the gelatin dissolves, then stir the dissolved gelatin thoroughly into the hot milk. Cool the milk mixture to 112°F and add the starter as directed above.

INCUBATION METHODS AND EQUIPMENT

All sorts of equipment ranging from hay- or feather-lined boxes to electric incubators have been recommended for the preparation of yogurt. Actually, yogurt can be made quite easily and successfully at home without special utensils. The important thing, as in bread making, is to maintain a correct and steady temperature during the period of incubation. Like yeast, the yogurt bacilli are very sensitive to temperature changes. Remember that the bacteria are inactive below 90°F and are killed at temperatures above 120°F. You must therefore find a suitable spot warm enough for the bacteria to thrive and thicken the milk to a semisolid consistency. A temperature of 112°F is ideal.

The easiest way to maintain a steady temperature during the incubation period is to use an electric yogurt maker, also called an electromatic incubator or culturizer. Electric yogurt makers can be purchased from health and specialty food shops or appliance stores and are available in several different brands, styles, and price ranges. Each includes a heating element and a set of jars with covers. Since the temperature is controlled for you, if you follow the manufacturer's instructions you can't go wrong.

Another very simple way of making yogurt is to use a wide-mouthed thermos. Prewarm the thermos by rinsing it with warm water. Pour in the lukewarm starter and milk mixture and seal at once. Leave undisturbed 4 to 6 hours or until the mixture sets. Then remove the lid and place the thermos in the refrigerator to chill. When chilled, transfer the yogurt to a glass jar or other suitable container and refrigerate. Since a thermos is designed to be an insulator, it will maintain the mixture at the same temperature at which it was poured in. This method of incubation is practically foolproof.

Although it is not quite so foolproof as an electric yogurt maker or thermos, a third way of making yogurt is based on the method that has been successfully employed throughout the Balkans, Middle East, Caucasus, and Central Asia for thousands of years. Pour the lukewarm milk and starter mixture into a clean earthenware or glass bowl. Cover with a large plate or a sheet of plastic, aluminum foil, or brown paper secured tightly with a rubber band. Wrap the bowl in a small woolen blanket or shawl and leave to set undisturbed in a warm place (110 to 115°F) free from drafts, such as a turned-off gas oven with a pilot light (the pilot light should provide enough warmth; if not, place a pan of hot water on the bottom rack), an oven that has been preheated to 120°F and then turned off, or an insulated picnic box that has been preheated by letting jars of warm water stand in it about 10 minutes. Note that the yogurt must not be disturbed—it will not tolerate agitation while it is forming.

The above are only a few of the many incubation methods used in the preparation of homemade yogurt. Follow any one of them or try some other method that appeals to you more. Just make sure that the temperature is kept between 110 and 115°F (ideally 112°F) during the process.

HOW LONG TO INCUBATE

Yogurt can take from a minimum of 4 to 6 hours to incubate in a thermos, quite possibly longer when using a dried culture. You must check periodically to see if the mixture has attained the proper consistency. Begin checking after about 6 hours (sooner if using a yogurt maker or a thermos), then check every hour or so. When the mixture has developed a creamy, custardlike texture and a slightly tart flavor it is ready. Refrigerate it at once. Take care not to overincubate the yogurt; otherwise it will become unpleasantly sour. Allow the yogurt to chill thoroughly before serving, preferably 24 hours.

You may sometimes notice a little watery substance (whey) on top of the yogurt after it has been refrigerated. This is a natural occurrence with both homemade and commercial yogurt. Do not try to stir it in; simply tip the container and pour it off, saving it if you wish to use it in place of water in cooking, since it is high in vitamin B_{12} and minerals.

To ensure a continuous supply of yogurt, remember to reserve a small quantity from each batch to serve as the starter for your next one. Stored in a tightly covered container, yogurt will keep in the refrigerator for about a week. For sweet, fresh-tasting yogurt make a new batch every four days. In this way you can conceivably go on making yogurt from your original culture almost indefinitely (some cultures have been perpetuated for over fifty years, a practice I do not recommend!). If, however, your yogurt should become too thin in texture or too bland in taste, simply begin again with a new starter of fresh yogurt or dried culture.

In the unlikely event that your efforts to make yogurt prove unsuccessful, it may be due to one or more of the following reasons: (1) your equipment was not absolutely clean; (2) the bacteria in the starter had previously been killed by pasteurization (be sure to use live yogurt); (3) the milk contained residues of antibiotics that had been given to cows for disease (though it is unlawful to sell such milk); (4) the milk or starter was too old (begin again with fresh ingredients); (5) the milk was not heated sufficiently to kill the bacteria in it; (6) the milk was too hot or too cold when the starter was added; (7) the starter was not mixed thoroughly into the milk; (8) the milk mixture was disturbed while incubating; (9) you did not allow for a long enough incubation period.

FLAVORED YOGURT

You can flavor your yogurt either before or after incubation. To flavor it beforehand, simply add 1/4 to 1/3 cup honey or other flavorings, such as 3 tablespoons chocolate syrup, 1 tablespoon instant coffee mixed with sugar to taste, or vanilla extract to taste, to the milk before heating it and proceed as directed above. By flavoring yogurt beforehand, however, you will be limiting its function; moreover, in my experience prior addition may delay or, possibly, even prevent coagulation.

On the other hand, if you make unflavored yogurt you have the option of serving it in a number of ways. You can enjoy a cup or so by itself as a snack or accompaniment to other foods and another cupful or two as a dessert mixed with fruit (sweetened or not as you wish) and still have a supply of unflavored yogurt left to cook with. Thus a single batch of yogurt will fulfill several functions and provide a variety of taste experiences.

YOGURT AND DIETING

With yogurt as a dieting aid, you do not have to give up all the pleasures of the table in order to shed excess pounds. One cup of unflavored yogurt made from partially skimmed milk contains about 120 calories compared to whole milk with 165, sour cream with 454, heavy cream with 838, and mayonnaise with 1,616. Even fruit-flavored commercial yogurts, which can contain more than twice the calories of low-fat yogurt (the exact amount varying according to the brand and kind), are still less fattening than a serving of apple pie or chocolate cake, although people who are trying to lose weight really should avoid them. While it is true that both unflavored yogurt and milk have similar nutritive value and calorie count, yogurt is more satisfying and filling. Judging from the figures above, substituting yogurt for higher calorie foods can be a great help in keeping weight under control. Many dishes actually taste better unencumbered by their traditional high-calorie accompaniments. For instance, try a baked potato with yogurt and chives rather than the usual lavishment of sour cream and butter, or stir yogurt instead of sour cream into a soup for a taste that is tarter, fresher, and more subtle. And how much more refreshing is a fruit compote when topped with a dollop of yogurt sprinkled with cinnamon in place of whipped cream. Also not to be overlooked is yogurt's wholesome food value, which can help you maintain your health and vitality while you wage your waistline war.

TIPS ON COOKING WITH YOGURT

- Always keep yogurt in the storage part of your refrigerator. Do not freeze, as freezing temperatures will kill the yogurt bacilli.

- Before heating yogurt allow it to reach room temperature.

- When cooking with yogurt it is best to employ low temperatures and brief cooking periods. Whenever possible, add it to a recipe toward the end of the cooking process, shortly before the dish is removed from the heat, to prevent separation. If, however, the yogurt must be added at the beginning of the cooking period, you must stabilize it first to prevent separation and curdling (see following instructions). When baking bread, cakes, and pastries this step is unnecessary, since flour is already included in the recipe.

- When cooking yogurt remember that unless the temperature is kept under 120°F, the bacilli will be killed. Your casserole, cake, bread, or whatever will, of course, retain yogurt's distinctive flavor, but its alleged medicinal qualities will be destroyed.

- Folding rather than stirring yogurt into other ingredients will help to retain its consistency.

- You can thicken yogurt by adding some powdered milk to it. Or if you are going to heat it, which will cause it to thin out, add a small amount of flour, cornstarch, or arrowroot dissolved in a little cold water.

- For a stiffer consistency try mixing yogurt with a beaten egg white.

- If yogurt appears to have thinned out from being overmixed or overstirred, try chilling it to help restore a measure of its former consistency. On the other hand, if you want yogurt with a more liquid consistency, simply beat it vigorously.

- Yogurt can often be substituted for milk, cream, buttermilk, or sour cream. If replacing milk or cream, you may need to use a slightly larger quantity of yogurt. When substituting it for buttermilk, thin it to the consistency of the latter with a little water. For a consistency similar to that of sour cream, use whole milk yogurt rather than low-fat yogurt.

- When substituting yogurt for milk, cream, sour cream, or buttermilk in baking, include 1/2 teaspoon baking soda per cup of yogurt.

- You can use yogurt or a mixture of yogurt and mayonnaise in place of mayonnaise in many recipes (page 88).

- Whipped cream can often be replaced by yogurt or a mixture of yogurt and whipped cream (see Yogurt Crème Chantilly, page 98).

- Stir yogurt into pan drippings to make gravy.

- Use it as a marinade for meats and poultry.

TO STABILIZE YOGURT

Extended cooking will cause yogurt made with cow's milk to curdle. Stabilizers such as egg white or cornstarch will prevent this from occurring.

1   quart unflavored yogurt
1   egg white, slightly beaten, or 1 tablespoon cornstarch or all-purpose flour dissolved in a little cold water
1/2   teaspoon salt

In a heavy enamel or stainless steel saucepan beat the yogurt vigorously until it attains an almost liquid consistency. Add the egg white, or cornstarch or flour dissolved in water, and salt. Stir thoroughly with a wooden spoon. Bring slowly to a boil, stirring continuously in one direction only (a traditional Middle Eastern technique, which probably discourages separation). Reduce the heat to very low and simmer gently, uncovered, about 10 minutes or until the mixture acquires a thick and creamy consistency.

The yogurt is now ready to be combined and cooked with meat and/or vegetables without any danger of curdling.

Appetizers

CHEESE AND HERB SPREAD

This spread, my own creation, is excellent served with rye, pumpernickel, or Armenian thin bread (lavash) as an accompaniment to cocktails or as a first course.

SERVES 4

- 6 ounces cream cheese or Neufchâtel cheese, at room temperature
- 1 cup finely crumbled feta cheese
- 1/2 cup or more unflavored yogurt
- 2 tablespoons finely chopped chives or scallions (include 2 inches of the green tops of the scallions)
- 2 tablespoons finely chopped fresh dill
- 2 tablespoons finely chopped fresh mint Salt to taste
- 1 small garlic clove, crushed, or to taste Tomato slices Cucumber slices Black olives (preferably Greek olives) Parsley sprigs

In a mixing bowl mash the cream cheese with a fork. Add the feta cheese and yogurt and beat vigorously with a wooden spoon until the mixture is well blended and fluffy. Beat in the chives, dill, mint, salt, and garlic. Taste and adjust the seasoning. Cover and chill.

Close to serving time, mound the cheese and herb mixture in the center of a platter. Arrange the tomato and cucumber slices, olives, and parsley sprigs in a decorative pattern around it.

VEGETABLE AND CHEESE APPETIZER

This is based on the classic Hungarian hors d'oeuvre called Liptauer.

SERVES 6

- 1/2 pint low-fat cottage cheese, drained
- 1/2 cup unflavored yogurt
- 2 teaspoons caraway seeds, crushed or whole
- 1 tablespoon capers, minced (optional)
- 3/4 teaspoon dry mustard Salt and freshly ground black pepper to taste
- 1/2 small cucumber, peeled, seeded, and finely chopped
- 1/2 small green pepper, seeded, deribbed, and finely chopped
- 4 scallions, finely chopped, including 2 inches of the green tops
- 1/2 cup finely chopped parsley Sweet Hungarian paprika Salad greens

Force the cheese through a ricer or fine sieve into a mixing bowl. Add the yogurt, caraway seeds, capers (if desired), mustard, and salt and pepper and stir until well blended. Add the cucumber, green pepper, scallions, and parsley and mix gently but thoroughly. Taste and adjust the seasoning. Cover and chill 1 hour. Transfer to a serving dish. Sprinkle with the paprika and garnish with the salad greens. Serve with rye or pumpernickel bread.

VARIATION Omit the caraway seeds and capers. Use 1/4 cup minced parsley and 2 tablespoons minced fresh dill rather than parsley alone.

PACIFIC ISLANDS COCKTAIL DIP

Although this unusual dip is authentically made with sour cream, I prefer it made with equal amounts of sour cream and yogurt, for it is lighter and less rich.

MAKES ABOUT 1-1/2 CUPS

1/2 cup unflavored yogurt

1/2 cup sour cream

1/4 cup finely chopped fruit chutney (preferably homemade)

1/2 tablespoon finely chopped mild white onion

1/4 teaspoon five-spice powder* or to taste

1/4 cup salted peanuts, finely chopped

Combine all the ingredients except the nuts in a bowl. Mix until thoroughly blended. Cover and chill. Just before serving stir in the nuts.

*Available at Oriental markets.

BLUE CHEESE DIP

MAKES ABOUT 1-1/2 CUPS

1/4 cup Roquefort, gorgonzola, or other blue cheese

6 ounces cream cheese or Neufchâtel cheese, at room temperature

1/2 cup unflavored yogurt

2 tablespoons finely chopped chives or scallions (include 2 inches of the green tops of the scallions)

2 tablespoons salted pistachio nuts, finely chopped
Salt to taste

In a small bowl mash the blue cheese with a fork. Add the cream cheese and mix until smooth. Add the yogurt, chives, pistachio nuts, and salt and blend thoroughly. Taste and adjust the seasoning. Cover and chill. Serve with raw vegetable sticks or crackers.

MUSHROOM DIP

This is my adaptation of a Persian recipe and a wonderful dish with which to welcome a guest.

MAKES ABOUT 2-1/2 CUPS

- 2 tablespoons butter
- 4 ounces mushrooms, finely chopped
- 4 scallions, finely chopped, including 2 inches of the green tops
- 3 ounces cream cheese or Neufchâtel cheese, at room temperature
- 1/2 cup unflavored yogurt
- 1 small garlic clove, crushed
  Salt to taste
- 2 tablespoons finely chopped parsley, fresh dill, or fresh coriander

In a heavy skillet heat the butter over moderate heat. Add the mushrooms and scallions and sauté until golden brown, stirring frequently. Remove from the heat and let cool to room temperature.

In a bowl mash the cream cheese with a fork. Add the yogurt and garlic and blend until smooth. Add the sautéed mushrooms and scallions and sprinkle with the salt. Mix well. Taste and adjust the seasoning. Cover and chill. Garnish with the parsley, dill, or coriander. Serve with crackers.

EGGPLANT PURÉE

Redolent of garlic, sharpened by lemon juice, and suffused with the smoky flavor of eggplant, this celebrated hors d'oeuvre enjoys popularity from the Balkans to the Caucasus. It tastes best when the eggplant is broiled over an open fire.

SERVES 4

- 1 large eggplant (about 2 pounds)
- 2 tablespoons freshly squeezed and strained lemon juice
- 2 tablespoons olive oil
- 1/2 cup unflavored yogurt
- 1 medium garlic clove, crushed, or to taste
  Salt and freshly ground black pepper to taste
- 1 tablespoon finely chopped parsley or fresh dill
  Green pepper rings (optional)

Cut the stem and hull from the top of the eggplant and discard. Using a longhandled fork, prick the skin of the eggplant in several places, then insert the fork through it and broil, preferably over charcoal, turning it frequently until the flesh is very soft and juicy and the skin charred.

When the eggplant is cool enough to handle, gently squeeze it to remove the bitter juices. Peel off the skin, remove the badly charred spots, and slit the eggplant open. Scoop out the seeds and discard. Place the eggplant pulp, lemon juice, oil, yogurt, garlic, and salt and pepper in the container of an electric blender. Cover and blend until smooth and creamy. If you do not have a blender, place the eggplant pulp in a bowl, immediately pour the lemon juice over it, and mash it thoroughly into a smooth purée. Gradually beat in the oil, then add the yogurt, garlic, and salt and pepper and mix thoroughly. Taste and adjust the seasoning. Transfer to a serving bowl, cover, and chill. Serve sprinkled with the parsley and garnished with the green pepper rings, if desired.

EGGPLANT SALAD VARIATION   Line a serving platter with romaine lettuce leaves. Mound the chilled eggplant purée in the center. Surround with tomato wedges and top with rings of mild onion and green pepper. Sprinkle with the parsley. This goes especially well with grilled lamb and often accompanies *shish kebab*.

CURRIED VEGETABLE APPETIZER

Serve this spirited combination as a dip with Indian unleavened bread (chapati) *or sesame crackers.*

SERVES 6

- 2 tablespoons peanut oil
- 1 medium onion, finely chopped
- 1 medium garlic clove, crushed
- 1 teaspoon curry powder or to taste
- 1 teaspoon chili powder or to taste
- 2 medium tomatoes, peeled, seeded, and chopped
- 1 cup peeled, seeded (if seeds are large), and diced cucumbers
- 2 cups unflavored yogurt
- 2 tablespoons finely chopped fresh coriander or parsley
  Salt and freshly ground black pepper to taste

In a heavy skillet heat the oil over moderate heat. Add the onion and garlic and sauté until soft but not browned. Add the curry powder and chili powder and cook 1 minute, stirring constantly. Remove from the heat and cool. Add the remaining ingredients and mix gently but thoroughly. Taste and adjust the seasoning. Cover and chill before serving.

SPINACH-YOGURT APPETIZER

Variations of this appetizer turn up throughout the Middle East and Caucasus.

SERVES 4

- 1 pound spinach
- 1/4 cup water
- 2 tablespoons sunflower seed, corn, or olive oil
- 1 small onion, finely chopped
- 1 cup unflavored yogurt
- 1 small garlic clove, crushed
- 1 tablespoon finely chopped fresh mint, or 1/2 teaspoon crushed dried mint
  Salt and freshly ground black pepper to taste
- 2 tablespoons finely chopped toasted walnut meats (optional)

Wash the spinach thoroughly under cold running water, discarding the tough stems and bruised leaves. Combine the spinach and water in a saucepan and bring to a boil over high heat. Reduce the heat to low, cover, and simmer 8 minutes. Drain, and when cool enough to handle, squeeze the spinach dry and chop coarsely.

In a heavy skillet heat the oil over moderate heat. Add the onion and sauté until golden, stirring frequently. Add the spinach and sauté 2 to 3 minutes. Remove from the heat.

Combine the yogurt, garlic, mint, and salt and pepper in a mixing bowl and beat until well blended. Add the sautéed onion and spinach mixture and blend thoroughly. Taste and adjust the seasoning. Transfer to a serving bowl, cover, and refrigerate until well chilled. Sprinkle with the walnuts, if desired. Serve with Armenian thin bread *(lavash)* or sesame crackers.

SHRIMP DIP

A tempting dip, made quickly and eaten just as fast.

MAKES ABOUT 1-1/2 CUPS

- 1 cup shrimp, cooked, shelled, and deveined
- 4 ounces cream cheese or Neufchâtel cheese, at room temperature
- 1/4 cup unflavored yogurt
- 1 tablespoon finely chopped mild white onion
- 1 teaspoon curry powder or to taste
- 1 tiny garlic clove, crushed
  Salt to taste
- 1 parsley sprig

Combine all the ingredients except the parsley sprig in the container of an electric blender. Cover and whirl until thoroughly blended and smooth. Taste and adjust the seasoning. Transfer to a serving bowl. Cover and chill. Garnish with the parsley sprig and serve with crackers or crisp raw vegetables.

YOGURT CHEESE APPETIZER

In the Middle East this is a favorite breakfast dish and restaurant appetizer as well as a classic after-school snack.

SERVES 6 TO 8

- 1 recipe Yogurt Cheese, page 148
- 1 tablespoon olive oil
  Paprika
- 2 teaspoons finely chopped fresh dill or mint
  Armenian thin bread *(lavash)* or sesame crackers
  Black olives (preferably Greek olives) (optional)
  Sliced cucumbers (optional)

Spread the cheese in a shallow serving dish. Sprinkle the surface evenly with the olive oil and paprika. Garnish the edges with the dill. Serve chilled as a dip with Armenian thin bread or sesame crackers and, if desired, a side dish of black olives and sliced cucumbers.

NOTE You may substitute carrot, cucumber, green pepper, and celery sticks for the olives and cucumbers.

PERSIAN YOGURT CHEESE WITH CUCUMBERS

Persians have been partial both to yogurt and this dish for many centuries.

SERVES 6

 1   recipe Yogurt Cheese, page 148
 2   medium cucumbers, peeled, seeded (if seeds are large), and finely chopped
1/4 cup very finely chopped red onion
 4   radishes, grated
1/2 cup finely chopped walnuts
1/4 cup dried currants
 1   tablespoon finely chopped fresh dill
 1   tablespoon finely chopped fresh mint
     Salt to taste
     Lettuce leaves

Combine all the ingredients except the lettuce leaves and mix thoroughly. With an ice cream scoop, shape the mixture into balls and arrange on a serving platter lined with the lettuce leaves. Serve chilled.

CHICKEN LIVER MOUSSE

Yogurt replaces the traditional heavy cream in this superb continental hors d'oeuvre, which may be served with sherry, Madeira, or champagne.

MAKES I POUND

 2   tablespoons butter
 1   pound chicken liver, cut into 1/2-inch pieces
 2   tablespoons chopped shallots or scallions (use only the white parts of the scallions)
 3   tablespoons Cognac or Madeira
1/2 cup unflavored yogurt
1/8 teaspoon ground allspice
1/8 teaspoon crushed dried thyme
1/2 teaspoon salt
1/8 teaspoon freshly ground black pepper
 4   tablespoons butter, melted
     Parsley sprigs

In a heavy skillet melt the 2 tablespoons butter over moderate heat. Add the chicken livers and sauté about 3 minutes or until lightly browned outside but still pink inside. Remove from the heat and pour the contents of the skillet into the container of an electric blender. Add the shallots or scallions, Cognac or Madeira, yogurt, allspice, thyme, salt, and pepper. Blend at medium speed until a smooth paste is formed. Add the melted butter and blend a few seconds more. Taste and adjust the seasoning. Pack the liver mousse into an attractive serving bowl. Cover with aluminum foil and chill thoroughly. Garnish with the parsley and serve, accompanied with crackers.

STUFFED CUCUMBER BOATS

SERVES 4 TO 6

4 to 6 small cucumbers
    Salt
1 recipe Blue Cheese Dip, page 10
2 tablespoons finely chopped parsley

Peel the cucumbers and cut them in half lengthwise. Scoop out the seeds with a grapefruit spoon and discard. Sprinkle the cucumber boats with the salt. Place them upside down on paper towels to drain for 30 minutes. Dry the cucumber boats with fresh paper towels and fill with the blue cheese mixture. Arrange on a serving platter and sprinkle with the parsley. Serve chilled with buttered thinly sliced pumpernickel. Thinly sliced tomatoes or cooked beets dressed with olive oil and lemon juice make an attractive garnish for the platter.

VARIATIONS   Other good fillings for the cucumber boats include Cheese and Herb Spread, page 9 (omit the last 4 ingredients), and minced cooked shrimp, lobster, or crab meat, moistened with Yogurt Mayonnaise, page 88.

CARIBBEAN STUFFED AVOCADOS

SERVES 6

8 ounces cooked jumbo shrimp, shelled, deveined, and diced
4 ounces cooked lobster meat, diced
4 ounces cooked crab meat, diced
1/2 cup thinly sliced celery heart
2 scallions, finely chopped, including 2 inches of the green tops
6 pimiento-stuffed green olives, thinly sliced
1/2 cup unflavored yogurt
2 tablespoons olive oil
1 tablespoon freshly squeezed and strained lemon or lime juice or to taste
    Salt and freshly ground black pepper to taste
3 large ripe avocados
    Boston or leaf lettuce leaves

Combine the shrimp, lobster, crab, celery, scallions, and olives in a mixing bowl. Beat together the yogurt, olive oil, lemon juice, and salt and pepper with a fork or whisk until well blended. Pour over the seafood mixture. Toss gently but thoroughly. Cover and chill. Close to serving time, halve the unpeeled avocados lengthwise. Remove the pits. Place each avocado half on an individual salad plate lined with lettuce leaves and fill with the seafood mixture.

STUFFED EGGS

Stuffed eggs gain an unusual flavor when prepared with yogurt instead of mayonnaise or sour cream.

SERVES 6

6	hard-cooked eggs
1/4	cup unflavored yogurt
1	tablespoon finely chopped chives
1	tablespoon finely chopped parsley
1	tablespoon freshly squeezed and strained lemon juice
1/2	teaspoon curry powder or to taste
	Salt, freshly ground black pepper, and ground cayenne pepper to taste
	Pimiento-stuffed olives, sliced

Halve the eggs lengthwise. Remove the yolks and mash them in a small bowl with the yogurt until perfectly smooth. Add the remaining ingredients except the olives and mix thoroughly. Taste and adjust the seasoning. Press the mixture through a pastry tube with a star-shaped tip, or use a spoon to fill the egg whites. Garnish the centers of the eggs with the sliced olives. Serve chilled.

VARIATION   Mash the egg yolks with 2 tablespoons each yogurt and mayonnaise. Add 1 tablespoon Dijon-style mustard and salt to taste and mix well. Fill the egg whites as above. Sprinkle finely chopped toasted blanced almonds over the centers of the eggs and serve.

SAVORY CHEESECAKE

Offer this smooth and creamy cheesecake, based on a French recipe, as an accompaniment to cocktails.

MAKES ABOUT 16 SERVINGS

1/3	cup fine French bread crumbs, lightly toasted
3	tablespoons freshly grated Parmesan cheese
28	ounces cream cheese, at room temperature
4	eggs
3/4	cup unflavored yogurt

Combine the bread crumbs and Parmesan cheese. Sprinkle the inside of a buttered metal cheesecake pan 8 inches wide and 3 inches deep with the mixture. Shake the pan so that the bottom and sides are thoroughly coated with the crumb mixture. Shake out the excess crumbs.

In a large mixing bowl combine the cream cheese, eggs, and yogurt. Beat until thoroughly blended and smooth. Turn the batter into the prepared pan and shake gently to level it. Place the pan in a slightly larger pan, making certain that the edges of the pans do not touch. Pour boiling water into the larger pan to a depth of 2 inches. Bake in a preheated 300°F oven 1 hour and 40 minutes or until the center of the cake is firm. When done, turn off the oven and allow the cake to remain inside 1 hour longer.

Lift the cheesecake out of the larger pan and place it on a wire rack to cool 2 hours or until it reaches room temperature. To unmold, place a flat plate over the cake pan and invert. Carefully remove the cake pan. Gently place a serving plate over the cake and invert again, being careful not to exert pressure on the cake. Serve at room temperature, or cover and chill well before serving.

SAVORY NUT CHEESECAKE VARIATION
Spread 1 cup blanched almonds or hazelnuts in a shallow pan and bake in a preheated 350°F oven about 15 minutes or until golden brown, stirring occasionally and watching closely to prevent burning. Cool, then coarsely grind the nuts in a blender. Prepare the pan and mix the batter as for Savory Cheesecake, preceding. Add the ground nuts to the batter and mix thoroughly. Turn into the crumb-coated pan and proceed as directed for savory cheesecake.

CHEESE AND BACON QUICHE

Serve this versatile pie either as an appetizer or as a luncheon main course accompanied with a green salad.

SERVES 6

1 Partially Baked Pie Pastry, page 150
3 large eggs
3/4 cup milk
3/4 cup unflavored yogurt, at room temperature
1/2 teaspoon salt or to taste
1/8 teaspoon ground white pepper (preferably freshly ground)
1/8 teaspoon ground nutmeg (preferably freshly ground) or to taste
6 slices bacon, cooked crisp and crumbled
4 ounces Gruyère cheese, grated
1/4 cup freshly grated Parmesan cheese (optional)

Prepare the pastry as directed in the recipe and set aside. In a large bowl beat the eggs, then beat in the milk, yogurt, salt, pepper, and nutmeg until well blended. Mix in the bacon. Spread the cheese evenly over the bottom of the partially baked pastry. Pour the egg mixture over the cheese. Bake in a preheated 375°F oven about 35 minutes or until the custard is set and a knife inserted into it comes out clean. Serve at once.

SPINACH AND CHEESE PIE

A Greek-inspired creation worth every minute of the time it takes to prepare.

SERVES 4 TO 6

1 Partially Baked Pie Pastry, page 150
1 pound spinach
1/4 cup water
3 tablespoons butter
3 scallions, finely chopped, including 2 inches of the green tops
2 eggs
2 egg yolks
1/2 cup unflavored yogurt
1/2 cup milk
1 tablespoon finely chopped parsley
1 tablespoon finely chopped fresh dill or basil
  Salt and freshly ground black pepper to taste
1 cup finely crumbled feta or grated Gruyère cheese
1/3 cup freshly grated Parmesan cheese

Prepare the pastry as directed in the recipe and set aside. Wash the spinach thoroughly under cold running water, discarding the tough stems and bruised leaves. Combine the spinach and water in a saucepan and bring to a boil over high heat. Reduce the heat to low, cover, and simmer 8 minutes. Drain the spinach. When it is cool enough to handle, squeeze the spinach dry and chop finely.

In a heavy skillet melt 2 tablespoons of the butter over moderate heat. Add the scallions and sauté until golden, stirring frequently. Stir in the spinach and remove from the heat. In a mixing bowl beat together the eggs and egg yolks, then beat in the yogurt, milk, parsley, dill or basil, and salt and pepper. Stir in the scallions and spinach and feta or Gruyère cheese. Turn the mixture into the pastry-lined pan. Dot with the remaining 1 tablespoon butter and sprinkle with the Parmesan cheese. Bake in a preheated 400°F oven 10 minutes. Reduce the heat to 350°F and bake about 30 minutes or until set. Remove the pie from the oven and allow to cool 5 minutes before cutting it.

TURKISH ZUCCHINI-CHEESE TURNOVERS

Savory pastries constitute one of the most interesting features of Middle Eastern food. These turnovers make a charming appetizer to offer with cocktails, or they can be served as an accompaniment to soup or salad.

MAKES ABOUT 5 DOZEN

Filling

2	medium zucchini
	Salt
2	eggs, slightly beaten
1	cup grated Gruyère cheese
1/2	cup finely crumbled feta or freshly grated Parmesan cheese
1	tablespoon finely chopped parsley
1	tablespoon finely chopped fresh mint or dill
	Freshly ground black pepper to taste
1	tablespoon all-purpose flour

Pastry

1/2	pound butter
2	tablespoons olive oil
2	eggs, beaten separately
1	cup unflavored yogurt
1/4	teaspoon baking soda
1/4	teaspoon salt
4	cups sifted all-purpose flour (approximately)

TO PREPARE THE FILLING   Grate the zucchini. Sprinkle with the salt and let stand about 20 minutes. Squeeze out as much liquid as possible. Combine with the eggs, Gruyère, feta, parsley, mint, and pepper and mix well. Sprinkle with the flour, mix again, and set aside.

TO PREPARE THE PASTRY   Melt the butter and add the oil. Let cool slightly, then add 1 beaten egg and the yogurt. Add the baking soda, salt, and enough flour to make a dough. Knead 5 minutes. Roll out the dough on a lightly floured board to 1/8-inch thickness. Cut into circles with a 3-inch cookie cutter. Place

about 1-1/2 teaspoons filling on the lower half of each circle. Dip a finger into cold water and moisten the edges. Fold over the other half to make a half moon and press the edges together. Brush with the second beaten egg. Place the turnovers 1 inch apart on a greased baking sheet. Bake in a preheated 400°F oven 15 to 20 minutes or until golden brown. Serve the turnovers warm.

GROUND MEAT TURNOVERS

MAKES ABOUT 5 DOZEN

2	tablespoons butter
1	medium onion, finely chopped
1	large garlic clove, finely chopped
8	ounces lean ground lamb or beef
1	small tomato, peeled, seeded, and finely chopped
1	teaspoon curry powder or to taste
	Salt and freshly ground black pepper to taste
2	tablespoons finely chopped parsley
	Pastry for Turkish Zucchini-Cheese Turnovers, preceding

In a heavy skillet melt the butter over moderate heat. Add the onion and garlic and sauté until soft but not browned, stirring frequently. Add the lamb or beef and sauté until browned, breaking it up with a fork. Add the tomato, curry powder, and salt and pepper. Cook about 10 minutes, stirring occasionally. Mix in the parsley and remove from the heat. Drain off the excess fat and liquid. Taste, adjust the seasoning, and set aside to cool.

Prepare, fill, and bake the pastry as directed in the recipe for Turkish zucchini-cheese turnovers. Serve warm.

Soups

CHILLED YOGURT AND CUCUMBER SOUP

This is a Persian interpretation of a traditional summer soup enjoyed throughout the Balkans, Middle East, and Caucasus.

SERVES 4

1/2 cup raisins or currants
2 cups unflavored yogurt
1/2 cup half-and-half
1 hard-cooked egg, chopped, or 1/4 cup chopped walnuts
1 medium cucumber, peeled, seeded (if seeds are large), and diced
4 scallions, chopped, including 2 inches of the green tops
Salt and ground white pepper (preferably freshly ground) to taste
6 ice cubes
2 tablespoons finely chopped fresh dill

Soak the raisins or currants in cold water 5 minutes. Place the yogurt in a large mixing bowl. Add the cream and 1 cup ice water and stir until thoroughly blended. Drain the raisins and add them to the yogurt mixture along with the egg or walnuts, cucumber, scallions, and salt and pepper. Stir in the ice cubes. Cover and chill 2 to 3 hours. Just before serving taste and adjust the seasoning. Serve in individual soup bowls, sprinkled with the dill.

TURKISH CHILLED TOMATO SOUP

SERVES 6

1-1/2 cups unflavored yogurt
1-1/2 tablespoons olive oil
1/4 cup freshly squeezed and strained lemon juice or to taste
1-1/2 teaspoons curry powder or to taste
Pinch crushed dried thyme
4-1/2 cups tomato juice
Salt to taste
Finely chopped chives or scallion tops

Spoon the yogurt into a large mixing bowl and beat until smooth. Add the olive oil, lemon juice, curry powder, and thyme and mix well. Gradually stir in the tomato juice until thoroughly blended. Season with the salt. Cover and chill. Serve in individual soup bowls or cups sprinkled with the chives or scallion tops.

CHILLED AVOCADO SOUP

SERVES 4

- 1 large avocado, peeled, pitted, and cut into large pieces
- 1 cup hot chicken broth
- 3 tablespoons freshly squeezed and strained lemon juice or to taste
- 3/4 teaspoon curry powder or to taste
- 1 teaspoon grated onion
- 1 tiny garlic clove, crushed (optional)
  Salt and ground white pepper (preferably freshly ground) to taste
- 1/2 cup unflavored yogurt
- 4 thin slices avocado

Place the avocado, chicken broth, 1 tablespoon of the lemon juice, curry powder, onion, garlic (if desired), and salt and pepper in the container of an electric blender. Blend until smooth. Turn into a bowl and allow to cool. Stir in the yogurt until thoroughly mixed. Taste and adjust the seasoning. Pour into individual soup bowls, cover, and chill. Garnish each serving with an avocado slice dipped in the remaining 2 tablespoons lemon juice.

CHILLED SPINACH-YOGURT SOUP

Here is a superbly refreshing hot-weather triumph from Armenia.

SERVES 6

- 1-1/2 pounds spinach
- 1/4 cup water
- 1 small garlic clove
- 1/2 teaspoon salt
- 3 cups unflavored yogurt
- 2 tablespoons finely chopped fresh mint, or 2 teaspoons crushed dried mint
- 1-1/2 cups ice water

Wash the spinach thoroughly under cold running water, discarding the tough stems and bruised leaves. Combine the spinach and water in a saucepan and bring to a boil over high heat. Reduce the heat to low, cover, and simmer about 5 minutes or until the spinach is barely wilted. Drain and cool the spinach, then squeeze it dry and chop finely.

Mash the garlic with the salt. In a deep bowl combine the yogurt with the mashed garlic and mint and stir until smooth. Add the spinach and mix well. Gradually stir in the ice water until thoroughly blended. Taste and adjust the seasoning. Cover and chill. Serve in individual soup bowls, adding 1 ice cube to each bowl.

NOTE More or less ice water may be used, depending on whether a thicker or thinner soup is desired.

CHILLED BROCCOLI-YOGURT SOUP
VARIATION Substitute 1-1/2 pounds cooked and puréed broccoli for the spinach, 1/2 teaspoon crushed dried basil for the mint, and 1-1/2 cups chicken broth for the ice water.

CHILLED ZUCCHINI-YOGURT SOUP

An excellent introduction to roasted or barbecued lamb.

SERVES 4

- 3 tablespoons butter
- 1 large onion, coarsely chopped
- 1-1/2 pounds zucchini, cubed
- 2 cups chicken broth
- 1 medium garlic clove, finely chopped
  Salt and freshly ground black pepper to taste
- 1 cup unflavored yogurt
- 1 tablespoon finely chopped fresh dill

In a heavy pot melt the butter over moderate heat. Add the onion and sauté until golden, stirring frequently. Add the zucchini and cook 5 minutes, stirring occasionally. Add the chicken broth, garlic, and salt and pepper. Cover and simmer 10 minutes or until the zucchini is tender. Purée the mixture in an electric blender or force through a fine sieve. Cool to room temperature. Stir in the yogurt until well blended. Taste and adjust the seasoning. Pour into individual soup bowls. Cover and chill. Serve garnished with the dill.

CHILLED BEET SOUP

SERVES 4

- 1 cup peeled and sliced cooked beets
- 1/4 cup chopped mild onion
- 1 medium potato, cooked, peeled, and cubed
- 2 tablespoons freshly squeezed and strained lemon juice
  Salt and freshly ground black pepper to taste
- 1 cup chicken or beef broth
- 1 cup unflavored yogurt
- 1 cup cracked ice
- 1/2 cup peeled, seeded, and finely diced cucumber (optional)
- 1 tablespoon finely chopped fresh dill

Put the beets, onion, potato, lemon juice, salt and pepper, chicken broth, and yogurt in the container of an electric blender. Blend on high speed until smooth. Add the cracked ice and blend 1 minute. Add the cucumber, if desired. Taste and adjust the seasoning. Serve chilled, garnished with the chopped dill.

VARIATION   Omit the yogurt and cracked ice. Turn the blended mixture into a saucepan. Stir in 1 cup additional broth and 1 teaspoon sugar. Simmer, partially covered, 10 minutes. Serve hot or chilled, garnishing each serving with a spoonful of unflavored yogurt and minced dill. If serving hot, omit the cucumber.

CHILLED BEET SOUP WITH SHRIMP, HAM, AND CUCUMBER

This lovely rose-colored soup, called chlodnik, *is of Polish origin but is widely appreciated in Russia as well.*

SERVES 4

8	ounces beets, peeled and coarsely grated
3-1/4	cups cold water
3	teaspoons red wine vinegar
2	teaspoons salt or to taste
1/2	teaspoon sugar
1/2	cup unflavored yogurt
1	medium cucumber, peeled, seeded (if seeds are large), and diced
1/2	cup chopped cooked shrimp
1/2	cup chopped cooked ham
2	scallions, finely chopped, including 2 inches of the green tops
2	tablespoons finely chopped fresh dill
1-1/2	tablespoons freshly squeezed and strained lemon juice or to taste
	Ground white pepper (preferably freshly ground) to taste
4	thin slices lemon
2	hard-cooked eggs, chilled and finely chopped

In an enameled or stainless steel saucepan bring the beets and cold water to a boil over moderate heat. Cook, uncovered, 10 minutes. Add 2 teaspoons of the vinegar, 1 teaspoon of the salt, and the sugar. Reduce the heat to low and simmer, partially covered, 25 minutes. Drain the beets in a fine sieve, reserving the cooking liquid. Set both aside separately, allowing them to cool to room temperature.

In a large bowl beat the yogurt until smooth. Gradually beat in the cooled beet liquid until well blended. Stir in the cooled beets, cucumber, shrimp, ham, scallions, 1 tablespoon of the dill, lemon juice, remaining 1 teaspoon each vinegar and salt, and pepper. Taste and adjust the seasoning. Cover and chill.

To serve, ladle the soup into a chilled soup tureen or individual soup bowls. Sprinkle with the remaining 1 tablespoon dill and garnish with the lemon slices and chopped eggs.

NOTE   Less vinegar and more lemon juice may be used, and the sugar may be omitted. Cooked cubed potato is sometimes added with the cucumber.

AUSTRIAN LEEK AND SPINACH SOUP WITH HAM

A rich and creamy soup to fortify the inner man on a cold evening.

SERVES 4

3	tablespoons butter
2	leeks (white parts only), thinly sliced
8	ounces spinach, washed thoroughly, stemmed, and coarsely chopped
3	tablespoons all-purpose flour
2-1/2	cups hot chicken broth
2	cups hot water
	Salt and ground white pepper (preferably freshly ground) to taste
8	ounces cream cheese or Neufchâtel cheese, at room temperature
1	cup unflavored yogurt
2	egg yolks
1	cup diced cooked ham
1/4	cup finely chopped chives

In a heavy pot melt 2 tablespoons of the butter over moderate heat. Add the leeks and spinach and sauté gently until soft, stirring frequently. Sprinkle with the flour and cook 1 minute, stirring. Add the chicken broth, water, and salt and pepper and cook over moderate heat, stirring constantly, until the mixture is slightly thickened. Reduce the heat, cover, and simmer 15 minutes.

Meanwhile, mash the cream or Neufchâtel cheese in a small bowl. Add the yogurt and egg yolks and beat until the mixture is well blended and smooth. In a small skillet melt the remaining 1 tablespoon butter over moderate heat. Add the ham and sauté, turning to color on all sides. Stir the yogurt mixture into the soup until thoroughly blended. Simmer 5 minutes, stirring constantly. Add the ham and serve hot, sprinkled with the chives.

MUSHROOM AND POTATO SOUP

SERVES 4

3   tablespoons butter
12   ounces mushrooms, trimmed (do not remove stems) and cut lengthwise into thin slices
1   medium onion, finely chopped
3   cups chicken broth
3   small boiling potatoes, peeled and thinly sliced
     Salt and freshly ground black pepper to taste
1/4 cup finely chopped scallions (include 2 inches of the green tops)
1   tablespoon finely chopped parsley
1/2 cup unflavored yogurt
1   tablespoon finely chopped fresh dill

In a heavy pot melt 2 tablespoons of the butter over moderate heat. Add the mushrooms and onion and stir until they are coated with the butter. Reduce the heat to low and simmer, partially covered, 20 minutes. Stir in the chicken broth, potatoes, and salt and pepper and bring the mixture to a boil over high heat. Reduce the heat to low and simmer, partially covered, about 25 minutes or until the potatoes are tender but still somewhat firm.

Meanwhile, melt the remaining 1 tablespoon butter in a small skillet. Add the scallions and parsley and sauté over low heat until the scallions are golden brown, stirring frequently. Remove from the heat and add to the soup.

In a small bowl beat the yogurt until smooth. Gradually beat in a little hot broth from the soup until well blended. Carefully stir the yogurt mixture into the pot and simmer just until heated through. Do not allow the soup to boil or it will curdle. Taste and adjust the seasoning.

Serve at once, sprinkled with the dill.

SOUTH AMERICAN PUMPKIN SOUP

This attractive soup is usually made with cream. It tastes, I think, even better with yogurt.

SERVES 4

1-1/4 pounds pumpkin, peeled and cubed
2-3/4 cups chicken broth
1/2   cup chopped onion
1/3   cup chopped scallions (white portions only)
       Salt and ground white pepper (preferably freshly ground) or ground cayenne pepper to taste
1   cup unflavored yogurt
4   thin slices tomato
       Unflavored yogurt
1/4   cup finely chopped scallions (green portions only)

In a heavy pot or saucepan combine the pumpkin, chicken broth, onion, and white portions of scallions. Bring to a boil over high heat. Reduce the heat to low, cover, and simmer about 20 minutes or until the pumpkin is tender. Force the mixture through a fine sieve or purée in an electric blender. Season with the salt and pepper. Cover and chill thoroughly. Stir in the yogurt until well blended. Taste and adjust the seasoning. Ladle the soup into chilled individual bowls or cups and top each serving with a tomato slice, a dollop of yogurt, and a sprinkling of chopped green scallion tops. Serve at once.

CREAM OF PUMPKIN SOUP

An elegant, delicate soup. Delicious hot, even better chilled.

SERVES 6

2	tablespoons butter
1/3	cup finely chopped onion
2	pounds pumpkin, peeled and cubed
1	quart chicken broth
1	small bay leaf
1/2	teaspoon crushed dried thyme
1	cup half-and-half
1	cup unflavored yogurt
	Salt and ground white pepper (preferably freshly ground) to taste
1/3	cup dry sherry
	Unflavored yogurt
1/4	cup finely chopped chives or scallion tops

In a heavy saucepan melt the butter over moderate heat. Add the onion and sauté until golden, stirring frequently. Add the pumpkin, chicken broth, bay leaf, and thyme. Reduce the heat to low, cover, and simmer about 20 minutes or until the pumpkin is very tender.

Remove the bay leaf. Force the mixture through a fine sieve or purée in an electric blender. Cool. Stir in the half-and-half and yogurt and simmer gently 5 minutes. Season with the salt and pepper. Stir in the sherry. Ladle the soup into individual bowls or cups. Serve hot or chilled, topping each serving with a dollop of yogurt and a sprinkling of chives or scallion tops.

LENTIL SOUP

Here is a soup, based on an Indian recipe, that deserves all the culinary superlatives.

SERVES 4

1	cup lentils
1	quart beef broth or water
2	tablespoons butter
1	medium onion, finely chopped
1	medium garlic clove, finely chopped
1-1/2	teaspoons curry powder or to taste
	Salt and freshly ground black pepper to taste
2/3	cup unflavored yogurt
	Plain or garlic-flavored croûtons (optional)

Combine the lentils and beef broth or water in a heavy pot. Bring to a boil and reduce the heat to low. Cover and simmer about 1 hour or until the lentils are very tender.

Meanwhile, in a small skillet melt the butter over moderate heat. Add the onion and garlic and sauté until golden, stirring frequently. Add the curry powder and cook, stirring, 1 minute. Add the contents of the skillet to the soup. Season with the salt and pepper. Cover and simmer 10 minutes. Purée the soup in an electric blender or force through a fine sieve. Return the soup to the pot and beat in the yogurt until thoroughly blended. Cook over low heat until the soup is heated through. Do not allow it to boil. Taste and adjust the seasoning. Serve with the croûtons, if desired.

VARIATION   One-half teaspoon ground cumin or turmeric or to taste may be substituted for the curry powder.

ARMENIAN YOGURT AND NOODLE SOUP

SERVES 4

3 cups unflavored yogurt
1 egg, beaten
3 cups chicken or beef broth or water
1 cup 1/4-inch-wide egg noodles, broken into small pieces
  Salt to taste
3 tablespoons butter
1 medium onion, finely chopped
1 tablespoon crushed dried mint

In a saucepan or pot beat together the yogurt and egg. Bring to a boil over moderate heat, stirring constantly in one direction. (The egg will prevent the yogurt from curdling.) Stir in the broth and the noodles. Season with the salt. Bring to a boil again, reduce the heat, and simmer about 10 minutes or until the noodles are tender.

Meanwhile, in a small skillet melt the butter over moderate heat. Add the onion and sauté until golden brown, stirring frequently. Stir in the mint. Remove from the heat and add the contents of the skillet to the soup. Stir and serve.

CHILLED SHRIMP AND TOMATO BISQUE

SERVES 4 TO 6

1 pound shrimp in their shells
3 cups water
2 tablespoons butter
1 small onion, finely chopped
2 tablespoons all-purpose flour
2 tablespoons tomato purée
1 teaspoon curry powder or to taste
1 cup half-and-half
  Salt and ground cayenne pepper to taste
1 cup unflavored yogurt
1 medium firm, ripe tomato, cut crosswise into 1-1/4-inch-thick slices
2 hard-cooked eggs, finely chopped

Shell and devein the shrimp. Place them in a sieve or colander and wash quickly under cold running water. In a saucepan bring the water to a boil over high heat. Add the shrimp and cook, uncovered, about 4 minutes or until they are pink and firm. Drain, reserving 2 cups of the cooking liquid. Put the shrimp through the finest blade of a food grinder and set aside.

In a heavy saucepan melt the butter over moderate heat. Add the onion and sauté until soft but not browned, stirring frequently. Add the flour, tomato purée, and curry powder and mix well. Gradually add the reserved cooking liquid, stirring constantly with a wire whisk until the sauce is slightly thickened and smooth. Reduce the heat to low and simmer 3 minutes. Add the ground shrimp, half-and-half, and salt and cayenne pepper and bring to a boil over moderate heat. Remove from the heat and cool to room temperature.

In a large bowl beat the yogurt until smooth. Gradually beat in the cooled soup until thoroughly blended. Taste and adjust the seasoning. Cover and chill.

Serve in individual soup bowls, garnished with the sliced tomato and chopped eggs.

INDONESIAN SHRIMP AND VEGETABLE SOUP

SERVES 6

- 1 small onion, finely chopped
- 1 medium garlic clove, finely chopped
- 1/2 teaspoon ground coriander
- 1/2 teaspoon ground cumin
- 1/2 teaspoon ground ginger
- 1 teaspoon salt or to taste
- 1/8 teaspoon ground dried chili pepper
- 2 tablespoons peanut oil
- 3 cups Coconut Milk, page 150
- 4 ounces green beans, trimmed and cut into 1-1/2-inch lengths
- 4 ounces carrots, peeled and sliced
- 4 ounces green peas, shelled
- 1/2 cup shredded cabbage
- 1 bay leaf
- 1 teaspoon grated lemon rind
- 1 cup unflavored yogurt
- 1 pound raw shrimp, shelled, deveined, and diced

In a mortar pound to a paste the onion, garlic, coriander, cumin, ginger, salt, and chili pepper. In a saucepan heat the oil over moderate heat. Add the paste and sauté gently 3 minutes, stirring almost continuously. Add the coconut milk and blend thoroughly. Bring to a boil. Add the green beans, carrots, green peas, cabbage, bay leaf, and lemon rind. Reduce the heat, cover, and simmer 20 minutes or until the vegetables are tender. Stir in the yogurt until well blended. Add the shrimp and simmer, uncovered, 5 minutes.

CHILLED SENEGALESE SOUP WITH YOGURT

SERVES 4

- 2-1/2 tablespoons butter
- 1 medium onion, finely chopped
- 1 stalk celery, sliced
- 1 medium tart apple, peeled, cored, and thinly sliced
- 2 teaspoons curry powder or to taste
- 1 tablespoon all-purpose flour
- 3 cups hot chicken broth
  Salt and ground white pepper (preferably freshly ground) to taste
- 1/2 cup unflavored yogurt, chilled
- 1/2 cup half-and-half, chilled
- 1/2 cup minced cooked chicken
- 3 tablespoons dry sherry (optional)
- 1 tablespoon finely chopped chives

In a heavy saucepan melt the butter over moderate heat. Add the onion, celery, and apple and sauté until soft but not browned. Add the curry powder and cook, stirring, 2 minutes. Add the flour and cook, stirring, 2 to 3 minutes. Gradually add the chicken broth, stirring constantly. Season with the salt and pepper. Reduce the heat to low and simmer 15 minutes. Purée the mixture in an electric blender or force through a fine sieve set over a large bowl. Cover and chill. Close to serving time, beat in the yogurt until thoroughly blended. Stir in the cream, chicken, and sherry, if desired. Taste and adjust the seasoning. Serve in chilled individual soup bowls and garnish with the chives.

CHILLED HAM AND SHRIMP SOUP WITH CUCUMBERS

This slightly tart soup, an adaptation of the Russian okroshka, *makes an excellent summer main course.*

SERVES 4

- 2 cups unflavored yogurt
- 2 cups milk
- 1 small cucumber, peeled, seeded (if seeds are large), and chopped
- 1 midget kosher dill pickle, chopped (optional)
- 3/4 cup diced cooked ham
- 3/4 cup diced cooked shrimp
- 3 scallions, finely chopped, including 2 inches of the green tops
- 3 tablespoons finely chopped parsley
- 3 tablespoons finely chopped fresh dill
- 1-1/2 tablespoons freshly squeezed and strained lemon juice or to taste
  Salt and freshly ground black pepper to taste
- 2 hard-cooked eggs, thinly sliced

Spoon the yogurt into a large mixing bowl. Gradually beat in the milk until thoroughly blended. Add the cucumber, dill pickle, ham, shrimp, scallions, parsley, dill, and lemon juice. Season with the salt and pepper. Mix gently. Taste and adjust the seasoning. Cover and chill. Serve in individual soup bowls, garnished with the sliced eggs.

NOTE   Instead of ham and shrimp, this soup is sometimes made with beef, ham, and tongue, veal, or chicken.

CHILLED BEEF SOUP WITH YOGURT

A fresh-tasting, herb-scented summer soup from Azerbaijan.

SERVES 4

- 2 small cucumbers
- 3 cups unflavored yogurt
- 1-1/2 cups ice water
- 12 ounces boiled lean beef, cubed
- 3 hard-cooked eggs, chopped
- 6 finely chopped scallions, including 2 inches of the green tops
  Salt to taste
- 1/2 cup finely chopped fresh herbs (dill, coriander, parsley, and mint)

Peel and quarter the cucumbers. Cut out the seeds if too large and discard. Slice the cucumbers crosswise into 1/4-inch-thick pieces and set aside.

Spoon the yogurt into a mixing bowl. Gradually beat in the ice water until well blended. Add the cucumbers, beef, eggs, scallions, and salt and mix gently. Taste and adjust the seasoning. Cover and chill. Serve in individual soup bowls, sprinkled with the chopped herbs.

NOTE   This soup may also be made without the beef.

MEATBALL SOUP WITH YOGURT

Here is another unusual and highly satisfying Azerbaijani soup, perfect for a winter meal.

SERVES 4 TO 6

8	ounces lean beef or lamb, ground twice
1	small onion, grated or very finely chopped
5	tablespoons finely chopped fresh dill
	Salt and freshly ground black pepper to taste
5	cups beef broth
1/3	cup uncooked long-grain white rice
1	cup drained canned chick-peas, rinsed
1	cup chopped spinach leaves
1/2	cup chopped sorrel (optional)
3	cups unflavored yogurt or to taste
1/4	cup finely chopped parsley
2	tablespoons finely chopped chives or scallions (include 2 inches of the green tops of the scallions)

In a mixing bowl combine the meat, onion, 1 tablespoon of the dill, and salt and pepper. Knead with your hands until the mixture is well blended. Taste and adjust the seasoning. Form into 1-inch balls.

In a heavy pot bring the broth to a boil over high heat. Season with salt and pepper. Add the meatballs and rice. Reduce the heat, cover, and simmer 20 minutes. Add the chick-peas, spinach, and sorrel (if desired) and simmer, covered, 10 minutes or until the meatballs and rice are tender.

In a deep bowl beat the yogurt until smooth. Gradually beat in a little of the soup broth until well blended. Slowly pour the yogurt mixture into the pot, stirring constantly. Add the parsley, chives, and remaining 4 tablespoons dill and continue stirring until thoroughly heated. Do not allow the soup to boil or it will curdle. Taste and adjust the seasoning. Serve hot.

CHILLED CHERRY SOUP

Fruit soups, so popular abroad, are neglected delights in America. A particular favorite in Hungary and northern Europe is cherry soup, which makes a splendid preamble to a summer meal.

SERVES 4 TO 6

1	pound sweet or sour cherries, stemmed and pitted
1	2-inch piece cinnamon stick
4	whole cloves (optional)
2	thin slices lemon
2	thin slices orange
2	cups water
1/4	cup sugar or to taste
	Pinch salt
1	tablespoon cornstarch
2	tablespoons water
1/4	cup unflavored yogurt
	Additional cherries for garnishing the soup

In an enameled saucepan combine the cherries, cinnamon stick, cloves, lemon slices, orange slices, and water. Bring to a boil over moderate heat. Reduce the heat, cover, and simmer about 10 minutes or until the cherries are very soft. Stir in the sugar and salt. Remove the cinnamon stick, cloves, and lemon and orange slices. Mix the cornstarch with the water and add to the soup. Simmer, stirring, 1 minute or until clear and slightly thickened. Purée the mixture through a sieve or in an electric blender. Add the yogurt and mix well. Pour into small individual soup bowls. Cover and chill. Serve garnished with the additional cherries.

VARIATIONS

· Rather than purée all the cherries, you may remove about 1 cup of the cherries and some of the liquid. Purée and return to the rest of the soup.

· Instead of mixing the yogurt with the soup, you may garnish each serving with a spoonful of yogurt.

· One-fourth cup dry red wine or Cherry Heering to taste may be added to the soup before mixing in the yogurt.

- Two cups each cherries and sliced peaches may be substituted for the cherries.

CHILLED BLUEBERRY SOUP VARIATION
Follow the recipe for Chilled Cherry Soup, preceding, substituting blueberries for the cherries.

CHILLED BERRY SOUP

This appealing Russian soup can either precede or follow the main course.

SERVES 4

2	cups hulled strawberries or raspberries, or 1 cup each hulled strawberries and raspberries
1/2	cup sugar or to taste
1/2	cup unflavored yogurt
2	cups ice water
1/2	cup dry red wine

Reserve 4 large berries for garnish. Rub the remaining berries through a fine sieve. Add the sugar and yogurt and mix well. Gradually stir in the water and wine until thoroughly blended. Taste and adjust the sweetening. Pour into small individual soup bowls. Cover and chill. Serve garnished with the reserved berries.

NOTE   For a thicker soup use only 1 cup ice water.

AUTUMN FRUIT SOUP

Here is a versatile Israeli soup with which to begin or end a meal.

SERVES 6

2	tart apples, quartered and cored
2	cups apple cider
2	Bosc or Bartlett pears, cored and thickly sliced
1	pound Italian purple plums, quartered and pitted
1	small juice orange
2	tablespoons sugar or to taste
1	teaspoon ground cinnamon
1/4	teaspoon ground cloves
1/2	cup seedless green grapes
1/2	cup Yogurt Crème Chantilly, page 98, or 1/2 cup unflavored yogurt sprinkled with cinnamon
1/4	cup toasted slivered blanched almonds, following

Grate the apples and combine them with the apple cider, pears, and plums in a heavy enameled saucepan. Grate the outer peel of the orange, then peel the orange and section it, removing the white membrane. Add the grated orange rind, orange sections, sugar, cinnamon, and cloves to the saucepan. Cover and simmer 20 minutes or until the fruit is tender. Serve hot or chilled, garnished with the grapes, yogurt crème Chantilly or yogurt sprinkled with cinnamon, and almonds.

TOASTED SLIVERED BLANCHED ALMONDS
Spread the almonds in a single layer on a rimmed baking sheet. Toast in a preheated 325°F oven, stirring occasionally, 10 to 15 minutes or until lightly browned, watching closely to prevent burning.

Salads

BULGARIAN TOSSED GREEN SALAD

Salads were known and appreciated in Bulgaria long before they gained popularity in Western Europe. This is a typical salad in Bulgaria, where yogurt is a staple item in the diet.

SERVES 4

1-1/2 quarts assorted salad greens (romaine, chicory, iceberg lettuce, and spinach)
1-1/2 cups peeled, seeded (if seeds are large), and sliced cucumber
1/2 cup sliced radishes
1/4 cup sliced scallions, including 2 inches of the green tops
1/2 recipe Yogurt French Dressing, page 87
1 tablespoon finely chopped fresh mint or basil (optional)

Combine the salad greens, cucumber, radishes, and scallions in a salad bowl. Add the yogurt French dressing and toss gently but thoroughly. Serve at once, sprinkled with the mint or basil, if desired.

SPINACH AND EGG SALAD

Spinach has a natural affinity with yogurt and is exceedingly good prepared in this Middle Eastern manner.

SERVES 4

1 pound spinach
1 small red onion, or
  3 scallions, finely chopped (include 2 inches of the green tops of the scallions)
2 hard-cooked eggs, chopped
1 recipe Yogurt French Dressing, page 87
8 black olives (preferably Greek olives), or
  4 slices crisp cooked bacon, crumbled

Wash the spinach carefully under cold running water. Remove and discard the stems and bruised leaves. Drain. Dry with paper towels and tear into bite-size pieces. Combine the spinach, onion, and eggs in a salad bowl. Add the yogurt French dressing and mix lightly but thoroughly, taking care not to mash the eggs. Taste and adjust the seasoning. Cover and chill. Serve garnished with the olives.

SWISS CHARD SALAD WITH YOGURT

SERVES 4

- 1   pound Swiss chard
- 1   teaspoon salt
- 1   recipe Garlic Yogurt French Dressing, page 87
- 1   tablespoon finely chopped parsley or fresh mint

Trim the stem ends of the chard. Cut off the stems and slice crosswise, then slice the leaves. Cook the stems 4 minutes in about 1/4 inch water to which the salt has been added. Add the leaves and cook 4 minutes or until just tender. Drain, pressing out the excess water.

In a mixing bowl combine the chard with the dressing and parsley or mint and mix well. Taste and adjust the seasoning. Transfer to a serving dish. Cover and chill before serving.

JAJIK
(Cucumber and Yogurt Salad)

Middle Easterners are notably fond of this classic summer salad, which is encountered in many variations throughout the region.

SERVES 4

- 2   cups unflavored yogurt
- 1   medium garlic clove
- 1/4 teaspoon salt
- 2   tablespoons finely chopped fresh mint, or 1 teaspoon crushed dried mint
       Salt and ground white pepper (preferably freshly ground) to taste
- 2   medium cucumbers, peeled, seeded, and diced
       Mint sprigs (optional)

Spoon the yogurt into a mixing bowl. Mash the garlic with the salt to a smooth paste. Mix with a few tablespoons of the yogurt, then add the mixture to the remaining yogurt in the bowl. Add the mint and salt and pepper. Blend well. Add the cucumbers and toss lightly but thoroughly. Taste and adjust the seasoning. Transfer to a serving dish, cover, and chill. Serve garnished with the mint sprigs, if desired.

VARIATION   Omit the garlic. Substitute 1 tablespoon minced fresh dill for the mint and add 3 minced scallions (include 2 inches of the green tops) with the cucumbers.

RAITA

This cool, fresh-tasting Indian salad provides an ideal counterpoint to the spicy curries it tradition- ally accompanies. It is sometimes prepared with just one vegetable, and the amounts suggested for each vegetable here can be varied according to personal preference.

SERVES 4

1-1/2 cups unflavored yogurt
1/3   cup peeled, seeded, and finely chopped cucumber
1/3   cup peeled and finely chopped radishes
1/3   cup seeded, deribbed, and finely chopped green pepper
1/3   cup peeled, seeded, and finely chopped tomato or beet
3   scallions, finely chopped, including 2 inches of the green tops
1/8   teaspoon ground cumin or to taste
      Salt to taste

Combine the yogurt and vegetables in a mixing bowl. Add the cumin and salt and mix lightly but thoroughly. Taste and adjust the seasoning. Transfer into a serving dish. Cover and chill.

ASPARAGUS AND EGG SALAD

One of the great gifts of spring is fresh asparagus, and here is a splendid recipe from the Caucasus to celebrate its arrival.

SERVES 4

1-1/2 pounds fresh asparagus
2   hard-cooked eggs, chopped
1   recipe Garlic Yogurt Sauce, page 85
      Salad greens
1   tablespoon finely chopped parsley

Snap off the tough lower parts of the asparagus stalks. Tie the asparagus in bundles and drop them into a large saucepan of rapidly boiling salted water. Boil, uncovered, about 12 minutes or until just tender. Drain. Plunge into cold water, drain thoroughly, and cool. Cut into 1-1/2-inch pieces.

Combine the cooled asparagus, eggs, and garlic yogurt sauce in a mixing bowl. Toss gen- tly but thoroughly. Taste and adjust the season- ing. Transfer to a serving dish lined with the salad greens. Cover and chill. Serve sprinkled with the parsley.

COLE SLAW

SERVES 6

1   small head green cabbage
1   tablespoon finely chopped fresh dill
2   tablespoons finely chopped fresh mint
3   tablespoons olive oil
1   tablespoon freshly squeezed and strained
    lemon juice or white wine vinegar
1   medium garlic clove, crushed (optional)
    Salt to taste
1/3 cup or more unflavored yogurt

Remove the outer leaves and hard core from the cabbage and discard. Shred the cabbage finely. In a salad bowl combine the shredded cabbage, dill, and 1 tablespoon of the mint. Beat together the oil, lemon juice or vinegar, garlic (if desired), and salt with a fork or whisk until well blended and pour over the cabbage mixture. Toss lightly but thoroughly. Cover and chill. Close to serving time, fold in the yogurt until well blended. Taste and adjust the seasoning. Sprinkle with the remaining 1 tablespoon mint and serve.

VEGETABLE COLE SLAW VARIATION   Use 2 cups shredded cabbage, 1/2 cup chopped green pepper, 1/2 cup chopped radishes, 1/2 cup chopped carrot, and 1/4 cup minced mild onion. Omit the garlic.

BEET SALAD

Beets harmonize perfectly with yogurt, as in the following Middle Eastern salad.

SERVES 4 TO 6

1   pound beets, cooked and peeled
1   small mild white onion, or
    2 scallions, finely chopped (include
    2 inches of the green tops of the scallions)
1   recipe Yogurt French Dressing, page 87
2   tablespoons finely chopped parsley

Slice 2 of the beets and reserve. Dice the remaining beets. In a mixing bowl combine the diced beets, onion, and yogurt French dressing. Toss gently but thoroughly. Taste and adjust the seasoning. Transfer to a serving dish, cover, and chill. Serve bordered with the reserved sliced beets and sprinkled with the parsley.

VARIATION   Omit the onion and substitute Garlic Yogurt French Dressing, page 87, for the above dressing. One tablespoon finely chopped fresh mint or dill may replace the parsley.

MUSHROOM AND
GREEN PEPPER SALAD

*An excellent salad to serve with charcoal broiled
steak, lamb, or fish.*

SERVES 6

6	green peppers, or 3 green peppers and 3 red peppers
8	ounces mushrooms
1	recipe Garlic Yogurt French Dressing, page 87
2	tablespoons finely chopped parsley
1/8	teaspoon crushed dried thyme or oregano (optional)
	Salad greens
	Pimiento strips
2	hard-cooked eggs, quartered

Broil the peppers over an open fire (or place
them on a baking sheet and broil in the oven)
until the skins char and blister, turning the peppers so they color evenly on all sides. When they
are ready, peel off the charred skins and cut off
the stems. Cut the peppers in half. Remove and
discard the white membranes and seeds. Cut
the peppers into strips and place in a mixing
bowl.

Wipe the mushrooms with damp paper towels. Remove the stems and reserve for another
use. Slice the mushroom caps thinly and combine with the peppers. Add the garlic yogurt
French dressing, parsley, and thyme or oregano,
if desired, and toss gently but thoroughly. Taste
and adjust the seasoning. Transfer to a serving
dish lined with the salad greens. Cover and
chill. Serve garnished with the pimiento strips
and quartered eggs.

CAUCASIAN
POTATO SALAD

SERVES 4

2	medium boiling potatoes
2	hard-cooked eggs, coarsely chopped
1	medium cucumber, peeled, seeded (if seeds are large), and diced
1	medium tomato, seeded and diced
2	tablespoons finely chopped scallions, including 2 inches of the green tops
2	tablespoons finely chopped parsley
2	tablespoons finely chopped fresh dill
	Salt and ground white pepper (preferably freshly ground) to taste
1/2	cup each unflavored yogurt and sour cream, or 1 cup Yogurt Mayonnaise, page 88
	Salad greens
	Tomato slices
	Green pepper rings

Cook the potatoes in boiling salted water until
just tender. Drain. Peel when cool enough to
handle. Cube and place in a mixing bowl. Add
the eggs, cucumber, diced tomato, scallions,
1 tablespoon of the parsley, 1 tablespoon of the
dill, and salt and pepper. Add the yogurt and
sour cream or yogurt mayonnaise and toss gently but thoroughly. Taste and adjust the seasoning. Transfer to a serving dish lined with the
salad greens. Cover and chill. Serve sprinkled
with the remaining 1 tablespoon each parsley
and fresh dill and garnished with the tomato
slices and green pepper rings.

VEGETABLE SALAD WITH YOGURT

Yogurt blends superbly with the Mexican-style seasonings of this unusual salad. An ideal accompaniment to barbecued meats.

SERVES 4

2	medium potatoes, boiled in jackets
3	small zucchini, cooked and sliced
1/2	head small cauliflower, cooked and separated into florets
4	ounces green peas, shelled and cooked
1	recipe Yogurt French Dressing, page 87
1	medium garlic clove, crushed
1	teaspoon crushed dried oregano or to taste
1	teaspoon chili powder or to taste
	Dash ground cumin
	Lettuce leaves
1	tablespoon finely chopped scallion, including some of the green top

Peel and cube the potatoes while still warm. In a mixing bowl combine the potatoes, zucchini, cauliflower, and peas. In a small bowl mix together the yogurt French dressing, garlic, oregano, chili powder, and cumin. Blend well. Pour over the vegetables and mix gently but thoroughly. Taste and adjust the seasoning. Transfer to a serving dish lined with the lettuce. Sprinkle with the chopped scallion and serve.

NORTH AFRICAN LENTIL SALAD

An earthy and nourishing salad given excitement by a tart dressing flavored with garlic, cumin, and oregano.

SERVES 4

1	quart water
2	teaspoons salt
1	cup lentils
1/4	cup finely chopped red onion
1/4	cup diced green pepper
1/3	cup diced celery
1/3	cup seeded (if seeds are large) and diced cucumber
1/4	cup peeled, seeded, and finely chopped tomato
1/2	cup sliced pitted black olives
3	tablespoons finely chopped parsley
1/4	cup olive oil
1/4	cup freshly squeezed and strained lemon juice
1	medium garlic clove, crushed
1/2	teaspoon ground cumin
1/2	teaspoon crushed dried oregano
	Salt and freshly ground black pepper to taste
1	cup unflavored yogurt
	Romaine or leaf lettuce leaves
2	hard-cooked eggs, quartered
	Radish roses

In a heavy saucepan bring the water and 2 teaspoons salt to a boil over high heat. Add the lentils, reduce the heat to low, partially cover, and simmer about 30 minutes or until the lentils are just tender. Do not overcook. Drain thoroughly and place in a mixing bowl. Add the onion, green pepper, celery, cucumber, tomato, olives, and 2 tablespoons of the parsley. Beat together the oil, lemon juice, garlic, cumin, oregano, and salt and pepper with a fork or whisk until well blended. Pour over the salad and toss gently but thoroughly. Taste and adjust the seasoning. Cover and chill.

Shortly before serving, fold in the yogurt until well blended. Taste again for seasoning. Transfer to a serving dish lined with the lettuce leaves. Sprinkle with the remaining 1 tablespoon parsley, garnish with the eggs and radish roses, and serve.

PROVENÇAL LENTIL SALAD VARIATION
Substitute 2 teaspoons minced fresh basil (or 1/2 teaspoon crushed dried basil) for the cumin. One-half cup each lentils and beans (kidney, mung, or other beans), cooked separately, may be substituted for the lentils.

SPANISH VEGETABLE AND SEAFOOD SALAD

SERVES 6

2 medium potatoes, boiled in jackets
1 cup cooked green beans, cut into
1-1/2-inch lengths
1 cup cooked green peas
1 cup cooked asparagus tips, cut into
1-1/2-inch lengths
1 cup cooked cauliflower florets
1-1/2 cups diced cooked lobster meat
1-1/2 cups diced cooked shrimp
1/2 cup finely diced lean cooked ham
1 small mild onion, finely chopped
1/4 cup finely chopped parsley
1 tablespoon wine vinegar
1 tablespoon freshly squeezed and strained
lemon juice
1 recipe Yogurt Mayonnaise, page 88
Lettuce leaves
1 8-ounce jar sliced pickled beets,
drained well
3 hard-cooked eggs, sliced
Pimiento strips
Pimiento-stuffed olives, sliced

Peel and cube the potatoes while still warm.
In a large mixing bowl combine the potatoes,
green beans, peas, asparagus, cauliflower, lobster, shrimp, ham, onion, and parsley. Mix together the vinegar and lemon juice and sprinkle
over the above ingredients. Add the yogurt
mayonnaise and toss gently but thoroughly.
Taste and adjust the seasoning. Transfer to a
serving platter lined with the lettuce leaves.
Arrange the sliced beets around the salad, alternating them with the sliced eggs. Garnish the
top with the pimiento strips and olives. Cover
and chill before serving.

SWISS SALAD

SERVES 4

2 Belgian endives, trimmed and cut
lengthwise into strips
2 medium potatoes, cooked, peeled, and
diced
2 medium tart apples, peeled, cored, and
diced
1 cup julienne-cut lean cooked ham
12 shrimp, cooked, shelled, deveined, and
finely chopped
1 recipe Yogurt French Dressing, page 87
2 tablespoons finely chopped shallots or
scallions (include 2 inches of the green
tops of the scallions)
1 teaspoon Dijon-style mustard
Salt and ground white pepper (preferably
freshly ground) to taste
2 hard-cooked eggs, quartered
2 tablespoons finely chopped parsley

In a salad bowl combine the endives, potatoes,
apples, ham, and shrimp. Beat together the
yogurt French dressing, shallots, and mustard
until well blended. Pour over the salad.
Sprinkle with the salt and pepper. Toss gently
but thoroughly. Taste and adjust the seasoning.
Serve garnished with the quartered eggs and
parsley.

APPLE, CARROT, AND BEET SALAD

This is adapted from a Finnish recipe and, like the original, can be served as an appetizer or as a side dish to a main course featuring lamb, beef, or veal.

SERVES 4

- 1 cup peeled and finely diced crisp tart apple
- 1 cup peeled and finely diced carrots
- 1 cup peeled and finely diced cooked beets
- 2 scallions, finely chopped, including 2 inches of the green tops
- 4 tablespoons finely chopped parsley or fresh dill
- 3 tablespoons olive oil
- 1 tablespoon freshly squeezed and strained lemon juice or to taste
  Salt to taste
- 1/2 cup unflavored yogurt
  Lettuce leaves

In a mixing bowl combine the apple, carrots, beets, scallions, and 3 tablespoons of the parsley or dill. Mix together the oil, lemon juice, and salt and pour over the salad. Toss gently but thoroughly. Taste and adjust the seasoning. Fold in the yogurt until well blended. Taste again for seasoning. Transfer to a serving dish lined with the lettuce leaves. Cover and refrigerate 1 hour. Serve sprinkled with the remaining 1 tablespoon chopped parsley or dill.

APPLE, BEET, AND PINEAPPLE SALAD

It is surprising that a Russian salad would include pineapple, but the following combination is indeed derived from an authentic Russian recipe.

SERVES 4

- 1 cup diced fresh pineapple
- 1 cup peeled and diced cooked beets
- 1 cup peeled and diced crisp tart apple
- 2 scallions, finely chopped, including 2 inches of the green tops
- 2 tablespoons olive oil
- 1 tablespoon wine vinegar
  Salt to taste
- 1/2 cup unflavored yogurt
  Lettuce leaves
- 1 tablespoon finely chopped parsley or fresh mint

In a mixing bowl combine the pineapple, beets, apple, and scallions. Sprinkle with the oil, vinegar, and salt and toss gently but thoroughly. Taste and adjust the seasoning. Fold in the yogurt until well blended. Taste again for seasoning. Transfer to a serving dish lined with the lettuce leaves. Cover and chill. Sprinkle with the parsley or mint and serve with ham, pork, or poultry.

GREEN PASTA SALAD

The incomparable fragrance of basil permeates this Italian-inspired salad.

SERVES 6

12	ounces small shell or elbow macaroni
1/4	cup olive oil
1/2	bunch parsley, washed, drained, and stemmed
1/2	cup fresh basil leaves
1	large garlic clove, crushed
1	recipe Yogurt Mayonnaise, page 88
3	scallions, sliced, including 2 inches of the green tops
	Salt and freshly ground black pepper to taste
2	hard-cooked eggs, quartered
1	tablespoon finely chopped chives

Cook the pasta as directed on the package. Drain well and set aside to cool. Put the oil, parsley, basil, and garlic in the container of an electric blender. Cover and blend to a paste. Add the yogurt mayonnaise, scallions, and salt and pepper. Cover and blend into a pale green creamy sauce. Place the cooled pasta in a salad bowl. Add the green sauce and toss gently but thoroughly. Taste and adjust the seasoning. Cover and refrigerate several hours or overnight. Serve garnished with the eggs and sprinkled with the chives.

WILD RICE SALAD WITH MUSHROOMS

SERVES 4

2	tablespoons olive oil
8	ounces mushrooms, sliced
2	tablespoons freshly squeezed and strained lemon juice or to taste
2	cups cold cooked wild rice or long-grain white rice, or
	1 cup each wild rice and white rice
2	hard-cooked eggs, coarsely chopped
3	scallions, finely chopped, including 2 inches of the green tops
3/4	cup Yogurt Mayonnaise, page 88
1	large garlic clove, crushed
3/4	teaspoon Dijon-style mustard
	Salt and freshly ground black pepper to taste
	Romaine or leaf lettuce leaves
8	ounces cooked shrimp, shelled and deveined
8	cherry tomatoes
1	tablespoon finely chopped parsley

In a heavy skillet heat the oil over moderate heat. Add the mushrooms and lemon juice and sauté until the mushrooms are lightly browned, stirring frequently. Remove from the heat and cool. In a mixing bowl combine the rice, mushrooms, eggs, and scallions. Mix together the yogurt mayonnaise, garlic, mustard, and salt and pepper and pour over the salad. Toss gently but thoroughly. Taste and adjust the seasoning. Transfer to a serving dish lined with the lettuce leaves. Garnish with the shrimp and cherry tomatoes. Sprinkle with the parsley and serve.

NOTE   Cooked sliced ham, crab, or lobster tails may be substituted for the shrimp.

POLYNESIAN RICE SALAD WITH PINEAPPLE

For a festive touch serve this salad in a pineapple shell.

SERVES 4

1-1/2   cups cold cooked long-grain white rice or brown rice
1-1/2   cups shredded fresh pineapple
1   cup chopped lean cooked ham or shrimp
3/4   cup finely sliced celery
3   scallions, finely chopped, including 2 inches of the green tops
1/4   cup olive oil
3   tablespoons freshly squeezed and strained lemon or lime juice or to taste
        Salt and freshly ground black pepper to taste
3/4   cup unflavored yogurt
1/4   teaspoon curry powder or to taste
        Lettuce leaves
1/3   cup chopped macadamia nuts or toasted shredded coconut

In a mixing bowl combine the rice, pineapple, ham or shrimp, celery, and scallions. Beat together the oil, lemon juice, and salt and pepper with a fork or whisk until well blended and pour over the rice mixture. Toss gently but thoroughly. Taste and adjust the seasoning. Cover and chill. Close to serving time, fold in the yogurt, which has been mixed with the curry powder. Taste again for seasoning. Transfer to a serving dish lined with the lettuce leaves. Garnish with the macadamia nuts or coconut and serve.

LOBSTER, GRAPEFRUIT, AND AVOCADO SALAD PLATTER

SERVES 4

2   pink grapefruits
1   large avocado
        Juice of 1 lemon, freshly squeezed and strained
        Salad greens
1   pound cooked lobster meat
        Pitted black olives
        Pomegranate seeds (optional)
1   recipe Yogurt Mayonnaise or Avocado Yogurt Mayonnaise, page 88

Peel, seed, and section the grapefruits (remove the white membrane). Halve, peel, pit, and slice the avocado, and dip the slices into the lemon juice. Line a large serving platter with the salad greens. Place the lobster meat in the center of the platter. Surround with the grapefruit sections and avocado slices. Garnish with the olives and pomegranate seeds, if desired. Serve with the mayonnaise.

HAWAIIAN CRAB AND FRUIT SALAD PLATTER

SERVES 6

1 small pineapple
1 large avocado
  Juice of 1 lemon, freshly squeezed and strained
1 large papaya
  Romaine or leaf lettuce leaves
1 pound cooked crab meat
  Lime slices
1 cup macadamia nuts
1 recipe Hawaiian Dressing, page 87, or Avocado Yogurt Mayonnaise, page 88 (omit scallions or garlic)

Peel the pineapple, remove the eyes, and slice into 1/2-inch-thick rounds. Cut out the core and cut each slice in half. Halve, peel, pit, and slice the avocado, and dip the slices into the lemon juice. Peel and halve the papaya. Remove the seeds, then slice the flesh. Line a large serving platter or a tray with the romaine or leaf lettuce leaves. Arrange on them in an attractive pattern rows of crab meat and pineapple, avocado, and papaya slices. Garnish with the lime slices. Serve accompanied with a bowl of the macadamia nuts and a bowl of the yogurt dressing or mayonnaise.

SCANDINAVIAN MEAT SALAD

Although this salad is traditionally made with sour cream, it tastes equally good made with yogurt (without the additional calories!).

SERVES 6

1-1/2 cups julienne-cut lean boiled or braised lamb
1-1/2 cups julienne-cut lean cooked ham
2 cups julienne-cut cooked potatoes
1 medium crisp tart apple, peeled, cored, and cut in julienne
1 small mild onion, finely chopped
2 pickled gherkins, diced (optional)
3 tablespoons finely chopped parsley or to taste
1 recipe Yogurt French Dressing, page 87
  Lettuce leaves
3 hard-cooked eggs, quartered
1 16-ounce jar sliced pickled beets, drained well

In a mixing bowl combine the lamb, ham, potatoes, apple, onion, gherkins (if desired), and 2 tablespoons of the parsley. Add the yogurt French dressing and toss gently but thoroughly. Taste and adjust the seasoning. Transfer to a serving dish lined with the lettuce leaves. Sprinkle with the remaining 1 tablespoon parsley. Garnish with the quartered eggs and surround with the sliced beets. Cover and chill before serving.

MOLDED AVOCADO CREAM

This recipe is based on the renowned guacamole *of Mexico.*

SERVES 6

1	envelope (1 tablespoon) unflavored gelatin
1/4	cup cold water
1	cup unflavored yogurt
2	large avocados, peeled, pitted, and mashed
1	large tomato, peeled, seeded, and finely chopped
1/4	cup very finely chopped mild white onion
1	very small garlic clove, crushed to a smooth purée
2	teaspoons olive oil
2	tablespoons freshly squeezed and strained lime or lemon juice or to taste
1	teaspoon chili powder
	Salt to taste
1	pound shrimp, cooked, shelled, and deveined
	Salad greens
	Cherry tomatoes
	Pitted black olives
	Lime or lemon slices

In a saucepan soften the gelatin in the water. Stir over low heat until the gelatin is dissolved. Remove from the heat. Add the yogurt, avocados, tomato, onion, garlic, oil, lime juice, chili powder, and salt. Mix thoroughly. Taste and adjust the seasoning. Turn into a rinsed and chilled 3-1/2-cup ring mold. Cover with aluminum foil and chill at least 4 hours or until set.

To unmold, have ready a chilled round platter large enough to allow for the garnish. Run the pointed tip of a knife around the edges of the mold to release it. Dip the mold up to the rim into a basin of hot water for just a few seconds. Place the platter upside down over the mold. Hold the platter and mold together and invert. Shake gently to release the avocado cream. If it does not release, repeat the process. Carefully lift off the mold and refrigerate the avocado cream.

Shortly before serving, fill the center of the ring with the shrimp. Garnish the sides with the salad greens, cherry tomatoes, olives, and lime or lemon slices.

SALMON MOUSSE

For an elegant presentation of this mousse, use a fish-shaped mold. An electric blender will give superior results.

SERVES 4

- 1   envelope (1 tablespoon) unflavored gelatin
- 1/4   cup cold water
- 1/2   cup boiling water
- 1/2   cup mayonnaise (preferably homemade)
- 1-1/2   tablespoons grated mild onion
- 1   tablespoon freshly squeezed and strained lemon juice
- 1/4   teaspoon Tabasco sauce or to taste
- 3/4   teaspoon salt or to taste
- 1   16-ounce can salmon, drained, picked over, and very finely chopped
- 1   tablespoon finely chopped fresh dill
- 3/4   cup unflavored yogurt
-    Watercress
-    Lemon slices
- 1   recipe Cucumber Yogurt Sauce, page 86

In a mixing bowl soften the gelatin in the cold water. Add the boiling water and stir to dissolve the gelatin. Add the mayonnaise, onion, lemon juice, Tabasco sauce, and salt and mix well. Cover and chill until partially set. Add the salmon and dill and beat until thoroughly blended and smooth. This can be done very quickly and easily in an electric blender; in fact, the result will be smoother than beating by hand. Add the yogurt and mix well. Taste and adjust the seasoning. Turn into a rinsed and chilled 4-cup fish mold or other mold. Cover with aluminum foil and chill until set. Unmold as directed in the recipe for Molded Avocado Cream, preceding, and garnish with the watercress and lemon slices. Serve with the cucumber yogurt sauce.

Eggs

HERB OMELET

Here is an adaptation of an Italian omelet.

SERVES 1

3	eggs
3	tablespoons unflavored yogurt
1	tablespoon finely chopped parsley
1	tablespoon finely chopped chives
1/2	teaspoon finely chopped fresh basil, or 1/4 teaspoon crushed dried basil
1/4	teaspoon finely chopped fresh rosemary, or 1/8 teaspoon crushed dried rosemary
	Salt and freshly ground black pepper to taste
1	tablespoon butter
1	sprig parsley

In a mixing bowl beat the eggs with a fork or whisk. Add the yogurt, parsley, chives, basil, rosemary, and salt and pepper and mix well. In a small skillet melt the butter over high heat and swirl it around in the pan. Pour in the egg mixture and reduce the heat to moderate. Run a thin spatula under the egg mixture as soon as it begins to set and lift to allow the uncooked portion to flow underneath. When the mixture is set, fold it over. Transfer to a heated plate and serve at once, garnished with the parsley sprig.

PIZZA OMELET

A variation on a familiar theme.

SERVES 4

8	eggs
1/2	cup unflavored yogurt
	Salt and freshly ground black pepper to taste
	Tabasco sauce to taste
2	tablespoons butter
1/2	cup shredded Swiss cheese
1/2	cup freshly grated Parmesan cheese
1	teaspoon crushed dried oregano
4	thin slices tomato
4	thin slices Italian salami
4	anchovy fillets (optional)
1/4	cup thinly sliced scallions, including 2 inches of the green tops

In a large mixing bowl beat together the eggs, yogurt, salt and pepper, and Tabasco sauce with a wire whisk until well blended. In a large, heavy ovenproof skillet melt the butter over high heat. When the butter begins to foam, pour in the egg mixture. Reduce the heat to medium-low, cover, and cook about 10 minutes or until the edges of the omelet begin to get firm. Uncover and run a spatula around the edges of the omelet to keep it from sticking to the pan. Cover and cook about 10 minutes or until the center of the omelet is firm. Remove from the heat. Sprinkle the Swiss and Parmesan cheeses evenly over the omelet, then sprinkle the oregano evenly over the cheeses. Broil just until the cheese is melted. Arrange the tomato, salami, and anchovy fillets (if desired) over the top of the omelet. Sprinkle with the scallions. Serve at once, cut into wedges.

PERSIAN VEGETABLE AND HERB OMELET

One of Iran's national dishes, traditionally served on New Year's Day.

SERVES 4

6	eggs
1/2	cup finely chopped spinach leaves or romaine lettuce
1/4	cup finely chopped leek (include some of the green top)
1/4	cup finely chopped scallions (include some of the green tops)
1	cup finely chopped parsley
1/4	cup finely chopped fresh dill
1/4	cup finely chopped fresh mint
2	tablespoons finely chopped fresh coriander
2	tablespoons chopped walnuts
2	tablespoons dried currants
	Pinch saffron or ground turmeric (optional)
	Salt and freshly ground black pepper to taste
2	tablespoons butter
1	cup unflavored yogurt

In a large bowl beat the eggs well. Add the remaining ingredients except the butter and yogurt and mix well.

Melt the butter in an ovenproof dish and pour in the egg mixture. Bake, covered, in a preheated 350°F oven 30 minutes. Uncover and bake 15 to 25 minutes or until the eggs are set and the top forms a golden crust. Serve hot or chilled as an appetizer or side dish, accompanied with the yogurt.

APPLE OMELET

SERVES 2 OR 3

2	tablespoons butter
2	apples (preferably Golden Delicious), peeled, cored, and sliced
1	tablespoon light brown sugar
1	teaspoon ground cinnamon
4	eggs
	Salt to taste
1/2	cup unflavored yogurt

In a heavy 10-inch skillet heat 1 tablespoon of the butter over moderate heat. Add the apple slices, sprinkle with the sugar and cinnamon, and sauté until golden brown and glazed, turning frequently. Transfer to a bowl, gently stir in the yogurt, and set aside. Clean the skillet.

Using a fork or whisk, beat the eggs and salt in a mixing bowl until blended. Add the remaining 1 tablespoon butter to the skillet and place the skillet over medium-high heat. When the butter is hot but not burning, pour in the beaten eggs. Run a thin spatula under the eggs as soon as they begin to set and lift to allow the uncooked portion to flow underneath. When the eggs are almost set, spoon the apple and yogurt mixture into the center of the omelet. Carefully fold the omelet in half. Transfer to a heated plate and serve at once.

CZECHOSLOVAKIAN OMELET WITH CRANBERRIES

Cranberries impart a delightful sweetsour piquancy to this unusual omelet.

SERVES 3 OR 4

1	cup cranberries, picked over and washed
1	tablespoon cold water
7	tablespoons sugar
	Ground cinnamon to taste (optional)
4	eggs, separated
1/2	teaspoon salt
2	tablespoon butter
1	recipe Yogurt Crème Chantilly, page 98

In a small enameled or stainless steel saucepan combine the cranberries, water, and 6 table-spoons of the sugar. Bring to a boil over moderate heat, stirring constantly to dissolve the sugar. Reduce the heat to low, cover, and simmer 10 minutes. Sprinkle with the cinnamon, if desired, remove from the heat, and keep warm.

In a mixing bowl beat the egg whites and the salt until they are stiff but not dry. In another bowl beat the egg yolks and the remaining 1 tablespoon sugar thoroughly. Fold the yolk mixture carefully into the beaten whites.

In a heavy 10-inch skillet melt the butter over medium-high heat. When the butter is hot but not burning, add the egg mixture. Flatten the top with a large spatula and cook until the underside is lightly browned. Turn it over with the spatula and cook until lightly browned on the other side and cooked through. Transfer the omelet to a heated serving platter. Spoon the cooked cranberries onto the center of the omelet. Top with the yogurt crème Chantilly and serve at once, cut into wedges.

FLAMING CRANBERRY OMELET VARIATION
Prepare the Czechoslovakian Omelet, preceding. When the omelet is browned on both sides and cooked through, combine the cooked cranberries and yogurt crème Chantilly and spoon into the middle of the omelet. Fold the omelet in half and transfer to a heated platter. Dust the top with 1 teaspoon sifted confectioners' sugar. At table ignite 2 tablespoons heated cranberry or orange liqueur and spoon flaming over the omelet.

BALKAN EGGS WITH SPINACH

SERVES 4

2	pounds spinach
4	tablespoons butter
1	medium onion, finely chopped
	Salt and freshly ground black pepper to taste
6	eggs
1/4	cup freshly grated kasseri or Parmesan cheese (optional)
1	recipe Garlic Yogurt Sauce, page 85

Wash the spinach leaves thoroughly under cold running water, discarding the tough stems and bruised leaves. Drain but do not dry. Place the wet spinach leaves in a saucepan, cover, and cook over moderate heat until tender, stirring twice. Drain and chop coarsely.

In a heavy skillet with an ovenproof handle melt the butter over moderate heat. Add the onion and sauté until golden brown, stirring frequently. Add the spinach and salt and pepper and mix well. Beat the eggs well and pour over the vegetables. Poke holes in several places to allow the eggs to penetrate downward. Sprinkle the top evenly with the grated cheese, if desired. Bake in a preheated 450°F oven about 10 minutes or until the eggs are just firm. Serve with the garlic yogurt sauce.

GROUND MEAT AND GREEN BEANS WITH EGGS

Tradition and imagination have provided the cuisines of the Caucasus with an impressive range of enticing egg preparations. The recipe below makes a substantial main course.

SERVES 2 TO 4

8   ounces green beans, trimmed and halved
2   tablespoons butter
1   medium onion, finely chopped
8   ounces lean ground lamb or beef
1/4 cup finely chopped fresh dill
    Salt and freshly ground black pepper
    to taste
4   eggs
    Pinch salt
1   cup unflavored yogurt or Garlic Yogurt
    Sauce, page 85

Drop the beans into lightly salted boiling water and bring back to a boil. Reduce the heat and cook, uncovered, about 10 minutes or until the beans are tender but still somewhat firm, not mushy. Drain and keep warm. In a heavy skillet with an ovenproof handle melt the butter over moderate heat. Add the onion and sauté until soft but not browned, stirring frequently. Add the meat and cook until browned, breaking it up with a fork. Stir in the beans, dill, and salt and pepper and cook a few minutes. Beat the eggs with a pinch of salt. Pour over the contents of the skillet and mix well. Bake in a preheated 450°F oven about 10 minutes or until the eggs are firm. Serve at once, accompanied with the yogurt or garlic yogurt sauce.

HUNGARIAN EGGS WITH HAM AND CHEESE

Leftover ham in exalted form.

SERVES 6

6   eggs
1/4 teaspoon salt
1/2 cup unflavored yogurt
1   cup finely chopped lean cooked ham
1/2 cup grated Gruyère or Swiss cheese
2   tablespoons finely chopped chives or
    scallions (include 2 inches of the green
    tops of the scallions)
2   tablespoons finely chopped parsley, or
    1 tablespoon each finely chopped parsley
    and fresh dill
2   tablespoons butter, melted
1/4 cup finely chopped hazelnuts or blanched
    almonds
    Paprika

In a large bowl beat the eggs with the salt. Beat in the yogurt. Add the ham, cheese, chives, parsley, butter, and 2 tablespoons of the hazelnuts or almonds and mix well. Pour into a buttered 9-inch-square pan. Sprinkle evenly with the remaining nuts and the paprika. Bake in a preheated 350°F oven about 25 minutes or until set. Cut into small squares. Serve hot as an appetizer.

SHRIMP AND CHEESE CASSEROLE

This is an appetizing brunch dish served with a crisp salad and a chilled white wine.

SERVES 4

6	slices French bread, crusts removed
4	tablespoons butter, melted
4	ounces small cooked shrimp
1	cup grated Gruyère cheese
2	tablespoons finely chopped chives
2	tablespoons finely chopped parsley
3	eggs
1	cup milk
1/2	cup unflavored yogurt
1/2	teaspoon Dijon-style mustard
1/2	teaspoon salt or to taste

Cut each slice of bread in half diagonally. Brush on both sides with the butter. Arrange half of the bread in an 8-inch-square baking dish. Scatter half the shrimp over the bread. Sprinkle with half each of the cheese, chives, and parsley. Cover, making layers, with the remaining bread, shrimp, cheese, chives, and parsley. Beat the eggs until frothy. Add the milk, yogurt, mustard, and salt and blend thoroughly. Pour the egg mixture over the layers. Cover and chill several hours or overnight. Bake in a preheated 350°F oven about 35 minutes or until lightly browned and puffy. Serve at once.

MADRAS-STYLE EGG CURRY

Serve this with rice and curry condiments such as chopped peanuts, raisins or currants, grated coconut, chopped mild onion, and chutney.

SERVES 4

3	tablespoons butter
1	small onion, finely chopped
1	small garlic clove, finely chopped
2	teaspoons curry powder or to taste
1	teaspoon tomato paste
1	cup unflavored yogurt
1	teaspoon freshly squeezed and strained lemon or lime juice or to taste
	Salt to taste
6	hard-cooked eggs, cut in halves lengthwise
1	tablespoon chopped fresh coriander or parsley (optional)

In a heavy skillet melt the butter over moderate heat. Add the onion and garlic and sauté 5 minutes, stirring frequently. Blend in the curry powder and tomato paste, reduce the heat to low, and cook, stirring, 1 minute. Stir in the yogurt, lemon juice, and salt. Add the eggs and cook gently until heated through. Garnish with the coriander or parsley, if desired.

SPINACH-CHEESE SOUFFLÉ ROLL

An elegant Viennese specialty that, once tasted, is unlikely to be forgotten. Yogurt is a refreshing alternative to the sour cream used in the traditional recipe.

SERVES 8

Filling

1	pound spinach
1/3	cup cold water
2	tablespoons butter
4	scallions, finely chopped, including 2 inches of the green tops
	Salt and ground white pepper (preferably freshly ground) to taste
6	ounces cream cheese, at room temperature
3/4	cup unflavored yogurt
2	tablespoons finely chopped fresh dill
1	large garlic clove, crushed
1/4	cup freshly grated Parmesan cheese

Soufflé

4	tablespoons butter
6	tablespoons all-purpose flour
2	cups warm milk
4	eggs, separated
	Salt and ground white pepper (preferably freshly ground) to taste
	Watercress sprigs and cherry tomatoes for garnish

TO PREPARE THE FILLING   Wash the spinach thoroughly under cold running water, discarding the stems and bruised leaves. Drain. Chop the spinach and combine with the water in a large saucepan. Bring to a boil over high heat. Reduce the heat to low, cover, and simmer 5 minutes or until the spinach is wilted. Transfer to a colander and allow the spinach to drain and cool. Squeeze it dry and chop finely. Reserve.

In a small, heavy skillet melt the butter over moderate heat. Add the scallions and sauté gently until golden, stirring frequently. Add the spinach and salt and pepper and cook, stirring, 2 minutes. Remove from the heat and set aside.

In a small bowl mash the cream cheese with a fork, gradually adding the yogurt until the mixture is well blended and smooth. Add the spinach mixture, dill, garlic, and Parmesan cheese and mix thoroughly. Taste and adjust the seasoning and reserve.

TO PREPARE THE SOUFFLÉ   Butter a jelly roll pan and line it with waxed paper. Butter the paper and sprinkle with flour, shaking off the excess. Set aside.

In a heavy saucepan melt the butter over low heat. Add the flour and cook about 1 minute, stirring continuously. Remove from the heat, then gradually add the warm milk, stirring the mixture with a wire whisk until well blended and smooth. Return to the fire and cook over moderate heat, stirring constantly until the batter is very thick. Remove from the heat and stir in the egg yolks thoroughly, one at a time. Season with salt and pepper and set aside. Beat the egg whites until stiff. Fold gently but thoroughly into the batter. Spread the batter evenly into the prepared jelly roll pan. Bake in a preheated 325°F oven about 35 minutes or until the soufflé is lightly browned and firm. Turn the soufflé out onto a sheet of aluminum foil. Peel off the waxed paper. Cool about 3 minutes, then spread with the spinach mixture and roll up lengthwise in jelly roll fashion. With 2 large spatulas, transfer the roll to a rectangular serving platter. Garnish with the watercress sprigs and cherry tomatoes and serve.

Fish

GRILLED MARINATED SALMON STEAKS

SERVES 4

4	salmon steaks, each 3/4 inch thick
1/2	cup olive oil
1/4	cup freshly squeezed and strained lemon juice
3	sprigs dill
3/4	teaspoon salt
1/2	teaspoon ground white pepper (preferably freshly ground)
4	tablespoons butter, melted Lemon wedges
1	recipe Cucumber Yogurt Sauce, page 86

Arrange the salmon steaks in a shallow enameled or glass dish in one layer. In a small bowl mix together the oil, lemon juice, dill, salt, and pepper and pour over the salmon steaks. Cover and refrigerate 3 or 4 hours, turning the fish steaks once.

Drain the salmon steaks and dry them with paper towels. Arrange them in a buttered shallow baking dish just large enough to hold the fish comfortably in one layer. Brush the fish with half of the melted butter. Place the dish about 3 inches from the broiler flame and broil the steaks 5 minutes. Turn the steaks and brush the other side with the remaining melted butter. Broil about 5 minutes or until the fish flakes when tested with a fork. Do not overcook.

Transfer the salmon steaks to a heated serving platter and garnish with the lemon wedges. Serve with the cucumber yogurt sauce and, if you like, boiled parslied potatoes.

GHIVETCH
(Rumanian Fish Casserole)

In Rumania this type of ghivetch *is essentially the day's catch and part of the vegetable garden thrown into the stew pot.*

SERVES 6

1/2	cup olive oil
2	medium potatoes, peeled and cubed
1	medium eggplant, stemmed, hulled, and cubed
4	ounces young okra, trimmed of stem ends
4	ounces green beans, trimmed and cut into 1-1/2-inch lengths
1	large carrot, peeled and thinly sliced
1	medium green pepper, seeded, deribbed, and thinly sliced
1	cup shredded green cabbage (optional)
1	medium onion, cut lengthwise in half and thinly sliced
1	large garlic clove, finely chopped
2	medium ripe tomatoes, peeled, seeded, and chopped
1	bay leaf
1/4	teaspoon crushed dried thyme Salt and freshly ground black pepper to taste
2	pounds white-fleshed fish fillets, cut into serving pieces
1	tablespoon butter
1	cup unflavored yogurt, at room temperature

In a large, heavy casserole heat the oil over moderate heat. Add all the ingredients except the fish, butter, and yogurt and mix lightly. Cover and bake in a preheated 350°F oven 30 minutes. Season the fish with additional salt and pepper and arrange over the vegetables. Dot with the butter. Bake 30 minutes or until the fish and vegetables are tender. Remove the casserole from the oven and spread the yogurt on top. Bake 5 minutes. Discard the bay leaf. Serve hot or chilled.

YUGOSLAVIAN BAKED FISH

SERVES 6

1	3-pound whole white-fleshed fish, cleaned
1/3	cup olive oil
1	medium onion, thinly sliced
1	small green pepper, seeded, deribbed, and thinly sliced
2	large garlic cloves, finely chopped
1-1/2	tablespoons sweet Hungarian paprika
2	large ripe tomatoes, peeled, seeded, and finely chopped
2	tablespoons tomato paste
1/2	teaspoon crushed dried thyme
2	tablespoons finely chopped parsley Salt and freshly ground black pepper to taste
3/4	cup dry white wine or water
2	tablespoons all-purpose flour
1/2	cup unflavored yogurt, at room temperature

Wash the fish under cold running water. Drain and pat dry inside and out with paper towels. Place in an oiled shallow baking dish.

In a heavy skillet heat the oil over moderate heat. Add the onion, green pepper, and garlic and sauté until soft. Add the paprika and cook, stirring, 1 minute. Add the tomatoes and cook a few minutes, then stir in the tomato paste, thyme, parsley, salt and pepper, and wine or water. Remove from the heat and spoon the mixture evenly over the fish. Bake in a preheated 400°F oven about 30 minutes or until the fish flakes easily when tested with a fork, basting occasionally with the pan juices.

Transfer the fish to a heated serving platter and keep warm. Pour the pan juices into a small saucepan. Stir in the flour. Add the yogurt and blend well. Taste and adjust the seasoning.

Cook over low heat, stirring just until the sauce thickens and is heated through. Serve with the fish.

NORWEGIAN BAKED COD WITH MUSHROOMS

Although this dish is traditionally made with cod, the most Norwegian of all fish (and sour cream rather than yogurt), other fish can be substituted.

SERVES 6

2	pounds cod or any white-fleshed fish fillets, cut into serving pieces
1/4	cup all-purpose flour
3	teaspoons sweet Hungarian paprika Salt and freshly ground black pepper to taste
5	tablespoons butter
4	shallots or scallions, finely chopped (include 2 inches of the green tops of the scallions)
12	ounces mushrooms, sliced
2	tablespoons finely chopped fresh dill
2	tablespoons finely chopped parsley
1	cup unflavored yogurt, at room temperature
1/2	cup freshly grated Parmesan cheese Fine dry bread crumbs

Wash the fish fillets under cold running water and dry with paper towels. Roll them in the flour seasoned with 2 teaspoons of the paprika and salt and pepper. Shake off the excess flour. Set aside.

In a heavy skillet melt 4 tablespoons of the butter over moderate heat. Add the shallots or scallions and sauté until soft but not browned, stirring frequently. Add the mushrooms and sauté, stirring, until golden brown. Remove from the heat and add the dill, parsley, and additional salt and pepper. Mix well.

Arrange half the mushroom mixture in a buttered baking dish. Cover with the fish. Place the remaining mushroom mixture over the fish. Spread the yogurt over the mushrooms.

Sprinkle with the cheese and remaining 1 teaspoon paprika. Top with a thin layer of bread crumbs and dot with the remaining 1 tablespoon butter. Bake in a preheated 375°F oven about 20 minutes or until the fish flakes easily when tested with a fork. Serve immediately.

MEDITERRANEAN FISH RAGOUT

A richly seasoned, hearty one-dish meal to be eaten with thick slices of crusty fresh bread. Any white-fleshed fish or several different kinds of fish can be used.

SERVES 6

- 2 pounds white-fleshed fish fillets, cut into serving pieces
- 3 tablespoons olive oil
- 1 medium onion, cut lengthwise in half and thinly sliced
- 1 large garlic clove, finely chopped
- 2 medium tomatoes, peeled, seeded, and finely chopped
- 2 tablespoons tomato paste
- 1 cup clam juice or water
- 1 cup dry white wine
- 4 medium potatoes, peeled and thickly sliced
- 1/2 cup thinly sliced celery or green pepper
- 1/4 cup finely chopped parsley
- 1/2 teaspoon crushed dried basil
- 1/2 teaspoon crushed dried thyme or oregano
- 1 bay leaf
  Salt and freshly ground black pepper to taste
- 1 cup unflavored yogurt, at room temperature

Wash the fish under cold running water and dry with paper towels. In a large, heavy casserole heat the oil over moderate heat. Add the onion and garlic and sauté until soft, stirring frequently. Add the tomatoes, tomato paste, clam juice or water, wine, potatoes, celery or green pepper, parsley, basil, thyme or oregano,

bay leaf, and salt and pepper. Cover and simmer 15 minutes. Add the fish and simmer, covered, 20 minutes or until the fish and potatoes are tender. Remove and discard the bay leaf. Stir in the yogurt and simmer just until heated through. Taste, adjust the seasoning, and serve.

MALAYSIAN LOBSTER AND CUCUMBER CURRY

Thanks to its long coastline, Malaysia enjoys a variety of fresh fish and shellfish in contrast to the dried fish so common in much of Southeast Asia. Well-seasoned curries are an important part of Malaysian cookery. Here is an adaptation of a traditional recipe.

SERVES 4

- 4 tablespoons butter
- 1 large onion, finely chopped
- 2 medium garlic cloves, finely chopped
- 2 tablespoons blanched almonds, ground
- 1-3/4 teaspoons peeled and very finely chopped ginger root
- 1 teaspoon ground coriander
- 1/4 teaspoon ground cumin
- 1/2 teaspoon ground dried chili pepper
- 3/4 teaspoon ground turmeric
- 1-1/2 teaspoons salt or to taste
- 1 small tomato, peeled, seeded, and finely chopped
- 1 tablespoon cornstarch
- 1-1/2 cups Coconut Milk, page 150
- 1 pound cooked lobster meat, cubed
- 1 cup unflavored yogurt, at room temperature
- 1 medium cucumber, peeled, seeded (if seeds are large), and cubed
- 1 tablespoon freshly squeezed and strained lime or lemon juice

In a saucepan melt the butter over moderate heat. Add the onion and garlic and sauté until golden brown, stirring frequently. Stir in the almonds, ginger, coriander, cumin, chili pepper, turmeric, salt, and tomato. Reduce the heat to low, cover, and simmer 5 minutes. Sprinkle with the cornstarch. Gradually add the coconut milk, stirring constantly until the mixture thickens. Stir in the yogurt until well blended. Add the lobster, cover, and simmer 10 minutes. Stir in the cucumber and lime or lemon juice and simmer 5 minutes. Serve at once with rice.

SHELLFISH POLYNESIA

SERVES 4

4	tablespoons butter
4	ounces mushrooms, sliced
1	small onion, finely chopped
1	small tart apple, peeled, cored, and finely chopped
1	pound shrimp, shelled and deveined
4	ounces lobster meat, cubed
4	ounces crab meat or bay scallops
1/2	teaspoon peeled and finely chopped ginger root
	Salt and freshly ground black pepper to taste
1-1/2	cups chicken broth
3/4	cup Coconut Cream, page 150
4	teaspoons cornstarch
3	tablespoons water
1/2	cup unflavored yogurt, at room temperature
1	tablespoon freshly squeezed and strained lime juice

In a heavy skillet heat 2 tablespoons of the butter over moderate heat. Add the mushrooms and onion and sauté until soft but not browned, stirring frequently. Add the apple and cook until soft. Remove to a platter and set aside. Add the remaining 2 tablespoons butter to the skillet and heat. Add the shrimp, lobster, and crab meat or scallops and sauté, stirring, 5 minutes. Return the mushrooms, onion, and apple to the skillet. Add the ginger root and salt and pepper and mix well. Stir in the chicken broth and coconut cream. Mix the cornstarch with the water until smooth and add to the skillet,

stirring constantly until thickened. Remove from the heat and stir in the yogurt and lime juice. Serve with steamed rice.

POLYNESIAN SHRIMP CURRY IN PAPAYA SHELLS

Seafood is a cornerstone of the Polynesian cuisine. This dish is as wonderful to eat as it is to look at.

SERVES 6

4	tablespoons butter
1	small onion, finely chopped
1/4	cup seeded, deribbed, and chopped green pepper
2	medium garlic cloves, finely chopped
1	cup unflavored yogurt, at room temperature
1	teaspoon freshly squeezed and strained lemon juice
2	teaspoons curry powder
1/4	teaspoon ground ginger
	Dash chili powder
	Salt and ground white pepper (preferably freshly ground) to taste
2	pounds shrimp, cooked, cleaned, and cut in halves lengthwise
3	papayas
	Hot cooked rice

In a heavy skillet melt the butter over moderate heat. Add the onion and green pepper and sauté until soft but not browned, stirring frequently. Add the garlic and sauté a few minutes. Stir in the sour cream, yogurt, lemon juice, curry powder, ginger, chili powder, salt and pepper, and shrimp. Cook over low heat just until heated through. Taste and adjust the seasoning. Remove from the heat and keep warm.

Peel the papayas. Cut them in halves lengthwise and remove the seeds. Place a mound of rice on each of 6 individual plates and top each with a papaya half. Fill the papaya halves with the shrimp curry. Serve at once accompanied with chutney, macadamia nuts, and other curry condiments of your choice.

VARIATIONS You may broil the filled papaya halves just before serving until golden brown on top. Saffron rice may be substituted for the plain rice.

CRAB MEAT AND RICE STEW

SERVES 4

- 1   pound cooked crab meat
- 1/2 cup dry sherry
- 2   tablespoons butter
- 4   scallions, finely chopped, including 2 inches of the green tops
- 1/4 cup diced green pepper
- 1   large garlic clove, finely chopped
- 1   large tomato, peeled, seeded, and diced
- 2   cups clam juice
     Salt and freshly ground black pepper to taste
- 1   cup uncooked long-grain white rice
- 1   teaspoon finely chopped fresh rosemary, or 1/2 teaspoon crushed dried rosemary
- 1   cup unflavored yogurt, at room temperature

Combine the crab meat and sherry in a bowl. Cover and refrigerate 1 hour. In a heavy saucepan melt the butter over moderate heat. Add the scallions, green pepper, and garlic and sauté until lightly browned, stirring frequently. Add the tomato, clam juice, and salt and pepper. Bring to a boil, then add the rice and rosemary. Reduce the heat to low, cover, and simmer 20 minutes. Stir in the yogurt and the crab and sherry mixture. Cover and simmer 5 minutes. Taste and adjust the seasoning and serve.

SCALLOP CASSEROLE

SERVES 4

- 1-1/2 pounds sea or bay scallops
- 3/4 cup dry white wine
- 1   tablespoon freshly squeezed and strained lemon juice
- 6   ounces mushrooms, sliced
- 1   small green pepper, seeded, deribbed, and diced
- 3-1/2 tablespoons butter
     Salt and freshly ground black pepper to taste
- 2   tablespoons all-purpose flour
- 1/2 cup shredded Gruyère or Swiss cheese
- 1/2 cup freshly grated Parmesan cheese
- 1/2 cup unflavored yogurt, at room temperature

Wash the scallops and drain. If sea scallops are used, slice them thickly. Leave bay scallops whole. In a saucepan bring the scallops, wine, lemon juice, mushrooms, and green pepper to a boil over moderate heat. Reduce the heat, cover, and simmer 8 minutes. Drain, reserving the liquid.

In a saucepan melt 2 tablespoons of the butter. Add the salt and pepper and flour and cook gently, stirring, until well blended and bubbly. Gradually stir in the reserved scallop liquid. Cook until thickened. Add the Gruyère or Swiss cheese and 1/4 cup of the Parmesan. Cook over low heat, stirring, until well mixed. Stir in the yogurt until well blended. Remove from the heat and stir in the scallop mixture. Taste and adjust the seasoning. Turn into a buttered 1-1/2-quart casserole or divide among 4 buttered individual casseroles. Sprinkle with the remaining 1/4 cup Parmesan. Dot with the remaining 1/2 tablespoon butter. Place under a broiler until lightly browned.

Poultry

SPITTED CHICKEN WITH SOUR PLUM SAUCE

The food of the Caucasus, which encompasses the cuisines of Armenia, Azerbaijan, and Georgia, is at once earthy and sophisticated, exotic and exquisite. In this unique Georgian outdoor treat the sour plum sauce provides a delightful accent of tartness—a perfect foil for the chicken.

SERVES 4

- 2 chickens (about 2 pounds each), split in half
- 1 cup unflavored yogurt
- 2 tablespoons chopped fresh herbs (basil, mint, coriander, and dill)
  Salt and freshly ground black pepper to taste
- 1/4 pound butter, melted, or as needed
  Sour Plum Sauce, following

Dry the chickens with paper towels. Place the yogurt in a large bowl. Add the chopped herbs and salt and pepper and mix well. Add the chickens, cover, and refrigerate 4 to 5 hours, turning the pieces over from time to time.

Remove the chickens from the yogurt marinade and put on a spit. Brush with butter and grill over glowing coals about 45 minutes or until the chickens are browned all over and cooked through, turning and brushing frequently with additional butter. Remove from the spit onto a heated serving platter. Serve with the sour plum sauce.

Sour Plum Sauce

- 2 cups sour plums
- 1 garlic clove, crushed to a purée
- 2 sprigs coriander, finely chopped
- 2 sprigs basil or mint, finely chopped
- 2 sprigs dill, finely chopped (optional)
- 1/4 teaspoon salt
  Ground cayenne pepper to taste

Wash the plums. Place them in a saucepan with just enough water to barely cover. Bring to a boil over high heat. Reduce the heat and cook, covered, about 20 minutes or until the plums are very soft. Drain, reserving the liquid. Cut out and discard the plum pits. Force the plums through a sieve, then stir in enough of the reserved liquid to obtain a medium-thick sauce. (Alternatively, put the plums and a little of their liquid in the container of an electric blender and blend until the mixture attains the desired consistency.) Return the sauce to the saucepan. Stir in the remaining ingredients and bring to a boil. Remove from the heat and allow to cool. Taste and adjust the seasoning.

CHICKEN TANDOORI

In northern India this renowned dish is roasted in a special clay oven over hot coals. While the chicken cooks, the dough for nan, *a flat bread, is slapped onto the sides of the oven to bake.*

SERVES 4

- 1 3-pound chicken, quartered
- 1 cup unflavored yogurt
- 2 large garlic cloves, crushed
- 1-1/2-inch piece ginger root, peeled and grated
- 1-1/2 teaspoons ground coriander
- 3/4 teaspoon ground cumin
- 1/4 teaspoon ground cardamom or aniseed
- 1/8 teaspoon ground cayenne pepper
- 1/4 cup freshly squeezed and strained lime or lemon juice
- 1-1/2 teaspoons salt
- 4 tablespoons butter, melted
  Paper-thin rings of mild onion
  Thin slices tomato
  Lime or lemon wedges

Dry the chickens with paper towels. In a large bowl combine the yogurt, garlic, ginger, coriander, cumin, cardamom, cayenne, lime juice, and salt and mix well. Add the chicken pieces and turn to coat them thoroughly with the mixture. Cover and marinate in the refrigerator at least 12 hours, turning the chicken pieces from time to time.

Remove the chicken pieces from the marinade and arrange on a greased rack in a shallow baking pan. Roast in a preheated 400°F oven 50 to 60 minutes or until golden brown all over but still tender inside, basting occasionally with the butter. Or broil the chickens over charcoal about 30 minutes or until tender, turning and basting frequently.

Transfer onto a heated serving platter and garnish with the onion rings, tomato slices, and lime wedges. Serve at once.

CHICKEN PAPRIKA

Here is an adaptation of the celebrated Hungarian paprikás czirke *that captures the essence of the original.*

SERVES 4

- 1 3-pound chicken, cut into serving pieces
- 2 tablespoons butter
- 1 medium onion, finely chopped
- 1 medium garlic clove, finely chopped
- 1 cup chicken broth (more if needed)
- 1 teaspoon salt or to taste
- 1 to 1-1/2 tablespoons sweet Hungarian paprika
- 1 medium green pepper, seeded, deribbed, and thinly sliced
- 1 large tomato, peeled, seeded, and thinly sliced
- 2 tablespoons all-purpose flour
- 2 tablespoons water
- 3/4 cup unflavored yogurt, at room temperature

Pat the chicken pieces dry with paper towels. In a large, heavy skillet melt the butter over moderate heat. Add the onion and garlic and sauté until soft but not browned, stirring frequently. Add the chicken pieces, a few at a time, and sauté briefly until golden all over but not browned. As the pieces are done, transfer them to a plate and keep warm. When all are done, pour 1/2 cup of the chicken broth into the skillet, scrape up any bits sticking to the pan, and stir in the salt and paprika. Return the chicken to the skillet. Pour the remaining 1/2 cup chicken broth into the skillet. Lay the green pepper and tomato slices on top of the chicken. Cover and simmer about 30 minutes or until the chicken is tender, adding more broth if necessary. Mix the flour with the water and a little of the hot chicken sauce. Add to the skillet and cook, stirring, until thickened. Stir in the yogurt. Taste and adjust the seasoning. Cover and simmer until just heated through. Do not allow to boil. Serve over noodles or rice.

CHICKEN WITH TARRAGON

SERVES 4

1 2-1/2- to 3-pound chicken, cut into serving pieces
1-1/2 tablespoons butter
1-1/2 tablespoons corn oil
1 small onion, finely chopped
1 medium garlic clove, finely chopped
2 tablespoons all-purpose flour
2 tablespoons tomato paste
1-1/2 cups hot chicken broth
Salt and freshly ground black pepper to taste
1 tablespoon finely chopped fresh tarragon, or
1-1/2 teaspoons crushed dried tarragon
1 cup unflavored yogurt
1/3 cup freshly grated Parmesan cheese (optional)

Dry the chicken pieces with paper towels. In a large, heavy skillet heat the butter and oil over moderate heat. Add the chicken pieces, a few at a time, and sauté, turning them to brown on all sides. Remove the chicken to a plate and keep warm. Add the onion and garlic to the skillet and cook until soft, stirring frequently. Stir in the flour and tomato paste. Gradually add the chicken broth, stirring, until the mixture comes to a boil and thickens. Return the chicken to the skillet. Add the salt and pepper. Cover and simmer 25 minutes. Add the tarragon, cover, and simmer 10 minutes or until the chicken is tender. Remove the chicken to a heated serving dish. Gradually fold the yogurt into the sauce and heat over low heat, stirring. Do not allow it to boil. Pour over the chicken and sprinkle with the cheese, if desired. Serve with noodles or rice.

VARIATION Rabbit can also be prepared in the above manner.

POULET VALLÉE D'AUGE
(Chicken and Apples in Cider)

The heart of the cider- and Calvados-producing region of Normandy lends its name to this inspired creation.

SERVES 6

2 2-1/2-pound chickens, cut into serving pieces
2 tablespoons butter
2 tablespoons corn oil
1/3 cup warmed Calvados or other apple brandy
1/3 cup finely chopped onion
2 tablespoons finely chopped parsley
1/4 teaspoon ground cinnamon
1/4 teaspoon ground nutmeg (preferably freshly ground)
1/4 teaspoon ground cloves
Salt and freshly ground black pepper to taste
4 medium tart apples, peeled, cored, and thickly sliced
3/4 cup apple cider or more
1 cup unflavored yogurt, at room temperature
2 egg yolks

Pat the chicken pieces dry with paper towels. In a large, heavy skillet heat the butter and oil over moderate heat. Add the chicken pieces, a few at a time, and sauté gently, turning to brown on all sides. Pour off the excess fat from the skillet. Add the Calvados or other apple brandy and ignite. When the flame has subsided, add the onion, parsley, cinnamon, nutmeg, cloves, salt and pepper, apples, and cider. Cover and simmer about 30 minutes or until the chicken is tender, adding more cider if necessary. Remove the chicken to a heated serving platter and keep warm. Combine the yogurt with the egg yolks in a bowl. Stir with a whisk until well blended and smooth. Gradually stir a little of the hot juices from the skillet into the yogurt mixture. Slowly pour the mixture into the skillet. Stir constantly over low heat until the sauce begins to thicken. Do not allow to boil. Taste and adjust the seasoning. Spoon some of the sauce over the chicken and serve the rest separately.

VARIATION   This dish is sometimes flavored with thyme or marjoram instead of cinnamon, nutmeg, and cloves.

SOUTH INDIAN CHICKEN CURRY

Considering its extraordinary range of flavors, Indian food can be surprisingly simple to prepare. Here is a rich-tasting but not overwhelming dish, punctuated with nuts and exotically spiced.

SERVES 4

1	3-pound chicken, cut into small serving pieces
4	tablespoons peanut oil
1	medium onion, finely chopped
1	teaspoon ground coriander
1/2	teaspoon ground turmeric
1/8	teaspoon ground cinnamon
1/8	teaspoon ground cloves
1/8	teaspoon ground cayenne pepper
1/8	teaspoon ground cardamom
1/2	teaspoon peeled and grated ginger root
2	medium garlic cloves, crushed
1	tablespoon diced green pepper
1/2	cup grated unsweetened coconut
1	teaspoon salt or to taste
1	cup unflavored yogurt, at room temperature
1	cup water
1/2	tablespoon butter
1/4	cup unsalted cashew nuts
2	tablespoons freshly squeezed and strained lime juice or to taste
	Mint sprigs (optional)

Pat the chicken pieces dry with paper towels. In a large, heavy skillet heat the oil over moderate heat. Add the chicken pieces, a few at a time, and sauté, turning to brown on all sides. Transfer them to a plate and keep warm. Add the onion to the skillet and sauté until golden. Add the coriander, turmeric, cinnamon, cloves, cayenne pepper, cardamom, ginger, and garlic and sauté 2 minutes or so. Stir in the green pepper, coconut, salt, yogurt, and water. Add the browned chicken pieces, cover, and simmer about 25 minutes or until the chicken is tender.

Meanwhile, in a small skillet melt the butter. Add the cashew nuts and sauté gently until golden brown, stirring frequently. When the chicken is done, stir in the sautéed nuts and lime juice. Transfer onto a heated serving dish. Garnish with the mint sprigs, if desired, and serve.

CHICKEN ENCHILADAS

This robust Mexican dish is a delicious way to outwit inflation.

SERVES 6

1	4-ounce can peeled green chili peppers
4	tablespoons corn oil
1	medium onion, finely chopped
1	small garlic clove, finely chopped
3	medium tomatoes, peeled, seeded, and finely chopped
1/4	teaspoon crushed dried oregano
	Salt to taste
1-1/2	cups shredded cooked chicken
4	ounces mild Cheddar cheese, grated
1	cup unflavored yogurt
12	corn tortillas

Drain and rinse the green chili peppers. Remove the seeds. Chop the peppers finely. Take care not to touch your face while handling the peppers, and wash your hands well when finished.

In a heavy skillet heat 1 tablespoon of the oil over moderate heat. Add the onion and garlic and sauté until golden, stirring frequently. Add the chili peppers, tomatoes, oregano, and salt. Simmer over low heat about 30 minutes or until the mixture thickens. Remove from the heat and set aside.

Combine the chicken, cheese, yogurt, and additional salt. Heat the remaining 3 tablespoons oil and dip in the tortillas, one at a time, just until they become limp (they must not be crisp). Drain on paper towels. Fill each tortilla with a little of the chicken mixture and roll it up. Arrange the rolls seam sides down and close together in a greased shallow baking dish. Pour the sauce over them. Bake in a preheated 350°F oven about 20 minutes or until thoroughly heated.

SIAMESE CHICKEN

Thailand, one of the most exotic countries of the Orient, has warm weather most of the year. The Thai diet is thus understandably light, but quite spicy in order to stimulate the appetite.

Serve this variation of a traditional Thai dish over cooked Chinese egg noodles.

SERVES 6

3	whole chicken breasts, boned and halved
1/4	cup finely chopped shallots or onion
2	medium garlic cloves
1/4	cup unsalted peanuts, ground
1	teaspoon ground coriander
2	teaspoons grated lemon rind
1/4	teaspoon ground dried chili pepper
1	teaspoon salt
2	tablespoons butter
1-1/2	cups Coconut Cream, page 150
1	tablespoon soy sauce
1	cup unflavored yogurt, at room temperature

Pat the chicken breasts dry with paper towels. In a mortar pound to a paste the shallots or onion, garlic, peanuts, coriander, lemon rind, red pepper, and salt. Coat the chicken breasts with the spice mixture, reserving any remaining mixture.

In a deep skillet melt the butter over moderate heat. Add the chicken and sauté 2 minutes or so on each side. Add the coconut cream, soy sauce, and any remaining spice mixture. Cover and simmer gently 20 minutes. Stir in the yogurt and simmer 5 minutes or until the chicken is tender. Taste and adjust the seasoning.

CORNISH GAME HENS IN MUSHROOM, TOMATO, AND WINE SAUCE

An easy way to fame as a cook.

SERVES 4

2 Cornish game hens (about 1 pound each), thawed and cut in halves lengthwise
Salt and freshly ground black pepper
3 tablespoons butter
1 medium onion, finely chopped
8 ounces mushrooms, thinly sliced
1/2 cup dry white wine
2 medium tomatoes, peeled, seeded, and diced
1 large garlic clove, minced
1 tablespoon finely chopped fresh basil, or 3/4 teaspoon crushed dried basil
2 teaspoon finely chopped fresh marjoram, or 1/2 teaspoon crushed dried marjoram
1 teaspoon finely chopped fresh thyme, or 1/4 teaspoon crushed dried thyme
1/2 cup unflavored yogurt, at room temperature
1 tablespoon all-purpose flour

Dry the hens with paper towels. Sprinkle lightly with salt and pepper. Arrange in a baking dish just large enough to hold them comfortably in one layer. Roast, uncovered, in a preheated 400°F oven 20 minutes.

Meanwhile, in a heavy skillet melt the butter over moderate heat. Add the onion and mushrooms and sauté until lightly browned, stirring frequently. Remove from the heat and stir in the wine, tomatoes, garlic, basil, marjoram, thyme, and salt and pepper to taste. Spoon the mixture over the hens. Reduce the oven temperature to 350°F. Cover the dish and bake 25 minutes or until the hens are tender. Remove the hens to a heated serving platter and keep warm.

Transfer the mushrooms and juices from the baking dish to a small saucepan. Blend the yogurt and flour until smooth. Add to the saucepan and simmer until thickened and hot, stirring constantly. Taste and adjust the season-

ing. Pour into a heated sauceboat and serve at once with the hens.

CURRIED CHICKEN

My adaptation of a Caribbean recipe.

SERVES 4

1 3- to 3-1/2-pound chicken, cut into serving pieces
2 tablespoons butter
1 tablespoon peanut oil
2 medium onions, finely chopped
1 cup chicken broth (more if needed)
2 medium garlic cloves, finely chopped
1 teaspoon ground coriander
1 teaspoon ground cumin
1 teaspoon ground turmeric
3 whole cloves
1 1/2-inch piece cinnamon stick
1 bay leaf
1/8 teaspoon crushed dried thyme
1/4 teaspoon dried hot red pepper flakes or to taste
Salt and freshly ground black pepper to taste
2 medium tomatoes, peeled, seeded and finely chopped
1/2 cup unflavored yogurt

Dry the chicken pieces with paper towels. In a large, heavy skillet heat the butter and oil over moderate heat. Add the chicken pieces, a few at a time, and sauté, turning until golden all over. Transfer the sautéed chicken to a heatproof casserole. Add the onions to the fat remaining in the skillet and sauté until lightly browned, stirring frequently. Stir in the chicken broth, garlic, coriander, cumin, turmeric, cloves, cinnamon stick, bay leaf, thyme, pepper flakes, and salt and pepper. Pour over the chicken. Cover and simmer 25 minutes, adding a little more broth if necessary. Stir in the tomatoes and yogurt. Taste and adjust the seasoning. Cover and simmer 15 minutes. Remove the cloves, cinnamon stick, and bay leaf before serving.

BURMESE CHICKEN

The cuisine of Burma offers fascinating eating for the adventurous. Easily prepared yet intriguingly flavored poultry dishes such as this one are the Burmese rule.

SERVES 4

3	pounds chicken breasts, skinned, boned, and cut into small pieces
1/4	cup peanut oil
1	medium onion, finely chopped
2	medium garlic cloves, finely chopped
1	teaspoon peeled and finely chopped ginger root
1	tablespoon curry powder or to taste
1-1/2	cups Coconut Milk, page 150
1	teaspoon salt or to taste
1	tablespoon cornstarch
1-1/2	tablespoons water
1	cup unflavored yogurt, at room temperature
2	cups cooked and drained Chinese egg noodles
2	hard-cooked eggs, chopped
1/4	cup thinly sliced scallions, including 2 inches of the green tops
1/4	teaspoon ground dried chili pepper

Dry the chicken pieces with paper towels. In a saucepan heat the oil over moderate heat. Add the onion, garlic, ginger, and curry powder and sauté 4 minutes, stirring frequently. Add the chicken and sauté 8 minutes. Stir in the coconut milk and salt. Cover and simmer 20 minutes or until the chicken is tender. Mix the cornstarch with the water. Blend into the sauce in the pan, stirring constantly until thickened. Stir in the yogurt and simmer until heated. Taste and adjust the seasoning. Place the noodles in a heated serving dish. Top with the chicken and its sauce. Sprinkle with the chopped eggs, scallions, and chili pepper and serve at once.

TURKEY AND WILD RICE CASSEROLE

A happy solution for utilizing leftover turkey.

SERVES 4

1/2	cup wild rice
3	tablespoons butter
8	ounces mushrooms, sliced
1	small onion, finely chopped
1-1/2	cups diced cooked turkey
1/4	cup sliced blanched almonds
	Salt and freshly ground black pepper to taste
1	cup or more turkey or chicken broth
1/3	cup heavy cream
1/2	cup unflavored yogurt
3	tablespoons freshly grated Parmesan or Romano cheese

Wash the rice and cover with boiling water. Allow to soak 1 hour. Drain thoroughly.

In a heavy skillet melt 1-1/2 tablespoons of the butter over moderate heat. Add the mushrooms and onion and sauté until lightly browned, stirring frequently. Remove from the heat and transfer the sautéed vegetables to a mixing bowl. Add the rice, turkey, almonds, salt and pepper, and broth. Mix together the cream and yogurt until well blended. Add to the rice mixture and stir gently but thoroughly. Transfer to a greased casserole. Cover and bake in a preheated 350°F oven 1 hour or until the liquid in the pan is absorbed and the rice is tender. If necessary, more broth may be added. Remove the cover, sprinkle with the cheese, and dot with the remaining 1-1/2 tablespoons butter. Raise the oven temperature to 450°F. Bake, uncovered, 5 minutes.

TURKISH DUCK WITH RICE

SERVES 4 TO 6

1   5- to 6-pound lean duck, trimmed of as
     much fat as possible, and cut into serving
     pieces
1   cup unflavored yogurt
     Salt
6   tablespoons butter
1   large onion, finely chopped
     The liver and heart of the duck, chopped
2   tablespoons slivered blanched almonds
2   tablespoons chopped unsalted pistachio
     nuts
2   tablespoons pine nuts
2   cups long-grain white rice
1/2 cup seedless raisins
1/2 teaspoon ground cinnamon (optional)
     Freshly ground black pepper to taste

Dry the duck pieces with paper towels. Place
the yogurt in a large bowl. Season to taste with
the salt. Add the pieces of duck and allow them
to marinate in the yogurt 3 to 4 hours, then
drain well and dry with paper towels.

In a large, heavy casserole melt 2 tablespoons
of the butter over moderate heat. Add the onion
and sauté until soft but not browned, stirring
frequently. Add the well-drained pieces of duck
and sauté, turning to brown on all sides. Pour in
4 cups of water, season to taste with salt, and
bring to a boil. Reduce the heat to low, cover, and
simmer about 40 minutes or until the duck is
tender. Drain the duck and keep it warm.
Measure the broth and add enough water to
make 4 cups. Reserve.

In a heavy saucepan melt the remaining 4 tablespoons butter. Add the duck liver and heart,
almonds, pistachio nuts, and pine nuts. Sauté
gently until the nuts turn golden, stirring almost constantly. Add the rice and cook, stirring,
until the grains are coated with the butter. Add
the raisins, cinnamon, additional salt, pepper,
and the reserved duck broth and water. Bring to
a boil. Reduce the heat to low, cover, and simmer undisturbed about 25 minutes or until the
rice is tender and the liquid in the pan has been
absorbed.

To serve, arrange the duck pieces in the center of a heated platter. Surround with the rice.
Or mound the rice on the platter and top with
the duck.

Meat

TURKISH KEBABS WITH YOGURT

SERVES 4

1/3 cup olive oil
1 medium onion, finely grated
1 teaspoon crushed dried thyme
1 teaspoon salt
1/4 teaspoon freshly ground black pepper
2 pounds boneless leg of lamb, trimmed of excess fat and cut into 1- to 1-1/2-inch cubes
2 loaves Arab bread (pocket bread or *pita*), broken into large pieces, or 8 slices French bread
1 cup unflavored yogurt, at room temperature
Salt and freshly ground black pepper to taste
2 tablespoons butter
2 teaspoons paprika

Combine the oil, onion, thyme, 1 teaspoon salt, and 1/4 teaspoon pepper in a large bowl and mix well. Add the lamb cubes and turn them about to coat thoroughly with the mixture. Cover and let stand at room temperature 2 to 3 hours or in the refrigerator 5 to 6 hours, turning the meat from time to time.

Remove the lamb cubes from the marinade and thread them on long skewers, leaving a few inches exposed at each end. Broil, preferably over charcoal, about 15 minutes or until the lamb is richly browned outside and pink and juicy inside, turning and basting now and then with the marinade.

Arrange the pieces of bread on 4 heated dinner plates. Using a fork, push the lamb off the skewers onto the bread. Beat the yogurt until smooth. Season to taste with salt and pepper and spoon over the lamb. Heat the butter and

stir in the paprika. Dribble the paprika butter over the yogurt and serve at once.

NOTE Seasoned yogurt is sometimes substituted for the above marinade. The bread may be toasted or fried in butter, or you may use toasted English muffins.

VARIATION Instead of broiling the meat, sauté it gently in olive oil or butter until tender. Season with salt and pepper and keep warm. Sauté 4 ripe tomatoes, peeled, seeded, and minced, in a little butter until reduced to a purée. Spread over toasted or fried bread slices (see NOTE, preceding). Top with the lamb, then the yogurt. Garnish with the paprika butter as above.

VEAL SCALLOPS WITH APPLES

SERVES 6

2 pounds leg of veal, cut into 1/4-inch-thick slices and pounded until very thin
Salt and freshly ground black pepper to taste
1/2 cup all-purpose flour
4 tablespoons butter
2 medium Golden Delicious apples, cored but not peeled and cut crosswise into 1/4-inch-thick rings
1/4 cup corn oil
2 tablespoons Calvados (optional)
1/4 cup heavy cream
1/2 cup unflavored yogurt, at room temperature

Pat the veal scallops dry with paper towels. Season them with the salt and pepper. Dredge each scallop lightly with the flour. Set aside.

In a large, heavy skillet melt 2 tablespoons of

the butter over moderate heat. Add the apple rings and sauté, turning them frequently until golden brown on both sides. Remove the skillet from the heat and cover to keep the apple rings warm.

In another large, heavy skillet melt the remaining 2 tablespoons butter with the oil over medium-high heat. Add the veal scallops and sauté until tender, turning to brown on both sides. Transfer them to a heated serving platter and keep them warm while you prepare the sauce.

Pour off the fat remaining in the skillet. Add the Calvados, if desired, and cream to the skillet and bring to a simmer over low heat, stirring and scraping the brown particles that cling to the bottom and sides of the skillet. Add the yogurt and cook gently, stirring constantly, until heated through. Taste and adjust the seasoning and remove from the heat.

To serve, arrange the apple rings on top of the veal scallops and spoon the sauce over them.

VEAL RAGOUT

This is just one of many delicious ways in which Central Europeans serve veal. Once again yogurt makes an excellent substitute for the usual sour cream.

SERVES 6 TO 8

3	pounds boneless veal, cut into 1-inch cubes
6	tablespoons all-purpose flour
1	teaspoon salt
1/8	teaspoon paprika
8	tablespoons butter
2	tablespoons corn oil
18	boiling onions, peeled
2/3	cup chicken broth
8	ounces mushrooms, sliced
1	cup half-and-half or milk
1	cup unflavored yogurt, at room temperature
6	large mushroom caps
2	tablespoons finely chopped parsley

Dredge the veal cubes in a mixture of 4 tablespoons of the flour, salt, and paprika. In a large, heavy skillet heat 2 tablespoons of the butter and the oil over moderate heat. Add the veal cubes and sauté, turning to brown them on all sides. Transfer to a casserole. Add the onions to the skillet and sauté until lightly browned, stirring frequently. Add to the veal. Pour the chicken broth into the skillet and bring to a boil, scraping up the brown particles from the bottom. Pour over the veal and onions. Add 4 tablespoons of the remaining butter to the skillet and heat over moderate heat. Add the sliced mushrooms and sauté until golden, stirring frequently. Sprinkle with the remaining 2 tablespoons flour and cook, stirring, 1 minute. Add the half-and-half or milk and cook, stirring constantly, until the sauce thickens. Remove from the heat and spoon over the veal and onions. Cover and bake in a preheated 325°F oven 40 minutes. Stir in the yogurt. Taste and adjust the seasoning. Cover and bake 10 minutes or until the meat and onions are tender.

Meanwhile, in a small skillet melt the remaining 2 tablespoons butter over moderate heat. Add the mushroom caps and sauté until lightly browned, stirring frequently. Garnish the veal ragout with the sautéed mushroom caps. Sprinkle with the parsley and serve.

BEEF STROGANOV

Beef Stroganov is a simple yet sophisticated Russian dish that has achieved international fame while undergoing numerous variations. The authentic Stroganov is made with sour cream; however, this version using yogurt makes a very good dish indeed.

SERVES 4 TO 6

1-1/2 pounds tenderloin or top sirloin of beef, trimmed of fat
Salt and freshly ground black pepper to taste
1/4 cup all-purpose flour
6 tablespoons butter
4 ounces mushrooms, thinly sliced
1/2 cup finely chopped onion or scallions (include 2 inches of the green tops of the scallions)
1 medium garlic clove, finely chopped
1 tablespoon tomato paste
1 cup beef broth
1 cup unflavored yogurt, at room temperature
2 tablespoons finely chopped parsley or fresh dill

Cut the meat into thin strips about 2 inches long and 1/4 inch wide. Season with the salt and pepper and dredge in 3 tablespoons of the flour. In a heavy skillet melt 4 tablespoons of the butter over moderate heat. Add the meat strips and sauté, turning them to brown on all sides. Remove to a plate and keep warm. Add the remaining 2 tablespoons butter to the skillet and heat. Add the mushrooms, onion or scallions, and garlic and sauté until lightly browned, stirring frequently. Sprinkle the remaining 1 tablespoon flour over the vegetables and mix well. Stir in the tomato paste and broth and simmer a few minutes. Remove from the heat and stir in the yogurt until well blended. Return the meat to the skillet. Cover and simmer over low heat 2 or 3 minutes until heated through. Taste and adjust the seasoning. Sprinkle with the parsley or dill and serve.

PORK WITH PRUNES AND APRICOTS

SERVES 4

4 ounces dried pitted prunes
4 ounces dried apricots
1-1/3 cups dry sherry
1 pound pork tenderloin, cut into 1/2-inch-thick slices and pounded until thin
Salt and freshly ground black pepper to taste
1/4 cup all-purpose flour
3 tablespoons butter
2 tablespoons Calvados or brandy
1 cup unflavored yogurt, or 1/2 cup each yogurt and heavy cream
1 tablespoon cornstarch

In a heavy enameled or stainless steel saucepan combine the dried fruits and sherry. Cover and cook over low heat 15 to 20 minutes or until tender.

Meanwhile, pat the pork slices dry with paper towels. Season them with the salt and pepper. Dredge each slice lightly with the flour. In a large, heavy skillet melt the butter over moderate heat. Add the pork slices and sauté, turning to brown them on both sides. Heat the Calvados or brandy, ignite, and add to the skillet. When the flame subsides, cover the skillet and cook over low heat 15 minutes. Transfer the pork slices to a heated serving platter and keep warm while you prepare the sauce.

Pour off the fat remaining in the skillet. Drain and reserve the fruit. Add the sherry to the skillet. Bring to a simmer over low heat, stirring and scraping the brown particles that cling to the bottom and sides of the skillet. Mix together the yogurt and cornstarch until smooth and add to the skillet. Cook gently, stirring constantly, until the sauce is thickened and hot. Taste and adjust the seasoning. Spoon the sauce over the pork slices. Garnish the platter with the prunes and apricots and serve at once.

MEDITERRANEAN PORK WITH ZUCCHINI

SERVES 6

2   tablespoons corn oil
3   pounds lean boneless pork butt, trimmed of excess fat and cut into 1-inch cubes
2   medium onions, thinly sliced
2   cups beef broth
2   medium garlic cloves, finely chopped
3/4 teaspoon crushed dried basil
1/2 teaspoon crushed dried marjoram
1/4 teaspoon crushed dried thyme
    Salt to taste
1/4 teaspoon freshly ground black pepper
2   medium zucchini, trimmed and cut crosswise into thin slices
3/4 cup unflavored yogurt
1   tablespoon cornstarch

Pour the oil into a 9 × 13-inch baking dish. Place the dish in an oven while it preheats to 500°F. Add the pork and onions to the dish and bake, uncovered, about 20 minutes or until the meat is browned, stirring frequently. Combine the broth, garlic, basil, marjoram, thyme, salt, and pepper. Pour over the meat. Reduce the oven temperature to 350°F. Cover the dish and bake 15 minutes. Remove the baking dish from the oven and stir in the zucchini. Cover and bake about 20 minutes or until the meat and zucchini are tender. With a perforated spoon transfer the meat and zucchini to a heated serving dish and keep warm. Pour the juices from the baking dish into a small saucepan. Skim off the fat if necessary. Over high heat boil the juices, uncovered, until reduced to 1-1/4 cups. Mix the yogurt with the cornstarch until smooth. Stir into the pan juices and cook gently, stirring constantly, until thickened and hot. Taste and adjust the seasoning. Pour the sauce over the meat and zucchini and serve at once.

LEBANESE MEAT AND SPINACH STEW

The shish kebabs *of the Middle East have long been famous, but no less delectable are many lesser-known recipes, such as this rustic stew.*

SERVES 4

2   pounds spinach
3   tablespoons butter
1   medium onion, finely chopped
1   pound lean boneless lamb, beef, or veal, cut into 1-inch cubes
    Salt and freshly ground black pepper to taste
1-1/2 cups water
2   tablespoons freshly squeezed and strained lemon juice
1/4 cup pine nuts
1/2 teaspoon paprika
2   loaves Arab bread (pocket bread or *pita*), toasted and broken into bite-sized pieces
1   recipe Garlic Yogurt Sauce with Mint, page 85

Wash the spinach thoroughly under cold running water. Remove and discard the stems and bruised leaves. Drain. Coarsely chop the spinach leaves and set aside.

In a heavy casserole melt 2 tablespoons of the butter over moderate heat. Add the onion and sauté until soft but not browned, stirring frequently. Add the meat and sauté, turning to brown on all sides. Add the salt and pepper and water and bring to a boil over high heat. Reduce the heat to low, cover, and simmer 1 hour or until the meat is tender and most of the liquid in the casserole has been absorbed. If not, reduce it by fast boiling, uncovered. Stir in the spinach, cover, and simmer 10 minutes. Stir in the lemon juice, taste and adjust the seasoning, and turn off the heat.

In a small skillet melt the remaining 1 tablespoon butter. Add the pine nuts and sauté gently until golden brown, stirring frequently. Stir in the paprika and remove from the heat.

To serve, spread the pieces of toasted bread

in the bottom of a serving dish. Spoon the meat and spinach stew over them. Cover with the garlic yogurt sauce with mint. Garnish with the sautéed pine nuts and dribble the paprika butter remaining in the skillet over the top.

MEAT AND EGGPLANT WITH YOGURT

Here is a good example of what Middle Eastern cooks can do with eggplant (and yogurt!).

SERVES 4

2   tablespoons butter
1   medium onion, finely chopped
1   pound lean boneless lamb or veal, cut into 1-inch cubes
1-1/2 cups water
    Salt and freshly ground black pepper to taste
1   recipe Fried Eggplant, page 78
1   recipe Yogurt Sauce with Pine Nuts and Garlic, page 85
1/4 cup chopped fresh mint or parsley

In a heavy casserole melt the butter over moderate heat. Add the onion and sauté until soft but not browned, stirring frequently. Add the lamb or veal and sauté, turning to brown on all sides. Add the water and salt and pepper, cover, and simmer 1 hour or until the meat is tender and almost all of the liquid in the pan has been absorbed. If not, reduce it by fast boiling, uncovered.

To serve, transfer the meat to a serving dish. Arrange the eggplant slices over it. Spoon the yogurt sauce over the eggplant and garnish with the mint or parsley.

LAMB WITH MUSHROOMS AND DILL

Yogurt provides a perfect replacement for the sour cream called for in this northern European stew.

SERVES 6

3   tablespoons butter
2   pounds lean boneless leg of lamb, cut into 1-inch cubes
1   large onion, finely chopped
1/4 cup finely chopped fresh dill
    Salt and freshly ground black pepper to taste
1-1/2 cups beef broth
1   pound mushrooms, sliced
1   cup unflavored yogurt, at room temperature
1   tablespoon all-purpose flour

In a heavy casserole melt the butter over moderate heat. Add the lamb and onion and sauté until the meat turns brown, stirring frequently. Add 2 tablespoons of the dill, salt and pepper, and broth. Cover, reduce the heat to low, and simmer 45 minutes or until the lamb is almost tender, adding more broth if necessary. Add the mushrooms, cover, and simmer 15 minutes or until the lamb and mushrooms are tender. Combine the yogurt with the flour. Add to the casserole along with the remaining 2 tablespoons dill and mix well. Cook gently a few minutes until heated through. Taste and adjust the seasoning. Serve with noodles or rice.

MEDITERRANEAN BAKED LAMB SHANKS

Here is a flavorful way of preparing an economical cut of lamb.

SERVES 4

4	lean lamb shanks (about 12 ounces each)
2	large ripe tomatoes, peeled, seeded, and finely chopped
2	medium onions, finely chopped
2	medium garlic cloves, finely chopped
1	tablespoon freshly squeezed and strained lemon juice
1/4	cup finely chopped parsley
2	tablespoons finely chopped fresh basil, or 2 teaspoons crushed dried basil
	Salt and freshly ground black pepper to taste
1	cup dry white wine
1	tablespoon all-purpose flour
1	cup unflavored yogurt

Place the lamb shanks in an oiled baking dish large enough to hold them in one layer. Bake in a preheated 450°F oven 30 minutes, turning the shanks now and then to brown them evenly on all sides.

Remove the dish from the oven and spread the tomatoes over the lamb. Sprinkle with the onions, garlic, lemon juice, parsley, basil, and salt and pepper. Pour in the wine, cover, and return to the oven. Reduce the heat to 375°F and bake about 1 hour or until the meat is tender. Drain the pan juices into a small saucepan. Cook over high heat until reduced to about 3/4 cup. Combine the flour with the yogurt and add to the saucepan. Mix thoroughly and cook over low heat about 3 minutes or until heated through. Taste and adjust the seasoning. Transfer the lamb shanks to a warmed serving dish and spoon the sauce over them. Serve at once.

VARIATION   Crushed dried oregano or rosemary to taste may be substituted for the parsley and basil.

NORTH INDIAN LAMB CURRY

SERVES 6

1/4	cup peanut oil, or 4 tablespoons butter
1	large onion, thinly sliced
2	medium garlic cloves, crushed
2	teaspoons peeled and grated ginger root, or 1/2 teaspoon ground ginger
1	tablespoon ground coriander
1	tablespoon poppy seeds, crushed
3/4	teaspoon ground cumin
1/2	teaspoon ground cardamom
3/4	teaspoon ground turmeric
3/4	teaspoon paprika
1/8	teaspoon ground cayenne pepper or to taste
1/8	teaspoon ground nutmeg
1/8	teaspoon ground cloves
1/8	teaspoon ground mace
1/4	teaspoon saffron
2	pounds lean boneless leg of lamb, cut into 1-inch cubes
4	medium tomatoes, peeled, seeded, and chopped
1/2	cup unflavored yogurt, at room temperature
1-1/2	teaspoons salt or to taste
1/2	cup water
2	tablespoons finely chopped fresh coriander (optional)

In a heavy casserole heat the oil or butter over moderate heat. Add the onion and sauté until golden, stirring frequently. Add the garlic, ginger, coriander, poppy seeds, cumin, cardamom, turmeric, paprika, cayenne pepper, nutmeg, cloves, mace, and saffron and sauté gently 2 minutes, stirring almost constantly. Add the lamb and sauté 5 minutes, turning to brown on all sides. Stir in the tomatoes and yogurt, then the salt and water. Cover and simmer over low heat 45 minutes or until the meat is tender. Serve garnished with the coriander, if desired.

LAMB CURRY WITH LENTILS

Lentils, so popular in Mediterranean countries and throughout the Middle East, are surprisingly neglected in America. One of the most nutritious of legumes, they are widely cultivated in India, where they form an integral part of the daily diet. This dish is derived from an Indian recipe.

SERVES 6

1   large onion, finely chopped
1   large garlic clove, crushed to a purée
1-1/2 tablespoons curry powder or to taste
1-1/2 teaspoons salt or to taste
1/2 cup unflavored yogurt, at room temperature
1-1/2 pounds lean boneless leg of lamb, cut into 1-inch cubes
1-1/2 cups lentils
3   tablespoons butter
3   cups boiling water

In a large bowl combine the onion, garlic, curry powder, and salt and mix until well blended. Gradually stir in the yogurt and mix thoroughly. Add the lamb and toss until well coated with the mixture. Cover and let stand at room temperature about 2 hours or in the refrigerator 5 to 6 hours.

Wash the lentils in a sieve under cold running water. Place them in a saucepan and cover with water. Bring to a boil, drain, and set aside.

In a heavy casserole melt the butter over moderate heat. Add the lamb mixture, reduce the heat to low, and cook, partially covered, 15 minutes, stirring frequently. Stir in the lentils and boiling water. Cover and simmer 30 minutes or until the meat and lentils are tender. Taste and adjust the seasoning and serve.

GROUND MEAT ON SKEWERS

A natural for outdoor entertaining, this great Middle Eastern specialty is best when broiled over hot embers.

SERVES 4

2   pounds lean lamb or beef, ground twice
1   large onion, grated
1   egg
    Salt and freshly ground black pepper to taste
1/2 teaspoon ground cinnamon or allspice, or 1/4 teaspoon each ground cinnamon and allspice
4   loaves Arab bread (pocket bread or *pita*)
1   recipe Garlic Yogurt Sauce, page 85
2   tablespoons butter
1   tablespoon paprika

In a large mixing bowl combine the meat, onion, egg, salt, pepper, and cinnamon and/or allspice. Mix and knead until the mixture is well blended and smooth. Divide into 8 equal portions. With hands dipped in cold water, form each portion into a sausage shape about 1 inch in diameter and 4 inches long. Thread lengthwise on oiled skewers (preferably flat-edged sword-type skewers, which are slightly wider than those used for *shish kebab*), pressing and molding the meat to the skewers. Broil, preferably over charcoal, 12 to 15 minutes or until done to taste, turning the skewers frequently so the meat browns evenly on all sides.

Arrange the loaves of bread on 4 heated plates. Using a fork, push the meat off the skewers, placing 2 "sausages" on each piece of bread. Spoon the garlic yogurt sauce over them. Heat the butter and stir in the paprika. Dribble this over the yogurt and serve at once.

VARIATION   Wedges of tomato, onion, and green pepper can also be strung on skewers, broiled, and served with the meat. You may brush the Arab bread lightly with olive oil, heat it, and fold it around the broiled meat. Tuck in the broiled vegetables (or use raw green pepper strips and tomato wedges). Add the garlic yogurt sauce and eat sandwich fashion.

SWEDISH MEATBALLS

This recipe is usually made with sour cream, but it lends itself equally well to yogurt.

SERVES 4

1	thick slice white bread, trimmed of crust
1	tablespoon milk
1	small egg, slightly beaten
2	tablespoons butter
1	small onion, finely chopped
8	ounces lean beef, ground twice
8	ounces veal, ground twice
4	ounces pork, ground twice
1/4	cup finely chopped fresh dill
1/4	teaspoon ground nutmeg (preferably freshly ground) or allspice
1	teaspoon salt
1/4	teaspoon freshly ground black pepper
1	tablespoon corn oil
3/4	cup beef broth
1/2	cup unflavored yogurt, at room temperature
1-1/2	teaspoons all-purpose flour

In a large bowl soak the bread in the milk and egg. In a medium skillet melt 1 tablespoon of the butter over moderate heat. Add the onion and sauté until lightly browned, stirring frequently. Add to the bread mixture in the bowl along with the beef, veal, pork, 1-1/2 tablespoons of the dill, nutmeg or allspice, and salt and pepper. Knead well until thoroughly blended and smooth. With hands moistened in water, shape the mixture into 1-1/2-inch balls. Add the remaining 1 tablespoon butter and the oil to the skillet and heat. Add the meatballs and sauté, turning to brown on all sides. Add the broth, cover, and simmer 10 minutes. Combine the yogurt and flour. Carefully stir into the skillet with 1-1/2 tablespoons of the remaining dill. Taste and adjust the seasoning.

Simmer a few minutes until heated through. Sprinkle with the remaining dill and serve.

POLYNESIAN MEATBALLS

SERVES 4

1	pound lean beef, ground twice
1	small onion, grated
1/3	cup dry bread crumbs
1	egg, slightly beaten
1/2	teaspoon curry powder
1/8	teaspoon ground ginger
	Salt and freshly ground black pepper to taste
1/3	cup all-purpose flour (approximately)
1	tablespoon peanut oil or more
3/4	cup hot beef broth
1/4	cup dark rum
1/2	cup unflavored yogurt, at room temperature
1/3	cup sour cream, at room temperature
1/4	cup shredded unsweetened coconut
1/4	cup finely chopped macadamia nuts or salted cashew nuts

Combine the beef, onion, bread crumbs, egg, curry powder, ginger, and salt and pepper in a bowl. Knead well until thoroughly blended and smooth. Taste and adjust seasoning. With hands moistened in water, shape the mixture into 1-1/2-inch balls. Roll lightly in the flour.

In a heavy skillet heat the oil over moderate heat. Add the meatballs and sauté until lightly browned on all sides, adding more oil if necessary. Transfer to a plate and keep warm. Add 1 tablespoon flour to the drippings in the skillet and mix well. Pour in the broth and rum, season with additional salt and pepper, and stir constantly until the sauce is slightly thickened. Return the meatballs to the skillet. Cover and simmer 20 minutes, adding more broth if necessary. Carefully stir in the yogurt and sour cream. Taste and adjust the seasoning. Simmer briefly until just heated through. Do not allow to boil. Serve sprinkled with the shredded coconut and macadamia or cashew nuts.

STUFFED *KIBBEH* IN YOGURT SAUCE

Kibbeh, which most frequently consists of a mixture of ground lamb and bulghur is considered by the Lebanese to be their national dish. Preparing and eating it is not only a hallowed tradition; it is a countrywide addiction!

SERVES 4 TO 6

Stuffing

3	tablespoons butter
1/3	cup pine nuts
1	medium onion, finely chopped
1/2	pound lean boneless leg or shoulder of lamb, ground
1/4	teaspoon ground cinnamon or allspice Salt and freshly ground black pepper to taste

Exterior of Kibbeh *Balls*

1-1/2	cups fine bulghur
1	pound very lean boneless leg of lamb, ground 3 times
1	medium onion, finely chopped
1/4	teaspoon ground cinnamon or allspice (optional) Pinch ground nutmeg (preferably freshly ground) (optional) Ground cayenne pepper to taste
2	teaspoons salt or to taste Freshly ground black pepper to taste

Yogurt Sauce

4	cups unflavored yogurt
1	egg white, slightly beaten, or 1 tablespoon cornstarch or all-purpose flour dissolved in a little cold water
1/2	teaspoon salt
1/4	cup butter
2	large garlic cloves, crushed with 1/4 teaspoon salt
2	tablespoons crushed dried mint

TO PREPARE THE STUFFING In a small skillet heat 1 tablespoon of the butter over moderate heat. Add the pine nuts and sauté gently until golden brown, stirring almost constantly.

Remove to a plate and reserve. Add the onion and the remaining 2 tablespoons butter to the skillet and cook until soft but not browned, stirring frequently. Add the lamb and, breaking it up with a fork, cook until lightly browned. Stir in the reserved pine nuts, cinnamon or allspice, and salt and pepper and mix well. Taste and adjust the seasoning and set aside.

TO PREPARE THE EXTERIOR OF THE *KIBBEH* BALLS Cover the bulghur with cold water and allow it to soak 10 minutes. Drain in a colander lined with a double thickness of dampened cheesecloth. Enclose in the cheesecloth and squeeze dry. In a large bowl combine the bulghur with the lamb, onion, cinnamon, or allspice (if desired), nutmeg (if desired), cayenne pepper, salt, and black pepper. Moistening your hands now and then by dipping them into a bowl of lightly salted ice water, knead the mixture about 15 minutes or until well blended and smooth. Taste and adjust the seasoning. For a finer consistency you may grind the mixture twice, adding a tablespoon or two of ice water.

Keeping your hands moistened, shape the mixture into 1-1/2-inch balls and stuff each as follows: Hold a ball in the palm of your left hand. Place your right thumb in the center and press to make an opening. Continue pressing gently with your thumb all around the inside wall while rotating the ball in the palm of your left hand until it is hollowed out. Place a spoonful of stuffing inside the shell, pressing it down gently. With moistened hands reshape the *kibbeh* around the stuffing to enclose it securely and form the ball into an egg shape.

Stabilize the yogurt, egg white, or cornstarch or flour, and salt as directed on page 8. Gently lower the stuffed *kibbeh* balls into the stabilized yogurt and simmer 20 minutes or until cooked through. Do not allow the yogurt to boil.

Meanwhile, in a small skillet melt the butter. Add the crushed garlic and mint and sauté until the garlic turns golden, stirring constantly. Carefully stir the mixture into the *kibbeh* and yogurt. Taste and adjust the seasoning. Serve hot with cooked rice if desired.

MOUSSAKA
(Baked Eggplant, Ground Meat, and Tomato Casserole)

Although this famous dish is reputed to have origi-nated in the Balkans, it is esteemed throughout most of the Middle East and Caucasus as well and exists in a great many variations.

SERVES 6

2	medium eggplants
	Salt
3	tablespoons butter
1	large onion, finely chopped
2	medium garlic cloves, crushed
1	pound lean ground lamb or beef
2	medium tomatoes, peeled, seeded, and finely chopped
2	tablespoons finely chopped parsley
1/2	teaspoon crushed dried oregano
1/4	teaspoon ground cinnamon
	Salt and freshly ground black pepper to taste
1/2	cup all-purpose flour
1/3	cup olive oil or as needed
2	eggs, beaten
3/4	cup unflavored yogurt, at room temperature
1/3	cup freshly grated *kefalotiri*, Parmesan, or Romano cheese

Remove the stems and hulls from the eggplants. Peel the eggplants or not as you wish. Cut crosswise into 1/2-inch-thick slices. Layer on paper towels and sprinkle generously with salt. Weigh down with a heavy object and let stand 30 minutes.

Meanwhile, in a heavy skillet heat the butter over moderate heat. Add the onion and garlic and sauté until soft but not browned, stirring frequently. Add the meat and cook until lightly browned, breaking it up with a fork. Stir in the tomatoes, parsley, oregano, cinnamon, and salt and pepper. Cook, uncovered, about 10 minutes or until most of the liquid in the pan evaporates. Taste and adjust the seasoning. Remove from the heat and set aside.

Rinse the eggplant slices with cold water. Pat dry with fresh paper towels. Coat lightly with the flour. In a large, heavy skillet heat the oil over moderate heat. Add the eggplant slices and fry until lightly browned on both sides, adding more oil as necessary.

Arrange half the eggplant slices in the bot-tom of a shallow baking dish. Spread the meat mixture over them. Cover with the remaining eggplant slices. Mix together the beaten eggs and yogurt and pour over the top. Sprinkle with the cheese. Bake, uncovered, in a preheated 375°F oven 35 to 40 minutes or until the top-ping is golden and set.

VARIATIONS   Omit the oregano and cinna-mon. Add 2 tablespoons minced fresh dill, basil, or mint along with the parsley.

Six medium potatoes, peeled, sliced, and fried in corn oil, may be substituted for the fried eggplant.

MEXICAN STUFFED PEPPERS WITH YOGURT

SERVES 6

6 medium green peppers
2 tablespoons lard or butter
1 medium onion, finely chopped
2 medium garlic cloves, finely chopped
1 pound lean ground pork
1 cup walnuts, ground
1 medium tart apple, peeled, cored, and chopped
2 peaches, peeled, pitted, and chopped
1/3 cup seedless raisins
3 tablespoons finely chopped parsley
1 teaspoon ground cinnamon
1/2 teaspoon ground cloves
   Salt and freshly ground black pepper to taste
1 tablespoon sugar
1/4 cup dry sherry
1 cup hot water
6 ounces cream cheese, at room temperature
1/2 cup or more unflavored yogurt
1 small garlic clove, broiled (if desired) and finely chopped
1/4 teaspoon ground cumin
   Seeds from 1 pomegranate

Roast the peppers by impaling them one at a time on the tines of a long-handled fork and turning them over an open flame until the skins blacken and blister. Alternatively, place the peppers on a baking sheet and broil them about 3 inches from the heat, turning them so they color evenly on all sides. Wrap the roasted peppers in a damp towel and let them rest for a few minutes. Skin the peppers, cut out the stems and white membrane, and discard the seeds. Set aside.

In a large, heavy skillet melt the lard or butter over medium-high heat. Add the onion and garlic and sauté until soft but not browned, stirring frequently. Add the pork and cook until tender, stirring constantly with a fork to break up any lumps. Add 1/2 cup of the walnuts, apple, peaches, raisins, 1 tablespoon of the parsley, cinnamon, 1/4 teaspoon of the cloves, salt and pepper, sugar, sherry, and hot water. Simmer, uncovered, about 10 minutes or until the liquid has evaporated. Taste and adjust seasoning. Remove from the heat and keep warm.

In a bowl mash the cream cheese, gradually adding the yogurt until the mixture is well blended and smooth. Add the remaining 1/2 cup walnuts and 1/2 teaspoon cloves, garlic, cumin, and salt to taste. Mix thoroughly. (The sauce should have the consistency of whipped cream. If necessary, add a little more yogurt.) Taste and adjust the seasoning.

Fill the roasted peppers with the pork mixture. Spoon some of the sauce over the top of each pepper. Sprinkle with the pomegranate seeds and remaining 2 tablespoons parsley and serve.

VARIATION One-half cup chopped dried apricots steeped in sherry may be substituted for the peaches. (Not Mexican, but very good nonetheless.)

STUFFED ZUCCHINI IN YOGURT SAUCE

Stuffed vegetables constitute popular family meals and party pieces throughout the Balkans, Middle East, and Caucasus, and a good cook is expected to excel in their preparation. This particular recipe is a favorite in Syria and Lebanon.

SERVES 6

1	pound lean ground lamb or beef
2/3	cup uncooked long-grain white rice, washed and drained
1/2	teaspoon ground cinnamon
1	medium tomato, peeled, seeded, and finely chopped
	Salt
	Freshly ground black pepper to taste
12	zucchini, each 6 by 2 inches, or as many as needed
2	cups hot beef broth or water, salted to taste
4	cups unflavored yogurt
1	egg white, slightly beaten, or 1 tablespoon cornstarch or all-purpose flour dissolved in a little cold water
1	tablespoon butter
2	large garlic cloves, crushed with 1/2 teaspoon salt
2	teaspoons crushed dried mint

Combine the meat, rice, cinnamon, tomato, salt, and pepper in a bowl. Knead thoroughly until the mixture is well blended and smooth. Taste and adjust the seasoning. Set aside.

Cut about 1/2 inch off the stem ends of the zucchini. Shape into "lids" and reserve. These will later serve as covers. Using an apple corer (or a special squash corer), scoop out the center pulp and discard (or save for another use), leaving a 1/4-inch-thick shell all around. Lightly sprinkle the insides with additional salt and spoon the meat and rice mixture into the zucchini. Cover with the reserved lids and place side by side in a heavy casserole just large enough to hold the zucchini comfortably. Pour in the broth or water and bring to a boil. Cover and simmer about 30 minutes or until the liquid is absorbed and the zucchini are almost done. (If desired, the stuffed zucchini can be sautéed in 2 or 3 tablespoons butter before adding the broth.)

Stabilize the yogurt, egg white, or cornstarch or flour, and 1/2 teaspoon salt as directed on page 8. Pour the stabilized yogurt over the zucchini and simmer, uncovered, about 20 minutes or until the zucchini are very tender.

In a small skillet melt the butter over moderate heat. Add the crushed garlic and mint, mix well, and sauté a minute or so. Pour the mixture over the yogurt and stir thoroughly. Taste and adjust the seasoning. Serve hot.

Pasta

NOODLES WITH YOGURT CREAM SAUCE

Try this with poultry or veal as a pleasant change from potatoes.

SERVES 4

- 3 tablespoons butter
- 1/2 cup finely chopped shallots or scallions (include 2 inches of the green tops of the scallions)
- 2 tablespoons all-purpose flour
- 1 cup half-and-half
- 1 cup unflavored yogurt, at room temperature
- 1/4 teaspoon ground nutmeg (preferably freshly ground) or to taste
  Salt and ground white pepper (preferably freshly ground) to taste
- 8 ounces spinach noodles or medium egg noodles, cooked and drained
  Freshly grated Parmesan cheese

In a medium-sized, heavy saucepan melt the butter over moderate heat. Add the shallots or scallions and sauté until soft and golden, stirring frequently. Add the flour and cook, stirring, about 2 minutes. Gradually stir in the half-and-half, then the yogurt. Cook over low heat until the sauce is smooth, thickened, and heated through. Add the nutmeg and salt and pepper. Taste and adjust the seasoning.

Place the noodles in a heated serving dish and cover with the sauce. Toss gently until well coated with the sauce. Sprinkle with a few spoonfuls of the grated cheese and serve at once, accompanied with a bowl of additional cheese.

SPAGHETTINI WITH CURRY YOGURT SAUCE

This can enliven a dinner featuring grilled hamburgers, chops, or chicken.

SERVES 4

- 2 tablespoons butter
- 1 large onion, finely chopped
- 1 large garlic clove, finely chopped
- 2 teaspoons curry powder or to taste
- 1 tablespoon all-purpose flour
  Salt and ground white pepper (preferably freshly ground) to taste
- 2 cups unflavored yogurt, at room temperature, or
  1 cup each yogurt and sour cream
- 8 ounces spaghettini, cooked and drained

In a medium-sized, heavy saucepan melt the butter over moderate heat. Add the onion and garlic and sauté until golden and soft, stirring frequently. Add the curry powder and cook, stirring, 1/2 minute. Add the flour and salt and pepper and cook, stirring, 1 to 2 minutes. Stir in the yogurt or yogurt and sour cream and cook gently just until heated through.

Place the pasta in a heated serving dish and cover with the curry yogurt sauce. Toss gently until well coated with the sauce. Serve at once.

NOODLES AND SPINACH BAKE

Here is an Armenian version of a dish that is encountered throughout much of the Middle East, Balkans, and Russia. Serve it either as a luncheon main course or as an accompaniment to poultry or meat.

SERVES 6

1	pound spinach
1/4	cup olive oil or butter
1	medium onion, finely chopped
2	tablespoons finely chopped fresh dill
	Salt and ground white pepper (preferably freshly ground) to taste
8	ounces medium egg noodles
4	tablespoons butter
2	tablespoons all-purpose flour
1-1/2	cups milk
1	cup unflavored yogurt, at room temperature
8	ounces freshly grated Gruyère or Parmesan cheese

Wash the spinach thoroughly under cold running water, discarding the tough stems and bruised leaves. Do not dry. Chop the spinach and set aside.

In a heavy skillet heat the oil or butter over moderate heat. Add the onion and sauté until soft but not browned, stirring frequently. Add the spinach and dill, cover, and simmer about 10 minutes or until tender, stirring occasionally. Season with the salt and pepper. Remove from the heat and reserve.

Cook the noodles as directed on the package. Drain thoroughly. Return to the pan and toss gently but thoroughly with 2 tablespoons of the butter. Set aside.

In a small saucepan melt the remaining 2 tablespoons butter over low heat. Add the flour and cook about 2 minutes, stirring constantly. Gradually stir in the milk, then the yogurt. Cook gently until the sauce is smooth, thickened, and heated through. Stir in 3/4 cup of the cheese. Season to taste with additional salt and pepper. Remove from the heat.

In a buttered casserole arrange alternate layers of noodles, spinach, and cream sauce, beginning and ending with noodles. Sprinkle the top with the remaining cheese. Bake in a preheated 375°F oven about 45 minutes or until lightly browned.

MACARONI WITH EGGPLANT

SERVES 6

3	tablespoons butter
3	tablespoons all-purpose flour
3	cups milk
1	cup unflavored yogurt, at room temperature
	Salt and ground white pepper (preferably freshly ground) to taste
1	cup freshly grated Parmesan cheese
1	pound elbow macaroni, cooked and drained
1	recipe Fried Eggplant, page 78
1/2	pound mozzarella cheese, thinly sliced

In a medium-sized, heavy saucepan melt the butter over moderate heat. Add the flour and stir about 2 minutes. Gradually stir in the milk, then the yogurt and salt and pepper. Cook gently until the sauce is smooth, thickened, and heated through. Stir in the Parmesan cheese and remove from the heat.

In a buttered casserole place layers of macaroni, eggplant, mozzarella, and cheese sauce in that order until all are used up. Bake in a preheated 350°F oven about 45 minutes or until nicely browned on top.

AUSTRIAN NOODLES WITH HAM

SERVES 4

8 ounces wide egg noodles, broken into 1-inch pieces
5 tablespoons butter
1/3 cup finely chopped onion
3/4 cup unflavored yogurt, or 1/2 cup yogurt and 1/4 cup sour cream
3 eggs, slightly beaten
6 ounces lean cooked ham, diced
 Salt and ground white pepper (preferably freshly ground) to taste
1/4 cup bread crumbs

Cook the noodles in plenty of boiling salted water until almost tender. Drain and reserve.

In a small skillet melt 2 tablespoons of the butter over moderate heat. Add the onion and sauté until golden, stirring frequently. Add the noodles and the remaining 3 tablespoons butter and toss until the noodles are well coated with the onion and butter. Remove from the heat.

In a large mixing bowl beat the yogurt or yogurt and sour cream and eggs together with a wire whisk. Stir in the ham, the contents of the skillet, and the salt and pepper. Butter a 2-quart casserole and sprinkle with the bread crumbs. Turn the noodle and ham mixture into the casserole. Bake, uncovered, in a preheated 350°F oven about 40 minutes or until the top is golden brown and crisp and the mixture is firm.

NOODLES WITH MUSHROOMS, ZUCCHINI, AND HAM

A French-inspired creation that is quite out of the ordinary.

SERVES 4

4 tablespoons butter
10 ounces mushrooms, cut into 1/16-inch-thick slices
1 pound small zucchini, cut into 1/16-inch-thick slices
 Salt to taste
2 medium garlic cloves, finely chopped
4 ounces prosciutto, thinly sliced and cut in julienne
1/4 cup finely chopped parsley
1-1/2 teaspoons finely chopped fresh marjoram, or 1/2 teaspoon crushed dried marjoram
3/4 cup heavy cream
1/2 cup unflavored yogurt, at room temperature
8 ounces medium egg noodles, cooked and drained
 Ground white pepper to taste (preferably freshly ground)
2/3 cup freshly grated Parmesan cheese or more

In a large, heavy skillet heat the butter over high heat. Add the mushrooms and zucchini and sauté 4 minutes, stirring frequently. Sprinkle with the salt. Add the garlic and sauté, stirring often, 5 minutes or until the liquid in the pan evaporates. Add the prosciutto, parsley, and marjoram and continue to sauté 1 minute. Stir in the cream and cook 1 to 2 minutes. Remove from the heat and stir in the yogurt. Reduce the heat to low. Return the skillet to the heat and leave it there just long enough to reheat the contents. Toss in the noodles and remove from the heat. Add additional salt and the pepper. Sprinkle with the cheese and toss gently but thoroughly. Serve at once.

VARIATION Omit the garlic (or replace it with finely minced shallots or scallions) and substitute fresh tarragon for the marjoram.

GREEK MACARONI AND MEAT CASSEROLE

SERVES 6

- 3 tablespoons olive oil
- 1 medium onion, finely chopped
- 1-1/2 pounds lean ground beef or lamb
- 2 large tomatoes, peeled, seeded, and finely chopped
- 1/2 teaspoon crushed dried oregano
- 1/4 teaspoon ground cinnamon
- 1/8 teaspoon ground nutmeg (preferably freshly ground) (optional)
  Salt and ground white pepper (preferably freshly ground) to taste
- 1 cup freshly grated *kefalotiri* or Parmesan cheese
- 2 tablespoons butter
- 1 tablespoon all-purpose flour
- 1 cup milk
- 1 cup unflavored yogurt, at room temperature
- 1 egg yolk
- 1 pound elbow macaroni, cooked and drained

In a heavy skillet heat the oil over moderate heat. Add the onion and sauté until soft but not browned, stirring frequently. Add the meat and cook until browned, breaking it up with a fork. Add the tomatoes, oregano, cinnamon, nutmeg (if desired), and salt and pepper. Simmer gently 5 minutes, stirring occasionally. Add 1/2 cup of the cheese and mix well. Taste and adjust the seasoning. Remove from the heat and keep warm.

In a small saucepan melt the butter over moderate heat. Add the flour and stir about 2 minutes. Gradually stir in the milk and season with salt and pepper. Cook gently until the sauce is thickened and smooth. Blend the yogurt with the egg yolk and stir into the sauce. Heat but do not allow to boil. Remove from the heat and keep warm.

In a buttered 2-quart casserole spread half the macaroni. Spread the meat mixture over it and cover with the remaining macaroni. Pour the cream sauce over all and sprinkle with the remaining 1/2 cup cheese. Bake, uncovered, in a preheated 375°F oven about 35 minutes or until the top is golden brown.

STUFFED MACARONI SHELLS BAKED IN BROTH

Here is an unusual, flavorful, and economical Armenian dish.

SERVES 4

- 8 ounces large shell macaroni
- 12 ounces lean ground lamb, beef, or veal
- 1 medium onion, grated
- 1/2 teaspoon ground cinnamon
- 2 tablespoons finely chopped parsley
- 2 tablespoons finely chopped fresh dill (optional)
  Salt and freshly ground black pepper to taste
- 1 quart chicken broth, salted to taste
- 1 recipe Garlic Yogurt Sauce, page 85

Boil the shells in plenty of lightly salted boiling water until almost tender. Drain. Cover with cold water and let stand a few minutes. Drain well and set aside.

In a mixing bowl combine the meat, onion, cinnamon, parsley, dill (if desired), and salt and pepper. Mix together and knead with your hands until well blended and smooth. Taste and adjust the seasoning. Stuff each shell with a little of the meat mixture. Arrange the stuffed shells in a buttered shallow baking dish just large enough to hold them comfortably in one layer. Bake, uncovered, in a preheated 400°F oven 15 minutes or until lightly browned. Heat the chicken broth and add 2 cups to the baking dish. Reduce the heat to 350°F and bake 15 minutes. Add the remaining 2 cups broth and bake an additional 15 minutes. Serve with the garlic yogurt sauce.

NOTE The chicken broth may be flavored with 1 teaspoon tomato paste.

Vegetables

CAULIFLOWER FRIED IN EGG

Middle Easterners, particularly the Lebanese, are very fond of this excellent dish.

SERVES 4

- 1 medium cauliflower, trimmed and separated into florets
- 1 egg, beaten well with a pinch of salt Olive oil or corn oil for deep-frying
- 1 recipe Garlic Yogurt Sauce with Mint, page 85, or 1 recipe Avocado Yogurt Dressing, page 91

Drop the cauliflower into boiling salted water and cook briskly, uncovered, about 10 minutes or until almost tender. Drain in a colander, then pat dry with paper towels.

In a heavy saucepan or deep skillet heat 2 inches oil until it reaches a temperature of 375°F. Dip the florets, a few at a time, in the beaten egg and fry in the hot oil until golden brown on all sides. Remove with a perforated spoon and drain on paper towels. Serve with the garlic yogurt sauce or avocado dressing.

FRIED EGGPLANT

SERVES 4

- 1 large eggplant Salt
- 1/3 cup all-purpose flour
- 1/2 cup olive oil or corn oil (approximately)
- 1 recipe Garlic Yogurt Sauce, page 85, or 1 recipe Yogurt Sauce with Pine Nuts and Garlic, page 85

Remove the stem and hull from the eggplant. Peel lengthwise in 1/2-inch strips, leaving 1/2-inch strips of skin between, making a striped design. Cut crosswise into 3/8-inch-thick slices and lay on paper towels. Sprinkle liberally with the salt, weigh down with a heavy object, and let stand 30 minutes. Rinse and dry thoroughly with fresh paper towels. Coat lightly with the flour.

In a large, heavy skillet heat the oil over high heat. Reduce the heat to moderate, add the eggplant slices, and fry until lightly browned on both sides. Drain on paper towels and arrange on a serving platter. Serve chilled as an appetizer or side dish with the yogurt sauce.

BEETS IN DILL SAUCE

SERVES 6

- 1 pound beets
- 2 tablespoons butter
- 1 medium onion, finely chopped
  Salt and ground white pepper (preferably freshly ground) to taste
- 1 cup unflavored yogurt, at room temperature
- 2 tablespoons finely chopped fresh dill

Remove the tops from the beets, leaving 1 inch of the stems. Wash the beets. Cover with lightly salted boiling water. Cover and cook 30 minutes to 1 hour (longer for old beets) or until tender. Drain and slip off the skins. Dice the beets and set aside.

In a heavy skillet melt the butter over moderate heat. Add the onion and sauté until golden brown, stirring frequently. Add the beets and season with the salt and pepper. Carefully stir in the yogurt and cook briefly over low heat until just heated through. Taste and adjust the seasoning. Sprinkle with the dill and serve.

INDIAN SPINACH WITH YOGURT

SERVES 2

- 2 bunches spinach
- 1/3 cup water
- 2 tablespoons peanut oil
- 1 medium onion, finely chopped
- 1 medium garlic clove, crushed
- 1/4 teaspoon ground turmeric
- 1/2 teaspoon ground cumin
- 1/4 teaspoon ground dried chili pepper
- 1/2 teaspoon salt
- 1 cup unflavored yogurt, at room temperature
- 1 hard-cooked egg, chopped

Wash the spinach thoroughly under cold running water, discarding the tough stems and bruised leaves. Combine the spinach and water in a saucepan and bring to a boil over high heat. Reduce the heat to low, cover, and simmer about 8 minutes or until tender. Drain, and when cool enough to handle, squeeze the spinach dry and chop finely. Set aside.

In a heavy skillet heat the oil over moderate heat. Add the onion and sauté until golden, stirring frequently. Add the garlic, turmeric, cumin, chili pepper, and salt and sauté 1 minute, stirring. Add the spinach and sauté 2 minutes. Remove from the heat and stir in the yogurt. Taste and adjust the seasoning. Serve hot or chilled, garnished with the chopped egg.

MUSHROOM GOULASH

SERVES 4

  3   tablespoons butter
  1   medium onion, thinly sliced
  1   pound mushrooms, thinly sliced
1-1/2 teaspoons sweet Hungarian paprika
1/4   cup water
  1   medium tomato, peeled, seeded, and
      finely chopped
      Salt and ground white pepper (preferably
      freshly ground) to taste
  1   cup unflavored yogurt, at room
      temperature
  1   tablespoon all-purpose flour
  2   tablespoons finely chopped parsley

In a heavy casserole melt the butter over moderate heat. Add the onion and sauté until soft but not browned. Add the mushrooms and sauté until lightly browned, stirring constantly. Add the paprika and cook 1 minute, stirring. Add the water, tomato, and salt and pepper and mix gently. Cover and simmer about 10 minutes or until the mushrooms are just tender. Combine the yogurt and flour and carefully stir into the mushroom mixture. Cook over low heat until just heated through. Taste and adjust the seasoning. Sprinkle with the parsley and serve.

MASHED SWEET POTATOES OR YAMS

Baked or mashed sweet potatoes are very good simply served with a dollop of yogurt and a dusting of cinnamon. With this recipe, which involves only a little additional effort, they become an epicurean treat.

SERVES 6

  6   medium sweet potatoes or yams
  2   tablespoons butter
1/2   cup unflavored yogurt or enough to
      moisten the potatoes
  2   tablespoons dry sherry or dark rum
  2   tablespoons light brown sugar or to taste
1/2   teaspoon salt or to taste
1/3   cup chopped dates
1/3   cup toasted slivered blanched amonds or
      chopped walnuts
      Ground cinnamon
      A bowl of unflavored yogurt (optional)

Cook the unpeeled sweet potatoes or yams in boiling water to cover about 30 minutes or until tender. Drain, peel, and mash to a smooth purée. Add the butter, yogurt, sherry or rum, sugar, and salt and beat with a fork or whisk until very light. Taste and adjust the seasoning. Transfer to a serving dish. Garnish with the dates and nuts. Sprinkle with the cinnamon and serve. Pass a bowl of additional yogurt if desired.

HAWAIIAN SWEET POTATOES

Tops with roast ham or pork.

SERVES 4

2	medium sweet potatoes or yams
1/2	cup Coconut Cream, page 150
1/2	cup unflavored yogurt
2	tablespoons sugar
	Salt to taste
1	tablespoon butter
1/4	cup flaked unsweetened coconut

Cook the unpeeled sweet potatoes or yams in boiling water to cover about 30 minutes or until tender. Drain, peel, and mash to a smooth purée. Gradually beat in the coconut cream, yogurt, sugar, and salt. Turn into a buttered 9-inch pie plate. Bake in a preheated 400°F oven 20 minutes or until lightly browned.

Meanwhile, in a small, heavy skillet melt the butter over moderate heat. Add the flaked coconut and stir until lightly browned. Sprinkle over the sweet potatoes and serve hot or chilled.

PERUVIAN POTATOES WITH CHEESE SAUCE

SERVES 4

2	pounds small red-skinned new potatoes, boiled in jackets
8	ounces cream cheese, at room temperature
4	hard-cooked egg yolks
2	teaspoons finely chopped seeded fresh red or green chili pepper, or 1/4 teaspoon ground dried chili pepper or to taste
1/4	cup olive oil
1	cup unflavored yogurt
1/3	cup very finely chopped onion
	Salt to taste
8	pitted black olives
2	hard-cooked eggs, quartered

Peel the potatoes while still warm and arrange them in a serving dish. Set aside.

In a bowl mash the cream cheese, gradually adding the egg yolks until the mixture is well blended and smooth. Add the chili pepper. Beat in the oil, 1 teaspoon or so at a time, and then the yogurt. Add the onion and salt and mix thoroughly. Taste and adjust the seasoning. Spoon the sauce over the potatoes. Garnish with the olives and quartered eggs and serve.

VARIATION Substitute 1 teaspoon chili powder or to taste for the chili pepper.

COLOMBIAN POTATOES WITH CHEESE, TOMATO, AND ONION SAUCE

This sauce, known as chorreada, *is traditionally made with heavy cream and served over boiled potatoes or cooked green beans. It also goes well with cooked cauliflower or zucchini.*

SERVES 4

- 2 pounds red-skinned new potatoes, boiled in jackets
- 2 tablespoons butter
- 1 medium onion, finely chopped
- 4 scallions, sliced, including 2 inches of the green tops
- 2 large tomatoes, peeled, seeded, and chopped
- 1/2 cup unflavored yogurt, at room temperature
- 1 tablespoon finely chopped fresh coriander or parsley
- 1/2 teaspoon crushed dried oregano
- 1/4 teaspoon ground cumin
  Salt and freshly ground black pepper to taste
- 4 ounces mozzarella or Muenster cheese, freshly grated

Peel the potatoes while still warm and place them in a serving dish. Keep warm.

In a heavy skillet melt the butter over moderate heat. Add the onion and scallions and sauté until soft but not browned, stirring frequently. Add the tomatoes and cook, stirring, 5 minutes. Reduce the heat to low and add the yogurt, coriander or parsley, oregano, cumin, salt and pepper, and cheese. Cook, stirring constantly, until the cheese melts. Taste and adjust the seasoning. Spoon the sauce over the potatoes and serve at once.

PUMPKIN AND APPLES

The imaginative use of fresh and dried fruits in Caucasian cookery dates back to ancient times. Here is a delicious Armenian way to prepare pumpkin. The cinnamon yogurt sauce is not traditional but my own addition.

SERVES 6

- 2 pounds pumpkin, peeled, seeded, and cut into 1-inch pieces
- 2 medium tart apples, peeled, cored, and chopped
- 6 tablespoons sugar
- 1/2 cup water
- 4 tablespoons butter
  Pinch salt
- 1/3 cup toasted blanched almonds or hazelnuts, chopped
- 1 recipe Cinnamon Yogurt Sauce, page 86

Combine the pumpkin and apples in a heavy saucepan. Sprinkle with the sugar. Pour in the water. Dot with the butter. Season with the salt. Bring to a boil over high heat. Reduce the heat, cover, and cook gently about 20 minutes or until the pumpkin is tender, stirring several times and adding more water if needed. Transfer to a warmed serving dish. Sprinkle with the nuts and serve at once with the cinnamon yogurt sauce.

CURRIED BANANAS WITH YOGURT

SERVES 4

3 tablespoons butter
1 teaspoon curry powder
1/2 teaspoon ground turmeric
4 medium bananas, peeled and halved lengthwise
  Salt to taste
1/3 cup unflavored yogurt, at room temperature
2 tablespoons toasted sliced almonds (optional)

In a large, heavy skillet melt the butter over moderate heat. Add the curry powder and turmeric and cook 2 or 3 minutes, stirring constantly. Add the bananas and sprinkle with the salt. Cook, uncovered, 3 minutes. Turn and cook 2 minutes on the other side. Spoon the yogurt evenly over the bananas. Cook gently about 4 minutes or until just heated. Serve at once, sprinkled with the almonds, if desired.

GHIVETCH
(Rumanian Vegetable Casserole)

A fascinating combination of flavors and textures, ghivetch *exists in countless interesting variations throughout the Balkans, Middle East, and Caucasus. This version can be served as a vegetarian entrée or as an accompaniement to fish, poultry, or meat.*

SERVES 6

2 potatoes, peeled and cubed
1/2 head cauliflower, separated into florets
2 carrots, peeled and thinly sliced
1 small unpeeled eggplant, stemmed, hulled, and cubed
4 ounces green beans, trimmed and cut up
4 ounces green peas, shelled
1 sweet green or red pepper, seeded, deribbed, and thinly sliced
1 medium zucchini or yellow squash, cubed
2 medium onions, thinly sliced
4 large ripe tomatoes, peeled, seeded, and chopped
2 stalks celery, finely sliced
1 parsnip, diced (optional)
1/2 cup pitted and sliced greengage or sour plums, or
  1/2 cup sour grapes
  Salt and freshly ground black pepper to taste
1/4 cup finely chopped parsley or fresh dill
2 large garlic cloves, finely chopped
1/3 cup olive oil
1 cup unflavored yogurt

Arrange the vegetables and plums or grapes in layers in a 3-quart casserole, seasoning each layer with salt and pepper. Sprinkle with the parsley or dill and garlic. Pour the olive oil over all. Cover and bake in a preheated 350°F oven about 1 hour or until the vegetables are tender, adding a little water if the mixture seems dry. Serve hot or at room temperature, accompanied with the yogurt.

CAUCASIAN VEGETABLE PLATTER

The cooking of the Caucasus embraces some of the most extraordinary dishes to be found anywhere. Although variations of this colorful combination exist in neighboring countries, they rarely achieve the subtlety of the Caucasian version.

SERVES 4

- 1 medium eggplant
  Salt
- 2 large green peppers, seeded, deribbed, and cut into 1- to 1-1/2-inch pieces
- 2 medium carrots, peeled and sliced
- 1 medium tomato, seeded and cubed
- 1 large onion, finely chopped
  Sunflower seed oil or corn oil as needed
  Salt, freshly ground black pepper, ground cinnamon, and sugar to taste
- 1 medium tomato, cut into wedges
- 1/4 cup finely chopped fresh herbs (parsley, basil, mint, and dill)
  Unflavored yogurt

Remove the stem and hull from the eggplant, then peel and cube it. Sprinkle the eggplant cubes generously with salt and let stand 1/2 hour. Squeeze out the moisture and rinse under cold running water. Dry thoroughly with paper towels.

Fry the eggplant, green peppers, carrots, tomato, and onion separately in the oil until golden brown on all sides. Drain on paper towels. Place the vegetables in a bowl. Season them with the salt, pepper, cinnamon, and sugar and mix carefully. Mound the vegetables in the center of a serving platter. Garnish with the tomato wedges and sprinkle with the herbs. Serve warm or chilled, accompanied with a bowl of the yogurt.

Sauces

GARLIC YOGURT SAUCE

A traditional accompaniment to many Middle Eastern and Caucasian dishes, particularly lamb and vegetables.

MAKES 1 CUP

1	cup unflavored yogurt
1	medium garlic clove or to taste
1/4	teaspoon salt

Pour the yogurt into a small bowl. Crush the garlic with the salt to a smooth paste. Add to the yogurt and beat until well blended. Taste and adjust the seasoning. Cover and chill.

GARLIC YOGURT SAUCE WITH MINT
VARIATION   Add 1 tablespoon minced fresh mint or 1/2 teaspoon crushed dried mint.

GARLIC YOGURT SAUCE WITH MIXED HERBS
VARIATION   Add 1 teaspoon each minced fresh basil, mint, and parsley or fresh coriander.

YOGURT SAUCE WITH PINE NUTS AND GARLIC

In Lebanon and Syria this pleasantly sharp sauce is often served with lamb or eggplant.

MAKES 1 CUP

1/2	tablespoon butter
3	tablespoons pine nuts
2	large garlic cloves, crushed
1	cup unflavored yogurt

In a small skillet heat the butter over moderate heat. Add the pine nuts and sauté until golden brown, stirring frequently. Remove to a bowl. Add the garlic to the skillet and sauté until barely golden. Remove and add to the nuts with the yogurt. Mix well.

CINNAMON YOGURT SAUCE

This is a Caucasian classic that goes wonderfully well with baked yams or sweet potatoes, pumpkin, winter squash, or stuffed vegetables.

MAKES I CUP

- I   cup unflavored yogurt
- 2   teaspoons sugar or to taste (optional)
- I   teaspoon ground cinnamon

Combine the yogurt and sugar, if desired, in a small bowl. Blend thoroughly. Sprinkle with the cinnamon. Cover and chill.

CINNAMON YOGURT SAUCE WITH WALNUTS
VARIATION   Add 1/4 cup ground walnuts with the sugar.

CUCUMBER YOGURT SAUCE

MAKES ABOUT I-I/2 CUPS

- I   cup unflavored yogurt
- 1/2 cup peeled, seeded (if seeds are large), and finely chopped cucumber
- I   tablespoon grated mild onion
- I   tablespoon or more finely chopped fresh dill
       Salt to taste

Combine all the ingredients in a small bowl. Blend thoroughly. Taste and adjust the seasoning. Cover and chill.

HAWAIIAN DRESSING

MAKES ABOUT 1-1/4 CUPS

1/2 cup unflavored yogurt
1/2 cup sour cream
   Grated rind and freshly squeezed and
   strained juice of 1 lime
1/4 cup finely chopped fruit chutney
   (preferably homemade)

Combine all the ingredients in a small bowl.
Mix thoroughly. Cover and chill.

YOGURT FRENCH DRESSING

This is a basic dressing that you will use again and again.

MAKES ABOUT 1-1/4 CUPS

1 cup unflavored yogurt, chilled
2 tablespoons olive oil
2 tablespoons freshly squeezed and strained
   lemon juice or to taste
   Salt and ground white pepper (preferably
   freshly ground) to taste

Combine all the ingredients in a small bowl.
Beat until thoroughly blended. Taste and adjust
the seasoning.

NOTE For some salads lime juice or wine
vinegar may be substituted for the lemon juice.

YOGURT FRENCH DRESSING VARIATIONS

GARLIC YOGURT FRENCH DRESSING To
Yogurt French Dressing add 1 medium garlic
clove, crushed.

ONION YOGURT FRENCH DRESSING To
Yogurt French Dressing add 2 tablespoons
minced shallots, mild onion, or scallions.

HERB YOGURT FRENCH DRESSING To
Yogurt French Dressing add minced fresh or
crushed dried herbs such as basil, dill, chives,
parsley, tarragon, and oregano, alone or in
combination.

PAPRIKA YOGURT FRENCH DRESSING To
Yogurt French Dressing add 1/2 teaspoon sweet
Hungarian paprika or to taste.

CURRY YOGURT FRENCH DRESSING To
Yogurt French Dressing add 1 teaspoon curry
powder or to taste, 2 tablespoons minced scallions, and, if desired, 2 tablespoons minced
peeled and seeded tomato. Very good with
seafood, chicken, meats, or vegetables.

EGG AND OLIVE YOGURT FRENCH DRESSING
To Yogurt French Dressing add 2 hard-cooked
eggs, chopped, and 8 pimiento-stuffed green
olives, chopped.

YOGURT MAYONNAISE

A great substitute for conventional mayonnaise.

MAKES I CUP

1/2 cup unflavored yogurt
1/2 cup mayonnaise (preferably homemade)
1 tablespoon freshly squeezed and strained lemon juice or to taste
Salt to taste

Combine all the ingredients in a small bowl. Blend thoroughly. Taste and adjust the seasoning. Cover and chill.

NOTE More yogurt and less mayonnaise (or vice versa) may be used. Lime juice may be substituted for the lemon juice for some salads.

YOGURT MAYONNAISE VARIATIONS

GARLIC YOGURT MAYONNAISE To Yogurt Mayonnaise add 1 small garlic clove, crushed, or to taste. Mix until thoroughly smooth.

HERB YOGURT MAYONNAISE To Garlic Yogurt Mayonnaise, preceding, add 2 teaspoons minced chives, 1/2 teaspoon grated onion, 1/4 teaspoon each crushed dried basil, tarragon, and dill, 1/4 teaspoon paprika, and a dash curry powder. Mix well. Serve on salad greens.

GREEN YOGURT MAYONNAISE To Yogurt Mayonnaise add 2 tablespoons each minced spinach, watercress, parsley, and chives and 2 teaspoons each minced fresh tarragon and dill. Mix thoroughly. Excellent for fish salads.

CURRY YOGURT MAYONNAISE To Yogurt Mayonnaise add 1 teaspoon curry powder or to taste and 1 small garlic clove, crushed (optional). Mix well. Use for egg, artichoke, potato, rice, pasta, meat, or seafood salads.

EGG YOGURT MAYONNAISE To Yogurt Mayonnaise add 2 hard-cooked eggs, minced, 1 teaspoon Dijon-style mustard, and 1/8 teaspoon Tabasco sauce. Mix gently but thoroughly. Recommended for shellfish, avocado, or tomato salads.

SHRIMP YOGURT MAYONNAISE To Yogurt Mayonnaise add 1/2 cup cooked, shelled, and deveined shrimp, ground, 2 hard-cooked egg yolks, sieved, 1 tablespoon minced mild white onion, 1 tablespoon catsup, 1 tablespoon minced parsley, 1 tiny garlic clove, crushed, 1/2 teaspoon dry mustard, 1/4 teaspoon paprika, and Tabasco sauce to taste. Mix well. Serve over crisp wedges of lettuce, sliced tomatoes, or avocados.

AVOCADO YOGURT MAYONNAISE To Yogurt Mayonnaise add 1 small avocado, peeled, pitted, and mashed, 1 minced scallion or crushed garlic to taste (optional), 1 tablespoon fresh strained lemon or lime juice, and salt to taste. Mix well. Use on cooked cauliflower.

GREEN GODDESS DRESSING WITH YOGURT

Lively and well seasoned—a classic dressing for seafood.

MAKES ABOUT 1-1/4 CUPS

1/2   cup unflavored yogurt

1/2   cup mayonnaise (preferably homemade)

2   teaspoons anchovy paste, or 2 anchovy fillets finely chopped

1-1/2   tablespoons finely chopped chives or scallion (include some of the green part of the scallion)

2   tablespoons finely chopped parsley

1   small garlic clove, finely chopped

2   teaspoons freshly squeezed and strained lemon juice

1-1/2   teaspoons tarragon wine vinegar or to taste
    Salt and freshly ground black pepper to taste

Combine all the ingredients in a small bowl. Blend thoroughly. Taste and adjust the seasoning. Cover and chill.

RUSSIAN DRESSING WITH YOGURT

Recommended for vegetable, egg, or shellfish salads.

MAKES ABOUT 1-1/3 CUPS

1/2   cup unflavored yogurt

1/2   cup mayonnaise (preferably homemade)

3   tablespoons catsup or chili sauce

2   tablespoons finely chopped mild white onion, chives, or scallions (include some of the green part of the scallions)

1   tablespoon freshly squeezed and strained lemon or lime juice
    Salt to taste

In a small bowl combine all the ingredients and mix well. Taste and adjust the seasoning. Cover and chill.

VARIATION   Combine 1/2 cup unflavored yogurt, 1/2 cup mayonnaise, 1/3 cup finely chopped cooked beets, 1-1/2 teaspoons grated horseradish, 1 tablespoon caviar, and salt to taste. Mix gently but thoroughly. Chill and serve as above.

REMOULADE SAUCE WITH YOGURT

MAKES ABOUT 1-1/4 CUPS

1/2	cup unflavored yogurt
1/2	cup mayonnaise (preferably homemade)
1/2	teaspoon anchovy paste
1	small garlic clove, finely chopped
1/2	teaspoon Dijon-style mustard
1-1/2	teaspoons finely chopped fresh tarragon, or 1/2 teaspoon crushed dried tarragon
2	teaspoons finely chopped parsley
1	hard-cooked egg, finely chopped
1	teaspoon freshly squeezed and strained lemon juice or to taste
	Salt to taste

In a small bowl combine the yogurt, mayonnaise, anchovy paste, garlic, and mustard and blend thoroughly. Add the remaining ingredients and mix well. Taste and adjust the seasoning. Cover and chill.

THOUSAND ISLAND DRESSING WITH YOGURT

MAKES ABOUT 1-1/2 CUPS

2/3	cup unflavored yogurt
1/3	cup mayonnaise (preferably homemade)
3	tablespoons chili sauce or catsup
1	hard-cooked egg, finely chopped
2	tablespoons finely chopped pimiento-stuffed olives
1	tablespoon finely chopped green pepper
1	tablespoon finely chopped mild onion or chives
	Salt to taste

In a small bowl combine all the ingredients and mix well. Taste and adjust the seasoning. Serve over crisp wedges of lettuce and sliced tomatoes.

AVOCADO YOGURT DRESSING

A natural with shellfish as well as a choice dressing for lettuce and sliced tomatoes.

MAKES ABOUT 1-1/3 CUPS

- 1 medium ripe avocado, peeled, seeded, and cubed
- 1/2 cup or more unflavored yogurt
- 1 tablespoon finely chopped mild onion or scallion (include some of the green part of the scallion)
- 2 tablespoons finely chopped fresh coriander or parsley (optional)
- 1 teaspoon finely chopped fresh dill or to taste (optional)
- 1 tiny garlic clove, crushed
- 1 tablespoon freshly squeezed and strained lemon or lime juice or to taste
  Salt to taste

Combine all the ingredients in the container of an electric blender and blend until smooth, adding more yogurt if a thicker consistency is desired. Taste and adjust the seasoning. Serve chilled.

YOGURT BLUE CHEESE DRESSING

MAKES ABOUT 1 CUP

- 4 ounces cream cheese or Neufchâtel cheese, at room temperature
- 1 tablespoon crumbled Roquefort or other blue cheese
- 6 tablespoons or more unflavored yogurt
- 1 tablespoon finely chopped mild onion or chives
  Salt and freshly ground black pepper to taste

In a small bowl mash the cheeses, gradually adding the yogurt until the mixture is well blended and smooth. Add the remaining ingredients and mix thoroughly. Taste and adjust the seasoning. Cover and chill before serving.

FINNISH EGG-YOGURT SAUCE

Serve this as the Finns do, with seafood or over poached eggs on toast.

MAKES ABOUT 2-1/2 CUPS

- 2 tablespoons butter
- 2 tablespoons all-purpose flour
- 1 cup milk
- 1 cup unflavored yogurt, at room temperature
  Salt and ground white pepper (preferably freshly ground) to taste
- 4 hard-cooked eggs, finely chopped
- 2 tablespoons finely chopped fresh dill
- 1 tablespoon freshly squeezed and strained lemon juice or to taste

In a saucepan melt the butter over low heat. Add the flour and cook a minute or two, stirring constantly. Gradually add the milk, stirring until the sauce is smooth and thickened. Add the yogurt and season with the salt and pepper. Stir in the eggs, dill, and lemon juice. Simmer until just heated through. Taste and adjust the seasoning. Serve the sauce hot.

TOMATO YOGURT SAUCE

A flavorful sauce for pasta, vegetables, chicken, or veal.

MAKES ABOUT 2-1/2 CUPS

- 1/4 cup olive oil
- 1 large onion, finely chopped
- 2 medium garlic cloves, crushed, or to taste
- 4 large ripe tomatoes, peeled, seeded, and chopped
- 6 tablespoons tomato paste
- 1 tablespoon finely chopped fresh basil, or 1 teaspoon crushed dried basil
- 1 teaspoon crushed dried oregano
- 1 bay leaf
  Salt and freshly ground black pepper to taste
- 1/2 cup unflavored yogurt, at room temperature
- 2 tablespoons finely chopped parsley (optional)

In a saucepan heat the oil over moderate heat. Add the onion and sauté until soft but not browned, stirring frequently. Add the garlic and sauté, stirring, about 1 minute or so. Add the tomatoes, tomato paste, basil, oregano, bay leaf, and salt and pepper. Bring to a boil, stirring constantly. Reduce the heat to low, cover, and simmer 45 minutes. Remove and discard the bay leaf. Stir in the yogurt and parsley, if desired. Taste and adjust the seasoning. Simmer a minute or two longer until just heated through.

CHEESE YOGURT SAUCE

This keeps congenial company with vegetables, pasta, or hard-cooked eggs.

MAKES ABOUT 2 CUPS

1/2	teaspoon dry mustard
1/2	teaspoon cold water
2	tablespoons butter
2	tablespoons all-purpose flour
1	cup milk
3/4	cup unflavored yogurt, at room temperature
1	cup grated sharp Cheddar, Swiss, or Gruyère cheese
1/4	teaspoon paprika (optional) Salt and ground white pepper (preferably freshly ground) to taste

Combine the mustard with the cold water and let stand 10 minutes to develop flavor. In a saucepan melt the butter over low heat. Add the flour and cook a minute or two, stirring constantly. Gradually add the milk and then the yogurt, stirring until the sauce is smooth and thickened. Add the cheese, mustard mixture, paprika, and salt and pepper. Simmer, stirring, just until the cheese is melted.

MUSHROOM YOGURT SAUCE

In Russia this sauce (generally made with sour cream rather than yogurt) is a popular accompaniment to potato dishes and meat loaf.

MAKES ABOUT 2-1/2 CUPS

4	tablespoons butter
1	medium onion, finely chopped
2	cups sliced mushrooms Salt and freshly ground black pepper to taste
2	tablespoons all-purpose flour
1	cup hot beef broth
1/2	cup unflavored yogurt, at room temperature Dash paprika

In a saucepan melt 2 tablespoons of the butter over moderate heat. Add the onion and sauté until soft but not browned, stirring frequently. Add the remaining 2 tablespoons butter to the saucepan and heat. Add the mushrooms and sauté until golden, stirring frequently. Season with the salt and pepper. Sprinkle the flour over the mushroom mixture and sauté 1 minute or so, stirring. Gradually add the broth and simmer, stirring often, until the sauce is thickened. Remove from the heat and stir in the yogurt and paprika until well blended. Return the sauce to the heat and cook gently until just heated through. Do not allow the sauce to boil.

CURRY SAUCE

Here is a useful sauce for leftover meat, chicken, or vegetables.

MAKES ABOUT 2 CUPS

- 2 tablespoons butter
- 1 medium onion, finely chopped
- 1 medium garlic clove, finely chopped
- 2 teaspoons curry powder or to taste
- 1/2 teaspoon ground ginger
- 1 tablespoon all-purpose flour
- 1-1/2 cups hot chicken or beef broth
  Salt and freshly ground black pepper to taste
- 1 cup unflavored yogurt, at room temperature

In a heavy saucepan melt the butter over moderate heat. Add the onion and sauté until soft but not browned, stirring frequently. Add the garlic and sauté 2 or 3 minutes. Add the curry powder, ginger, and flour and cook, stirring, 2 minutes. Gradually add the broth and bring to a boil, stirring constantly. Season with the salt and pepper, cover, and simmer over low heat 15 minutes. Stir in the yogurt until well blended. Cook gently until just heated through. Taste and adjust the seasoning.

HAWAIIAN CURRY SAUCE

MAKES ABOUT 2 CUPS

- 1/4 cup peanut or corn oil
- 1 medium onion, finely chopped
- 2 medium tart apples, peeled, cored, and diced
- 1-1/2 teaspoons curry powder or to taste
- 1 teaspoon ground ginger
- 1 tablespoon all-purpose flour
- 1-1/2 cups Coconut Milk, page 150
  Salt to taste
- 2 tablespoons soy sauce
- 1 cup unflavored yogurt, at room temperature

In a heavy saucepan heat the oil over moderate heat. Add the onion and apples, cover, and simmer 10 minutes, stirring now and then. Add the curry powder, ginger, and flour and cook, stirring, 1 minute or so. Gradually add the coconut milk and bring to a boil, stirring constantly. Add the salt and soy sauce, cover, and simmer 15 minutes. Stir in the yogurt mixture until well blended. Cook very gently until just heated through. Taste and adjust the seasoning. The sauce is now ready to be combined with 2 cups cooked seafood, chicken, or meat and served on steamed rice or vermicelli.

Dessert Sauces and Dressings

SWEET YOGURT SAUCE

MAKES ABOUT 1 CUP

- 1   cup unflavored yogurt
- 2   tablespoons confectioners' sugar or honey or to taste
  - Few drops vanilla extract
- 1/4   teaspoon ground cinnamon (optional)

Pour the yogurt into a small bowl. Add the confectioners' sugar or honey and vanilla extract and beat until well blended. Sprinkle with the cinnamon, if desired, and serve over baked apples, stewed cherries, or other fruit desserts.

VARIATION   If preferred, the cinnamon may be blended with the other ingredients and the sauce sprinkled with minced walnuts.

YOGURT AND CURRANT JELLY SAUCE

A pale pink sauce, subtle enough to enhance mild-flavored fruits, pancakes, and crêpes without overpowering them.

MAKES ABOUT 3/4 CUP

- 3   ounces cream cheese or Neufchâtel cheese, at room temperature
- 1/4   cup unflavored yogurt
- 1/4   cup currant jelly
- 2   teaspoons crème de cassis or to taste (optional)

In a small bowl mash the cream cheese, gradually stirring in the yogurt until the mixture is well blended and smooth. Add the currant jelly and crème de cassis, if desired, and mix thoroughly. Cover and chill.

ORANGE YOGURT DRESSING

MAKES ABOUT 1-1/2 CUPS

- 2 eggs, slightly beaten
- 1/4 cup honey
- 1/2 cup freshly squeezed and strained orange juice
- 1 teaspoon freshly squeezed and strained lemon juice or to taste
- 2 teaspoons grated orange rind
- 1/2 teaspoon grated lemon rind
  Dash salt
- 1/2 cup unflavored yogurt
  Pinch ground cinnamon (optional)

Combine the eggs, honey, orange juice, lemon juice, orange rind, lemon rind, and salt in the top of a double boiler. Cook over hot, not boiling, water about 15 minutes or until thickened, stirring constantly. Remove from the heat, cover, and chill. Fold in the yogurt and cinnamon, if desired, until thoroughly blended. Serve on dessert fruit salads.

CHOCOLATE YOGURT SAUCE

Spoon over individual portions of cake, or use to ice a cake.

MAKES ABOUT 1-1/2 CUPS

- 6 1-ounce squares semisweet chocolate
- 1/2 cup unflavored yogurt
- 1/2 teaspoon ground cinnamon
- 1/4 cup milk
  Confectioners' sugar to taste

Melt the chocolate pieces over very low heat or over hot water, stirring constantly. Remove from the heat. Stir in the remaining ingredients until thoroughly blended.

VARIATION   Substitute 2 to 3 tablespoons apricot or chocolate-mint liqueur for the cinnamon. Use only 2 tablespoons milk.

YOGURT, LIME, AND CRÈME DE MENTHE DRESSING

A cool, elegant dressing for pineapple, pears, melon, or other fruits.

MAKES ABOUT 1-1/4 CUPS

- 1 cup unflavored yogurt
- 3 tablespoons freshly squeezed and strained lime juice or to taste
- 1-1/2 tablespoons green crème de menthe liqueur
- 1 mint sprig

In a small bowl combine the yogurt, lime juice, and crème de menthe liqueur. Blend thoroughly. Cover and chill. Serve garnished with the mint sprig.

YOGURT, HONEY, AND CRÈME DE MENTHE DRESSING VARIATION   Omit the mint sprig. Substitute 1 tablespoon honey for the lime juice. Blend and serve as above.

STRAWBERRY YOGURT SAUCE

This can grace fruit salads, pancakes, or crêpes.

MAKES ABOUT 3 CUPS

- 2 cups unflavored yogurt
- 1-1/4 cups strawberries, hulled, sliced, and sweetened, or
  - 1 10-ounce package frozen sweetened sliced strawberries, thawed
- 2 tablespoons strawberry liqueur (optional)
- 1/8 teaspoon almond extract (optional)

Combine all the ingredients in a bowl. Stir until thoroughly blended. Cover and chill.

APRICOT YOGURT SAUCE

Here is an exquisite sauce to serve on delicately flavored fruits such as bananas and pears, as well as on pancakes and crêpes.

MAKES ABOUT 3/4 CUP

- 3 ounces cream cheese or Neufchâtel cheese, at room temperature
- 1/4 cup unflavored yogurt
- 1/4 cup or more apricot preserves
- 2 teaspoons apricot liqueur or to taste

In a small bowl mash the cream cheese, gradually stirring in the yogurt until the mixture is well blended and smooth. Add the apricot preserves and apricot liqueur and mix thoroughly. Cover and chill.

YOGURT CRÈME CHANTILLY

I created this recipe in an effort to come up with an alternative to sweetened whipped cream that would be much lower in calories.

MAKES ABOUT 1-1/2 CUPS

- 1/2 cup chilled heavy cream
- 1-1/2 tablespoons confectioners' sugar or to taste, sifted
- 1/2 to 1 teaspoon vanilla extract
- 3/4 cup soft Yogurt Cheese, page 148 (omit the salt)

Pour the cream into a chilled bowl and beat until it begins to stiffen. Add the confectioners' sugar and vanilla extract and continue to beat until stiff. Fold in the yogurt cheese gently but thoroughly. You may serve this at once, or cover and refrigerate it up to several hours.

NOTE   One tablespoon rum, Grand Marnier, or apricot or other liqueur may be substituted for the vanilla extract.

CRÈME CHANTILLY VARIATIONS

BERRY YOGURT CRÈME CHANTILLY   Force 1/2 pint each strawberries and raspberries through a fine sieve, or whirl them in an electric blender until puréed. Strain. Add 1/2 cup sugar or to taste and 1-1/2 teaspoons orange flower water and mix well. Cover and chill. Just before serving, fold the puréed fruit mixture into the yogurt crème Chantilly, blending them together gently but thoroughly with a rubber spatula. Use as a filling or topping for angel or sponge cake, or serve with ice cream or as a dessert in chilled parfait or sherbet glasses, garnished with strawberries.

PINEAPPLE OR MANGO YOGURT CRÈME CHANTILLY   Place 1-1/2 cups finely chopped and drained fresh pineapple or mango in a bowl. Sprinkle with 1 tablespoon light or amber rum if desired. Cover and chill. Just before serving, using a rubber spatula, fold the fruit into the yogurt crème Chantilly, blending them together gently but thoroughly. Use as a topping for angel, sponge, or coconut cake, or serve as a dessert in chilled parfait or sherbet glasses.

APRICOT YOGURT CRÈME CHANTILLY   Fold 1/2 cup diced candied apricots, steeped in apricot brandy or kirsch, into the yogurt crème Chantilly along with 1/4 cup finely chopped toasted blanched almonds, blending them together gently but thoroughly with a rubber spatula. Serve with angel or sponge cake or ice cream.

KUMQUAT YOGURT CRÈME CHANTILLY   Fold 1/2 cup drained and finely diced preserved kumquats into the yogurt crème Chantilly, blending them together gently but thoroughly with a rubber spatula. Use as a topping for angel, sponge, or coconut cake, or serve with ice cream.

CHESTNUT YOGURT CRÈME CHANTILLY   Fold 1/2 cup broken preserved glazed chestnuts (*marrons glacés*), steeped in brandy, curaçao, or rum, into the yogurt crème Chantilly, blending them together gently but thoroughly with a rubber spatula. Use as a topping for cakes or serve with ice cream.

COCONUT YOGURT CRÈME CHANTILLY   Fold 1/2 cup lightly toasted shredded unsweetened coconut and 1 tablespoon light or amber rum into the yogurt crème Chantilly, blending them together gently but thoroughly with a rubber spatula. Use as a topping for cakes or dessert fruit salads.

Breads

YOGURT BREAD

A crusty, shortening-free bread with a sourdough-like flavor.

MAKES 2 LOAVES

1-1/2 cups warm water (110 to 115°F)
1-1/2 packages active dry yeast
  1   cup unflavored yogurt, at room
       temperature
  1   tablespoon salt
6-1/2 cups unsifted all-purpose flour
       (approximately)
       Cornmeal

Pour the water into a large mixing bowl and sprinkle with the yeast. Let the mixture rest 5 minutes, then stir to dissolve the yeast. Add the yogurt and salt to the dissolved yeast and mix well. Stir in 3 cups of the flour and beat with a large spoon until smooth. Add the remaining flour, a little at a time, mixing thoroughly.

Knead the dough in the bowl until it is no longer sticky. Turn it onto a lightly floured surface and knead thoroughly, sprinkling with flour as necessary, until the dough is fairly stiff. Form into a ball and place in a lightly oiled bowl, turning to grease the top. Cover loosely with a cloth and let rise in a warm place (85°F) free from drafts (such as an unlit oven with a pan of hot water on the bottom rack) about 1 to 1-1/2 hours or until the dough doubles in bulk.

Punch down the dough and divide into 2 equal parts. Shape each into a long or round loaf. Place on 2 baking sheets sprinkled with the cornmeal. Cover and let rise again in a warm place until doubled in bulk, about 1 to 1-1/2 hours.

With a sharp knife make diagonal slashes across each loaf, about 1/2 inch deep and 2 inches apart. Brush the loaves with water and bake in a preheated 400°F oven about 45 minutes or until golden brown, brushing again with water twice at intervals during the baking period. Remove from the pans and cool on a wire rack.

WHOLE WHEAT YOGURT BREAD

MAKES 2 LOAVES

1/3 cup warm water (110 to 115°F)
  1 package active dry yeast
  2 cups unflavored yogurt, at room
     temperature
  3 tablespoons butter, melted
  1 tablespoon salt
1/2 cup honey
  6 cups unsifted stone-ground whole wheat
     flour (approximately)

Pour the water into a large mixing bowl and sprinkle with the yeast. Let the mixture rest 5 minutes, then stir to dissolve the yeast. Add the yogurt, 2 tablespoons of the butter, salt, and honey. Gradually stir in 5 cups of the flour to make a soft dough. Spread 1/2 cup of the remaining flour on a board. Turn out the dough and knead vigorously about 10 minutes, adding more flour if necessary, until smooth and elastic. Place the dough in a lightly oiled bowl, turning to grease the top. Cover loosely with a cloth and let rise in a warm place (85°F) free from drafts (such as an unlit oven with a pan of hot water on the bottom rack) about 2 hours or until the dough is almost doubled in bulk.

Punch down the dough and divide into 2 equal parts. Shape each into a loaf and place in an 8 × 4-1/2-inch loaf pan that has been greased on the bottom only. Cover with a cloth and let rise again in a warm place until almost doubled in bulk, about 45 minutes. Brush the loaves with the remaining 1 tablespoon butter. Bake in a preheated 375°F oven about 45 minutes or until golden brown. Remove from the pans and cool on a wire rack.

GERMAN CHEESE BREAD

MAKES 2 LOAVES

3-1/2 to 3-3/4 cups unsifted all-purpose flour
1 package active dry yeast
3/4 teaspoon sugar
1-3/4 teaspoons salt
1/4 cup water
1-1/2 tablespoons butter
1/2 cup unflavored yogurt, at room temperature
3 eggs
6 ounces Muenster cheese, shredded
Half of 1 beaten egg
1-1/2 teaspoons milk

In a large bowl combine 2 cups of the flour, yeast, sugar, and salt and mix well. In a small saucepan heat the water and butter to the scalding point, stirring to melt the butter. Remove from the heat and stir in the yogurt. Cool to 120°F. Gradually add the yogurt mixture to the dry ingredients, blending well. Add the 3 eggs, 3/4 cup of the cheese, and 1/2 cup of the flour and beat thoroughly. Add enough of the remaining flour to make a stiff dough.

Turn the dough out onto a lightly floured surface and knead about 10 minutes until smooth and elastic. Place in a lightly oiled bowl, turning to grease the top. Cover loosely with a cloth and let rise in a warm place (85°F) free from drafts (such as an unlit oven with a pan of hot water on the bottom rack) about 1 hour or until the dough doubles in bulk.

Punch down the dough and divide into 2 equal parts. Shape each into a round loaf. Place on 2 greased baking sheets. Cover and let rise again in a warm place about 1 hour or until doubled in bulk. Mix together the beaten egg and milk and brush over the loaves. Top the loaves with the remaining cheese. Bake in a preheated 350°F oven about 30 minutes or until golden brown. Remove from the pans and cool on a wire rack.

PRUNE BREAD

MAKES 1 LOAF

1 cup unsifted all-purpose flour
1 cup unsifted whole wheat flour
1/2 teaspoon double-acting baking powder
1 teaspoon baking soda
1 teaspoon salt
1/2 teaspoon ground cinnamon
4 tablespoons butter
3/4 cup brown sugar, firmly packed
1 egg
1 cup unflavored yogurt
1 12-ounce package moist pitted prunes, chopped
2/3 cup chopped walnuts

Sift together the all-purpose flour and wheat flour, baking powder, baking soda, salt, and cinnamon in a bowl. Set aside. In a large mixing bowl beat the butter and brown sugar until creamy, then beat in the egg. Add the flour mixture alternately with the yogurt to the creamed mixture. With the last addition of flour add the prunes and nuts. Stir until blended. Turn into a greased 9 × 5-inch loaf pan. Bake in a preheated 350°F oven about 1 hour or until a food pick inserted in the center comes out clean. Remove from the oven and let stand in the pan 10 minutes, then turn out on a wire rack to finish cooling. Wrap with aluminum foil and store overnight. Serve the bread thinly sliced, spread with cream cheese if you wish.

INDIAN BREAD

Very good with curry dishes or spread with honey.

MAKES ABOUT 8 ROUND, FLAT BREADS

- 2 cups unsifted all-purpose flour
- 1/2 teaspoon baking soda
- 1/4 teaspoon salt
  About 3/4 cup unflavored yogurt, at room temperature
  Melted butter or margarine
  Corn oil

In a large mixing bowl sift together the flour, soda, and salt. Add enough yogurt to achieve a firm dough. Knead a few minutes, cover with a cloth, and let rest at room temperature about 15 minutes.

Form the dough into 2-inch balls. Roll out each ball about 1/2 inch thick. Brush the surface generously with the melted butter or margarine. Fold into a ball and roll out again to about 1/8 inch thick. Cook on a hot griddle, brushing with the oil on both sides and turning frequently until golden brown on both sides. Serve warm.

YOGURT SCONES

A centuries-old teatime treat throughout Scotland, Ireland, and northern England. Yogurt replaces the milk or cream used in the traditional recipe.

MAKES 24

- 1/2 cup currants or raisins
- 2-1/2 to 2-3/4 cups unsifted all-purpose flour
- 1/2 teaspoon salt
- 1/2 cup sugar
- 2 teaspoons double-acting baking powder
- 1 teaspoon baking soda
- 6 tablespoons butter
- 1 egg, beaten
- 1 cup unflavored yogurt
  Rind of 1/2 lemon, grated

Dredge the currants in 2 tablespoons of the flour and set aside. Sift the remaining flour with the salt, sugar, baking powder, and baking soda. Cut in the butter until the mixture resembles coarse meal. Add the beaten egg to the flour mixture along with the yogurt, currants, and lemon rind. Mix well. Divide the dough into 24 balls. Flatten to 1/2-inch-thick round cakes. Arrange on a lightly greased cookie sheet. Bake in a preheated 425°F oven about 12 minutes or until lightly browned. Cool on wire racks or serve warm with butter and jam.

YOGURT MUFFINS

MAKES 12 MUFFINS

2	cups unsifted all-purpose flour
1/3	cup sugar
2	teaspoons double-acting baking powder
1	teaspoon baking soda
1/2	teaspoon salt
1	egg, well beaten
3/4	cup unflavored yogurt
4	tablespoons butter, melted

Sift together the flour, sugar, baking powder, baking soda, and salt into a large bowl. Combine the egg, yogurt, and melted butter. Add to the dry ingredients and stir just until they are moistened. Do not beat; the batter should be lumpy. Spoon into well-greased muffin cups, filling each about 2/3 full. Bake in a preheated 400°F oven about 25 minutes or until the muffins are golden brown and a food pick inserted in the center comes out clean. Serve at once.

YOGURT MUFFIN VARIATIONS

BLUEBERRY YOGURT MUFFINS   Add 1 cup blueberries to the sifted dry ingredients.

APPLE YOGURT MUFFINS   Sift 1/2 teaspoon ground cinnamon (or 1/4 teaspoon each ground cinnamon and nutmeg) with the dry ingredients and stir 1/2 cup peeled and finely chopped apple into the batter.

BANANA YOGURT MUFFINS   Mix 3/4 cup mashed ripe bananas with the egg, yogurt, and melted butter.

CHEESE YOGURT MUFFINS   Omit the sugar and add 1/2 to 2/3 cup grated sharp Cheddar cheese to the sifted dry ingredients. Sprinkle with paprika before baking.

CRANBERRY YOGURT MUFFINS   Mix 3/4 cup finely chopped cranberries, 2 tablespoons sugar, and 3/4 teaspoon grated orange rind (optional). Add to the sifted dry ingredients.

YOGURT CORN BREAD OR CORN MUFFINS

MAKES 1 9 × 9-INCH CORN BREAD OR
12 MUFFINS

1	cup unsifted all-purpose flour
3/4	cup yellow cornmeal
2	to 4 tablespoons sugar
1	teaspoon double-acting baking powder
1	teaspoon baking soda
1	teaspoon salt
1	cup unflavored yogurt
1	egg, slightly beaten
3	tablespoons butter, melted

Sift together the flour, cornmeal, sugar, baking powder, baking soda, and salt into a large bowl. Make a well in the center and add the yogurt, egg, and melted butter. Stir to blend the liquid and dry ingredients. Turn the batter into a greased 9 × 9-inch pan or spoon into greased muffin cups, filling each 2/3 full. Bake in a pre-heated 425°F oven 25 to 30 minutes or until golden brown and cooked through.

Waffles, Pancakes, & Fritters

HAWAIIAN KUMQUAT WAFFLES

SERVES 4

1	10-ounce jar whole preserved kumquats in syrup
2	egg yolks
1	cup unflavored yogurt
1/3	cup melted butter
1	cup unsifted all-purpose flour
1/2	teaspoon double-acting baking powder
1/2	teaspoon baking soda
1/2	teaspoon salt
1	tablespoon sugar
2	egg whites
1/2	cup firmly packed brown sugar
4	tablespoons butter

Drain the kumquats, reserving 1/3 cup of the syrup. Remove and discard the seeds, then finely chop the kumquats. Set aside.

In a large bowl beat the egg yolks, then beat in the yogurt and melted butter. Add all but 1/4 cup of the minced kumquats. Combine the flour, baking powder, baking soda, salt, and sugar in a bowl and mix well. Stir the flour mixture into the egg yolk mixture until just blended.

Beat the egg whites until stiff peaks form. Fold into the batter. Bake in a preheated greased waffle iron until brown.

In a small saucepan combine the brown sugar, 4 tablespoons butter, and 1/3 cup reserved kumquat syrup. Bring to a boil over moderate heat. Reduce the heat and simmer, uncovered, stirring to dissolve the sugar. Add the remaining 1/4 cup minced kumquats and simmer a few minutes until the sauce is slightly thickened. Serve hot with the kumquat waffles.

BANANA WAFFLE VARIATION   Omit the kumquats, brown sugar, and 4 tablespoons butter. Add to the batter before folding in the egg whites 1/2 cup peeled and thinly sliced ripe banana and 1/2 teaspoon ground cinnamon, if desired. Serve with honey or a fruit syrup or sauce.

COCONUT WAFFLE VARIATION   Omit the kumquats, brown sugar, and 4 tablespoons butter. Add to the batter before folding in the egg whites 1/3 cup shredded coconut. Serve the waffles topped with papaya slices, garnished with lime wedges, and accompanied with coconut syrup.

YOGURT PANCAKES

These Middle Eastern pancakes are usually eaten with honey but are equally delicious served with maple syrup or yogurt mixed with sweetened berries or other fresh fruit.

SERVES 6

  4   egg yolks
1/4   cup sugar
  2   cups unflavored yogurt
  4   tablespoons butter, melted
1-1/2 cups sifted all-purpose flour
  2   teaspoons double-acting baking powder
  1   teaspoon baking soda
  1   teaspoon salt
  3   egg whites, beaten until stiff

In a large bowl beat the egg yolks well. Stir in the sugar, then the yogurt and butter. Sift together the flour, baking powder, baking soda, and salt. Add to the yogurt mixture, blending until smooth. Fold in the beaten egg whites. Drop by tablespoons onto a hot, lightly greased griddle or heavy skillet, turning to brown on both sides. Serve at once.

GERMAN APPLE PANCAKES

Enjoy these at brunch or with afternoon coffee.

SERVES 4

  1   tablespoon butter
  1   large Golden Delicious apple, peeled, cored, and cubed
  1   cup unflavored yogurt
1/2   teaspoon salt
  1   tablespoon milk
  3   egg yolks
  1   tablespoon sugar
3/4   cup sifted all-purpose flour (approximately)
  3   egg whites, stiffly beaten
  2   tablespoons Clarified Butter, page 151, or as needed
      Sugar and ground cinnamon to taste

In a small, heavy skillet melt the butter over moderate heat. Add the apple cubes and sauté until golden brown, turning frequently. Remove from the heat and set aside.

Combine the yogurt, salt, and milk in a bowl and stir well. Beat in the egg yolks and sugar. Gradually stir in the flour until the batter is the consistency of heavy cream. Add the sautéed apple cubes and mix gently but thoroughly. Fold in the egg whites.

In a large, heavy skillet heat 1 tablespoon of the clarified butter over medium-high heat, tilting the skillet to coat its surface. For each pancake drop about 1/3 cup of the batter into the hot butter, spacing the pancakes 3 inches apart. Cook until the undersides turn golden brown. Turn and brown the other sides. Cook the remaining pancakes, adding more butter as needed. Serve sprinkled with the sugar and cinnamon.

SOUTH PACIFIC FRUIT PANCAKES

Why not serve these for Sunday brunch? They are certainly worth getting up for!

SERVES 4

- 4 tablespoons butter
- 3 tablespoons brown sugar
- 2 teaspoons ground cinnamon
- 1 ripe papaya or mango, peeled, seeded, and cut in julienne
- 1 egg
- 1/2 cup unflavored yogurt
- 2/3 cup unsifted all-purpose flour (approximately)
- 1/2 teaspoon double-acting baking powder
- 1/4 teaspoon baking soda
- 1/4 teaspoon salt
- 2 tablespoons confectioners' sugar
  Butter as needed to cook pancakes

In a heavy skillet melt 4 tablespoons butter over moderate heat. Remove 1 tablespoon melted butter and reserve. Stir the brown sugar and 1-1/2 teaspoons of the cinnamon into the melted butter in the skillet. Add the papaya or mango and cook a few minutes, stirring gently until half-tender. Remove from the heat and set aside.

In a large bowl beat the egg well. Stir in the yogurt and the reserved 1 tablespoon melted butter. Sift together the flour, baking powder, baking soda, salt, and 1 tablespoon of the confectioners' sugar. Add to the egg mixture and blend until the batter is the consistency of heavy cream. Add the papaya or mango and mix lightly.

In a small, heavy skillet melt 1 tablespoon butter. Drop the papaya or mango batter, a large spoonful at a time, into the hot butter and cook until lightly browned on the bottom sides. Turn and lightly brown the other sides. Repeat until all the batter has been used, adding more butter to the skillet as necessary.

Mix together the remaining 1 tablespoon confectioners' sugar and 1/2 teaspoon cinnamon and sprinkle over the pancakes. Serve at once.

NOTE   Other fruit such as peaches, pineapple, or bananas are also delicious prepared in the above manner.

FLORENTINE CRÊPES

SERVES 4 TO 6

Crêpes

2 cups sifted all-purpose flour
4 eggs
1 cup milk
1 cup water
1/2 teaspoon salt
4 tablespoons butter, melted
 About 2 tablespoons melted butter for brushing the crêpe pan

Cheese Sauce

4 tablespoons butter
5 tablespoons all-purpose flour
2-1/4 cups hot milk
1/2 teaspoon salt
 Ground white pepper and nutmeg (both preferably freshly ground) to taste
1/2 cup unflavored yogurt, at room temperature
1 cup grated Swiss cheese

Spinach Filling

12 ounces spinach
1/4 cup water
 Salt to taste

Mushroom and Cheese Filling

2 tablespoons butter
6 ounces mushrooms, diced
3 tablespoons finely chopped shallots
8 ounces cream cheese, at room temperature
1 egg
 Salt and freshly ground black pepper to taste
1 tablespoon butter

TO MAKE THE CRÊPES Put the flour, eggs, milk, water, salt, and 4 tablespoons melted butter in the container of an electric blender. Cover and blend at high speed 1 minute. Scrape down the sides of the container with a rubber spatula and blend again about 15 seconds or until smooth. Or in a mixing bowl blend the eggs and

flour with an electric beater or wooden spoon, then beat in the milk, water, melted butter, and salt. Cover and refrigerate the batter 2 hours.

Warm a 6- to 7-inch crêpe pan or heavy skillet over high heat, testing it with a drop of cold water. When it splutters and evaporates instantly, the pan is ready. Brush the pan lightly with melted butter. Reduce the heat to medium. Stir the crêpe batter with a wire whisk or spoon. Remove the pan from the heat and, using a small ladle, immediately pour about 2 tablespoons of the batter into the pan (just enough batter to coat the bottom of the pan thinly). Quickly tilt the pan in all directions to allow the batter to cover the bottom completely. The batter will adhere to the pan and begin to firm up almost instantly. At once pour off any excess batter back into the bowl and note the correct amount for the next crêpe. The cooked crêpes should be no more than 1/16 inch thick. If the batter seems too heavy (that is, if it spreads too slowly in the pan), thin it by stirring in a little milk or water. Place the pan over medium heat and cook about 1 minute or until the underside of the crêpe is very lightly browned. If any holes appear in the crêpe, spoon on a little batter just to cover. Turn it over with a narrow spatula, using your fingers to help, and cook 30 to 60 seconds or until very lightly browned on the other side. Slide the crêpe onto a plate. Repeat with the remaining batter, greasing the pan lightly each time if it seems necessary and stacking the crêpes as they are cooked. Set aside.

TO MAKE THE CHEESE SAUCE In a medium-sized, heavy saucepan melt the butter over moderate heat. Stir in the flour and cook gently without coloring, about 2 minutes. Remove from the heat and add the milk, salt, and pepper and nutmeg. Boil, stirring, 1 minute. Reduce the heat to low and stir in the yogurt and all but 3 tablespoons of the cheese, which will be used near the end of the recipe. Taste and adjust the seasoning. Remove from the heat and keep warm.

TO MAKE THE SPINACH FILLING Wash the spinach thoroughly under cold running water, discarding the tough stems and bruised leaves. Combine the spinach and water in a saucepan and bring to a boil over high heat. Reduce the heat to low, cover, and simmer 8 minutes. Drain, and when cool enough to handle, squeeze the spinach dry and chop. Blend about 1/2 cup of the cheese sauce into the spinach. Taste and adjust the seasoning. Set aside.

TO MAKE THE MUSHROOM AND CHEESE FILLING In a heavy skillet melt the butter over moderate heat. Add the mushrooms and shallots and sauté until lightly browned, stirring frequently. Remove from the heat. In a mixing bowl mash the cream cheese. Beat in the egg and about 1/2 cup of the cheese sauce. Add the mushroom mixture and blend well. Season to taste with the salt and pepper.

TO ASSEMBLE AND BAKE THE CRÊPES
Place a crêpe in the bottom of a lightly buttered baking dish about 9 inches in diameter and 1-1/2 inches deep. Spread with a layer of the spinach filling. Cover with a crêpe, pressing it gently. Spread it with a layer of the mushroom and cheese filling. Continue with alternating layers of crêpes and the two fillings, ending the mound with a crêpe. Pour the remaining cheese sauce over the mound. Sprinkle with the remaining 3 tablespoons grated Swiss cheese. Dot with the 1 tablespoon butter. Bake in a preheated 375°F oven 25 to 30 minutes or until heated through and lightly browned on top. To serve, cut into pie-shaped wedges.

NOTE This dish can be assembled for the oven in the morning and refrigerated until about half an hour before serving. The crêpes themselves can be made several days in advance and frozen. Stack them between layers of waxed paper, wrap in aluminum foil, and freeze. When you are ready to use them, place the frozen crêpes, still in their foil wrapping, in a preheated 275°F oven until heated through.

MEXICAN CRÊPES

These crêpes are an example of the French influence on Mexican cookery. Similar to enchiladas*, they are more subtle in flavor.*

SERVES 4

1/2 recipe Crêpes, page 108
1 recipe Tomato Yogurt Sauce, page 92 (omit the parsley)
2 canned peeled green chilies, seeded
1/4 teaspoon crushed dried oregano
8 ounces sliced cooked ham
6 ounces Monterey Jack cheese, shredded

Place the tomato yogurt sauce, green chilies, and oregano in the container of an electric blender. Whirl until smooth. Pour about half of the sauce into 4 shallow, individual serving-size ovenproof dishes. Divide the ham and half of the cheese evenly among the crêpes. Roll up tightly to enclose the filling. Place 2 filled crêpes, seam sides down, in each dish. Pour over the remaining sauce and sprinkle the remaining cheese over the top. Bake, uncovered, in a preheated 350°F oven about 15 minutes or until the cheese is melted and the crêpes are heated through. Serve at once.

CHEESE BLINTZES

Here is an adaptation of the thin cheese-filled pancakes so popular in Jewish kitchens.

SERVES 4 TO 6

Pancakes

2 eggs
1/2 cup water
1/2 cup unflavored yogurt
1 tablespoon melted butter or margarine
1/8 teaspoon salt
3/4 cup sifted all-purpose flour
About 2 tablespoons melted butter for brushing the crêpe pan

Cheese Filling

1 pound pot cheese, crumbled farmers' cheese, or dry cottage cheese
6 ounces cream cheese, at room temperature
1 egg
3 tablespoons sugar or to taste
1/4 teaspoon salt
1/4 teaspoon ground cinnamon
1 teaspoon vanilla extract
4 tablespoons butter or more (preferably Clarified Butter, page 151)
1 cup unflavored yogurt or Yogurt Crème Chantilly, page 98
1 recipe Cherry sauce, page 119, or cherry preserves

TO MAKE THE PANCAKES   In a mixing bowl beat the eggs with the water and yogurt, using a rotary beater or wire whisk. Beat in the melted butter or margarine and salt. Gradually add the flour, beating constantly until the batter is smooth. Alternatively, put the flour, eggs, water, yogurt, melted butter or margarine, and salt in the container of an electric blender. Cover and blend at high speed 1 minute. Scrape down the sides of the container with a rubber spatula and blend again about 15 seconds or until smooth. Cover and let the batter rest at room temperature 30 minutes.

Cook the pancakes one at a time as directed in the recipe for Florentine Crêpes, page 108, but brown them on one side only.

TO PREPARE THE CHEESE FILLING   In a mixing bowl combine the cheeses, egg, sugar, salt, cinnamon, and vanilla extract. Beat until the mixture is well blended and smooth.

To make each blintz, place a rectangular mound of about 2 tablespoons cheese filling across the lower third of the *browned* side of each pancake. Fold over once, turn the sides in, and fold over once or twice more to form a small rectangular package. Set aside.

In a large, heavy skillet melt 4 tablespoons butter over medium-high heat. Fry the blintzes, seam sides down and without crowding, until golden brown. Turn carefully and fry until lightly browned on the other sides, adding more butter as necessary. Transfer to a serving platter and keep warm.

Spoon the yogurt or yogurt crème Chantilly onto each serving of blintzes and top with the cherry sauce or cherry preserves.

STRAWBERRY CRÊPES

This flaming dessert is none other than the New Orleans specialty Crêpes Fitzgerald, with yogurt substituted for the sour cream.

SERVES 4

Crêpes

1/2	cup sifted all-purpose flour
1	tablespoon sugar
1/8	teaspoon salt
2	eggs
1/2	cup milk
1/4	teaspoon vanilla extract
1/2	teaspoon finely grated orange rind
	About 2 tablespoons melted butter for brushing the crêpe pan

Filling

6	ounces cream cheese, at room temperature
1/2	cup unflavored yogurt
2-1/2	tablespoons sugar
2	teaspoons finely grated lemon rind

Strawberry Sauce

2	cups strawberries, hulled, or 26 ounces frozen unsweetened whole strawberries, thawed and drained
4	tablespoons butter
1/4	cup strawberry liqueur
2-1/2	tablespoons sugar
4	tablespoons butter
1/4	cup kirsch

TO MAKE THE CRÊPES   Put the flour, sugar, salt, eggs, milk, and vanilla extract in the container of an electric blender. Cover and blend at high speed 1 minute. Scrape down the sides of the container with a rubber spatula and blend again about 15 seconds or until smooth. Pour the batter into a bowl and stir in the orange rind. Alternatively, combine the flour, sugar, salt, and eggs in a mixing bowl. Stir well. Gradually mix in the milk and vanilla extract. Beat with a wire whisk or an electric beater until smooth. Rub the batter through a fine sieve into a bowl and stir in the orange rind. Cover and let the batter rest at room temperature 1 hour.

Cook the crêpes one at a time as directed in the recipe for Florentine Crêpes, page 108.

TO PREPARE THE FILLING   In a mixing bowl mash the cream cheese and beat vigorously until fluffy, then beat in the yogurt until the mixture is well blended and smooth. Stir in the sugar and lemon rind. Place about 1-1/2 tablespoons of the mixture across the lower third of each crêpe and roll up tightly. Reserve.

TO MAKE THE STRAWBERRY SAUCE   Purée the strawberries. In a small saucepan melt the butter over moderate heat. Add the puréed strawberries, the strawberry liqueur, and the sugar. Bring to a boil, stirring to dissolve the sugar. Cover the pan, remove from the heat, and set aside.

In a large, heavy skillet or chafing dish melt the 4 tablespoons butter over moderate heat. Add the filled crêpes and, turning them carefully with a spoon, cook about 3 minutes or until heated through. Pour the kirsch over the crêpes, allow it to warm, and then ignite it with a match. Slide the pan back and forth over the heat until the flame dies. Transfer the crêpes to a warmed serving platter. Pour the strawberry sauce over them and serve immediately.

NOTE   If you wish, you can make the crêpes in advance and freeze them. Stack them between layers of waxed paper, wrap in aluminum foil, and freeze. When needed, place the frozen crêpes, still in their foil wrapping, in a preheated 275°F oven until heated through.

POLYNESIAN FRUIT FRITTERS

A South Seas triumph.

SERVES 6

Batter

1	cup sifted all-purpose flour
1	tablespoon sugar
1	teaspoon double-acting baking powder
1	teaspoon baking soda
1/2	teaspoon salt
2	eggs
1/2	cup unflavored yogurt
1	teaspoon peanut or corn oil
1/2	teaspoon vanilla extract
1	teaspoon finely grated lemon rind

	Peanut or corn oil for deep-frying
2	pounds sliced fruit (bananas, pineapple, papayas, peaches, or pears)
1/2	cup flour
	Confectioners' sugar

TO MAKE THE BATTER Sift the 1 cup flour with the sugar, baking powder, baking soda, and salt. In a large bowl combine the eggs, yogurt, 1 teaspoon oil, vanilla extract, and lemon rind and beat until well blended. Gradually beat in the flour mixture until smooth.

In a deep-fryer or heavy saucepan heat 3 inches of the oil until it reaches a temperature of 375°F on a deep-frying thermometer. Coat the fruit with flour, shaking off the excess. Dip it in the batter and deep-fry 3 or 4 fritters at a time about 3 minutes or until golden brown, turning frequently. With a perforated spoon transfer the fritters onto paper towels to drain. Sprinkle with the confectioners' sugar and serve.

YOGURT FRITTERS IN SYRUP

In the Middle East these syrupy doughnuts are sold in bazaars during festivals.

SERVES 6

Syrup

1-1/2	cups sugar
3/4	cup water
1	tablespoon freshly squeezed and strained lemon juice
1-1/2	teaspoons each rose water and orange flower water*

Fritters

4	eggs
1	cup unflavored yogurt
2	cups all-purpose flour, sifted
2	teaspoons sugar
1	tablespoon double-acting baking powder
1	tablespoon baking soda

	Corn oil for deep-frying
1/4	cup finely chopped walnuts or unsalted pistachio nuts

TO MAKE THE SYRUP In a small saucepan bring the sugar, water, and lemon juice to a boil over high heat, stirring to dissolve the sugar. Reduce the heat and simmer, uncovered, about 15 minutes or until the syrup reaches a temperature of 220°F on a candy thermometer. Add the rose water and orange flower water. Remove from the heat and cool.

TO PREPARE THE FRITTERS Place the eggs and yogurt in a large bowl and beat until well blended. Combine the flour, sugar, baking powder, and baking soda. Add to the yogurt mixture and blend well.

*Available at Middle Eastern groceries and some gourmet shops.

In a deep-fryer or heavy saucepan heat 4 inches of the oil over moderate heat. Drop the dough mixture, a tablespoon at a time, into the hot oil, being careful not to crowd the pan. Fry the fritters until golden brown on all sides, turning frequently. Remove from the oil with a perforated spoon and drain on paper towels.

Dip the fritters in the syrup and mound on a platter. Garnish with the nuts before serving.

YOGURT DOUGHNUTS

MAKES ABOUT 3 DOZEN

4-1/3 cups sifted all-purpose flour
1/2 teaspoon ground cinnamon or nutmeg (nutmeg preferably freshly ground)
2 teaspoons double-acting baking powder
1 teaspoon baking soda
3/4 teaspoon salt
3 eggs
1-1/4 cups sugar
2 tablespoons butter, melted
1 cup unflavored yogurt
Corn oil for deep-frying

Confectioners' sugar

Sift together the flour, cinnamon or nutmeg, baking powder, baking soda, and salt. In a large bowl beat the eggs until thick and pale yellow. Gradually beat in the sugar. Add the melted butter and yogurt, then add the flour mixture and mix well. Cover and chill 1 hour. Turn out on a well-floured board and roll to a 1/3-inch thickness. Cut with a floured 3-inch doughnut cutter. Press the trimmings together, reroll, and cut.

In a deep-fryer or heavy saucepan heat 2 inches of the oil until it reaches a temperature of 375°F on a deep-fryer thermometer. Carefully drop the doughnuts, a few at a time, into the hot oil. Fry until golden brown on one side, then turn and lightly brown on the other side, about 3 minutes in all. With a perforated spoon transfer onto paper towels to drain. When cool, sprinkle the doughnuts with the confectioners' sugar.

VARIATION Instead of sprinkling the doughnuts with confectioners' sugar, you may frost them with this chocolate glaze: Melt 2 ounces unsweetened chocolate and 2 tablespoons butter over hot water. Combine with 1/4 cup hot milk, 1 cup sifted confectioners' sugar, and 1 teaspoon vanilla extract and beat with a fork until smooth. If desired, 1 or 2 teaspoons Grand Marnier may also be added.

Cakes, Pies, & Cookies

YOGURT SPICE CAKE

An aristocrat among spice cakes.

MAKES ABOUT 12 SERVINGS

1/4 pound plus 4 tablespoons butter, at room temperature
1-1/2 cups sugar
3 egg yolks
2-1/4 cups unsifted cake flour
1-1/2 teaspoons double-acting baking powder
1/2 teaspoon baking soda
1 teaspoon ground cinnamon
1/2 teaspoon ground nutmeg (preferably freshly ground)
1/2 teaspoon ground cloves
1/2 teaspoon salt
3/4 cup unflavored yogurt
3 egg whites

In a large bowl cream the butter until soft. Gradually add the sugar, beating until the mixture is very light. Add the egg yolks, one at a time, beating well after each. Sift together twice the flour, baking powder, baking soda, cinnamon, nutmeg, cloves, and salt. Add to the creamed mixture in 3 parts, alternating with the yogurt. Stir the batter after each addition until smooth. Beat the egg whites until stiff but not dry. Fold them gently into the batter. Turn into a greased 9 × 3-1/2-inch tube pan. Bake in a preheated 350°F oven about 1 hour and 15 minutes or until a food pick inserted in the center of the cake comes out clean. Cool in the pan on a wire rack 15 minutes. Cover with a rack and invert. Remove the pan. Cover the cake with a rack and invert to cool right side up.

YOGURT CAKE WITH RAISINS AND NUTS

MAKES ABOUT 12 SERVINGS

1/4 pound butter, at room temperature
1 cup sugar
2 eggs
2 cups unsifted all-purpose flour
1 teaspoon double-acting baking powder
1 teaspoon baking soda
1/8 teaspoon salt
1 cup unflavored yogurt
1 teaspoon vanilla extract
3 teaspoons ground cinnamon
1/2 cup seedless raisins
1/2 cup chopped walnuts

In a large bowl cream the butter and 3/4 cup of the sugar until thoroughly blended. Add the eggs, one at a time, beating well after each. Sift together the flour, baking powder, baking soda, and salt. Add to the creamed mixture alternately with the yogurt, mixing until well blended. Stir in the vanilla extract.

Turn half of the batter into a buttered 9 × 9-inch baking pan. Mix together the remaining 1/4 cup sugar, cinnamon, raisins, and walnuts. Sprinkle half of this mixture evenly over the batter. Cover with the remaining batter and sprinkle the rest of the raisin mixture over the top, pressing lightly with the back of a spoon.

Bake in a preheated 350°F oven about 45 minutes or until a food pick inserted in the center of the cake comes out clean. Remove from the oven and cool on a wire rack.

CHOCOLATE CAKE

Top this cake with Yogurt Crème Chantilly, page 98, or fill with apricot preserve and frost with Chocolate Yogurt Sauce flavored with apricot liquer, page 96.

MAKES 2 9-INCH LAYERS

4	ounces unsweetened chocolate
1/4	pound butter, at room temperature
2	cups sugar
2	eggs
1	cup hot water
1	teaspoon vanilla extract
1	cup unflavored yogurt
2	teaspoons baking soda
2	cups sifted all-purpose flour

Place the chocolate in a heatproof measuring cup. Set the cup in a small skillet of shallow hot but not boiling water over moderate heat until the chocolate is melted. Remove the cup from the heat and let the melted chocolate cool.

In a large bowl cream the butter and sugar until thoroughly blended. Add the eggs, one at a time, beating well after each. Stir in the melted and cooled chocolate, hot water, and vanilla extract. Combine the yogurt and baking soda. Add to the creamed mixture alternately with the flour, mixing well until blended. Turn the batter into 2 well-greased and lightly floured 9-inch layer cake pans. Bake in a preheated 350°F oven about 35 minutes or until a food pick inserted in the center comes out clean. Remove from the pan and cool thoroughly on wire racks.

JAM CAKE

MAKES 1 9-INCH 3-LAYER CAKE

1-1/4	cups strawberry preserves
1-1/4	cups seedless blackberry jam
1/2	pound butter, at room temperature
1	cup sugar
5	egg yolks, slightly beaten
3	cups unsifted all-purpose flour
1	tablespoon baking soda
3	teaspoons ground cinnamon
2	teaspoons ground allspice
1	cup unflavored yogurt
5	egg whites
1	recipe Yogurt Crème Chantilly, page 98 (optional)

Combine the strawberry preserves and blackberry jam and rub them through a fine sieve into a small bowl. Set aside.

In a large bowl cream the butter and sugar until thoroughly blended. Beat in the egg yolks, then stir in the sieved jam mixture. Sift together the flour, baking soda, cinnamon, and allspice. Add to the creamed mixture in 3 parts, alternating with the yogurt and beginning and ending with the flour. Stir the batter after each addition until smooth.

Beat the egg whites until stiff enough to hold a shape. With a rubber spatula, fold them into the batter gently but thoroughly. Turn the batter into 3 buttered 9-inch layer cake pans. Bake in a preheated 350°F oven about 45 minutes or until a food pick inserted in the center comes out clean. Remove from the oven and let the cakes cool in the pans 5 minutes. Remove from the pans and cool thoroughly on wire racks. Fill and frost as desired, or serve with the yogurt crème Chantilly.

YOGURT LEMON CAKE

MAKES ABOUT 15 SERVINGS

Cake

1/4	pound butter, at room temperature
1-3/4	cups sugar
2	eggs
2-1/2	cups unsifted all-purpose flour
1/2	teaspoon baking soda
1/8	teaspoon salt
1	cup unflavored yogurt
2	teaspoons grated lemon rind
1-1/2	tablespoons freshly squeezed and strained lemon juice

Glaze

1/4	cup freshly squeezed and strained lemon juice
1	tablespoon water
1/2	cup sugar

Confectioners' sugar

In a large bowl cream the butter and sugar until thoroughly blended. Add the eggs, one at a time, beating well after each. Sift the flour with the baking soda and salt. Add to the creamed mixture alternately with the yogurt, mixing until well blended. Stir in the lemon rind and lemon juice. Pour the mixture into a greased 13 × 9 × 2-inch baking pan dusted with flour. Bake in a preheated 350°F oven 35 to 40 minutes or until a food pick inserted in the center of the cake comes out clean.

Meanwhile, prepare the glaze: In a small bowl combine the 1/4 cup lemon juice, water, and sugar. Let stand, stirring occasionally. When the cake is done, remove it from the oven and let stand 5 minutes in the pan. Turn out on a wire rack and brush all over the top and sides of the hot cake with the lemon glaze until absorbed. Let stand until cool. Sift the confectioners' sugar generously over the cake.

YOGURT CAKE WITH LEMON-ROSE SYRUP

A moist, delicate Middle Eastern cake.

MAKES ABOUT 24 SERVINGS

Syrup

1/2	cup sugar
1/2	cup mild honey
1-1/3	cups water
2	tablespoons freshly squeezed and strained lemon juice
1/2	teaspoon grated lemon rind
1-1/2	tablespoons rose water*

Cake

1/4	pound butter, at room temperature
2	cups sugar
2	eggs
2-1/2	cups unsifted all-purpose flour
1/2	teaspoon baking soda
1/8	teaspoon salt
1	cup unflavored yogurt
1	teaspoon vanilla extract
24	toasted whole blanched almonds (approximately)
1	recipe Yogurt Crème Chantilly, page 98 (optional)

TO PREPARE THE SYRUP   Combine the sugar, honey, water, lemon juice, and lemon rind in a small saucepan. Bring to a boil over moderate heat, stirring constantly to dissolve the sugar. Reduce the heat to low and cook, uncovered, 15 minutes. Add the rose water and simmer 2 minutes longer. Remove from the heat and cool to lukewarm.

Meanwhile, in a large bowl cream the butter and sugar until thoroughly blended. Add the eggs, one at a time, beating well after each. Sift the flour with the baking soda and salt. Add to the creamed mixture alternately with the yogurt, mixing until well blended. Stir in the vanilla extract.

*Available at Middle Eastern groceries and some gourmet shops.

Pour the mixture into a greased 13 × 9 × 2-inch baking pan dusted with flour. Bake in a preheated 350°F oven 40 to 45 minutes or until a food pick inserted in the center of the cake comes out clean. Remove from the oven and cool on a wire rack 5 minutes. Pierce the surface all over with a small skewer and slowly spoon the syrup evenly all over the hot cake. Score the top of the cake into diamonds or squares and place a toasted almond in the center of each. Cool to room temperature. Serve with the yogurt crème Chantilly, if you like.

YOGURT ORANGE CAKE WITH COCONUT TOPPING

This delicious cake is enhanced by a crunchy, broiled topping.

MAKES ABOUT 12 SERVINGS

Cake
1/4	pound butter, at room temperature
1	cup sugar
2	eggs
2	cups unsifted all-purpose flour
3	teaspoons baking soda
1/2	teaspoon salt
1	cup unflavored yogurt
2	teaspoons finely grated orange rind
1/4	cup freshly squeezed and strained orange juice

Topping
3/4	cup shredded coconut
1/3	cup walnuts, finely chopped
1/2	cup firmly packed brown sugar
3	tablespoons butter, melted
1/4	cup heavy cream
1/3	teaspoon vanilla extract

In a large bowl cream the butter and sugar until thoroughly blended. Add the eggs, one at a time, beating well after each. Sift the flour with the baking soda and salt. Add to the creamed mixture alternately with the yogurt, mixing until well blended. Stir in the orange rind and orange juice. Pour the mixture into a greased 13 × 9 × 2-inch baking pan dusted with flour. Bake in a preheated 350°F oven 40 to 45 minutes or until a food pick inserted in the center of the cake comes out clean. Remove from the oven and cool on a wire rack.

Meanwhile, prepare the topping: Combine the coconut, walnuts, brown sugar, and melted butter in a bowl. Mix together the cream and vanilla extract and pour over the coconut mixture. Blend thoroughly. Spread evenly over the cake. Place the cake briefly under the broiler until the topping is lightly browned and bubbly, watching closely to prevent burning.

VALENCIAN FRUITCAKE

MAKES 1 9 × 3-1/2-INCH CAKE

- 2 cups unsifted all-purpose flour
- 1 teaspoon double-acting baking powder
- 1/2 teaspoon baking soda
- 1/4 teaspoon salt
- 1-1/2 cups pitted dates, chopped
- 3/4 cup blanched almonds or walnuts, coarsely chopped
- 1/4 pound butter, at room temperature
- 1-3/4 cups sugar
- 2 eggs
- 1 teaspoon vanilla extract
- 3/4 cup unflavored yogurt
  Grated rind and freshly squeezed and strained juice of 2 oranges

Sift the flour with the baking powder, baking soda, and salt. Combine a few tablespoons of this mixture with the chopped dates and nuts in a bowl. Stir well and set aside.

In a large bowl cream the butter and 1 cup of the sugar until thoroughly blended. Add the eggs, one at a time, beating well after each. Stir in the vanilla extract. Add the flour mixture alternately with the yogurt, mixing until well blended. Stir in the date and nut mixture and orange rind and mix well. Turn into a greased 9 × 3-1/2-inch spring-form pan dusted with flour. Bake in a preheated 350°F oven about 45 minutes or until a food pick inserted in the center of the cake comes out clean.

Meanwhile, combine the remaining 3/4 cup sugar and the orange juice in a small saucepan. Bring to a boil over high heat, stirring to dissolve the sugar. Remove from the heat and set aside.

When the cake is done, remove it from the oven and place it on a wire rack. Quickly prick the top all over with a small skewer. Gradually brush the hot glaze over the cake until it is thoroughly absorbed. Allow the cake to cool in the pan, then remove it from the pan.

VARIATION   Bring the orange juice and sugar to a boil as above. Boil 3 minutes. Remove from the heat and cool 10 minutes. Stir in 1/4 cup Grand Marnier or other orange-flavored liqueur or light rum. Brush over the cake as directed.

BANANA CAKE

Enjoy this deservedly popular cake either plain or frosted.

MAKES 2 9-INCH LAYERS

- 1/4 pound butter, at room temperature
- 1-1/2 cups sugar
- 2 eggs
- 1 teaspoon vanilla extract
- 2-1/4 cups unsifted all-purpose flour
- 2 teaspoons double-acting baking powder
- 3/4 teaspoon baking soda
- 1/2 teaspoon salt
- 2/3 cup unflavored yogurt
- 1 cup mashed very ripe bananas (about 3 bananas)
- 1/2 cup coarsely chopped nut meats (walnuts, pecans, or toasted blanched almonds)

In a large mixing bowl cream the butter and sugar until thoroughly blended. Add the eggs, one at a time, beating well after each. Beat in the vanilla extract. Sift together the flour, baking powder, baking soda, and salt. Add to the creamed mixture in 3 parts, alternating with the yogurt and beginning and ending with the flour. Stir the batter after each addition until smooth. Stir in the bananas and nuts, mixing until just blended. Turn into 2 well-greased 9 × 1-1/2-inch round cake pans dusted with flour. Bake in a preheated 350°F oven about 35 minutes or until a food pick inserted in the centers of the cakes comes out clean. Remove from the oven and let cool in the pans 10 minutes. Remove from the pans and cool thoroughly on wire racks.

APRICOT BANANA CAKE VARIATION   Add 1/2 cup chopped dried apricots with the nuts.

SOUFFLÉED CHEESECAKE WITH STRAWBERRIES

Dieters, don't stop here!

MAKES 10 TO 12 SERVINGS

24 ounces cream cheese, at room temperature
6   eggs, separated
1   cup sugar
2   tablespoons all-purpose flour
1   cup unflavored yogurt
1   teaspoon freshly squeezed and strained lemon juice
1   teaspoon vanilla extract
1-1/2 teaspoons grated lemon rind
1-1/2 teaspoons grated orange rind
1/4 teaspoon cream of tartar
1   quart strawberries, hulled

In a large mixing bowl beat the cream cheese with the egg yolks until the mixture is very smooth. Beat in the sugar, flour, yogurt, lemon juice, vanilla extract, lemon rind, and orange rind.

Beat the egg whites with the cream of tartar until they stand in soft, stiff peaks. Fold into the cheese mixture. Pour into an ungreased 9 × 3-1/2-inch spring-form pan. Bake in a preheated 325°F oven about 1 hour and 30 minutes or until the center of the cake is firm.

Remove the cake from the oven and allow it to cool at room temperature 2 hours before removing it from the pan. Serve at room temperature or chilled, accompanied with a bowl of the strawberries.

VARIATION Instead of serving the cheesecake with a bowl of strawberries, you may top it with a strawberry-currant glaze: Starting at the outer edge, form a ring of strawberries, placing them upright side by side and close together. Continue with additional berries, arranging them in concentric circles working toward the center until the top is completely covered. In a small saucepan melt 1/2 cup red currant jelly, stirring until smooth. Spoon or brush the jelly over the strawberries.

CHEESECAKE WITH CHERRY SAUCE

Lower in calories than the preceding recipe, but tempting and opulent-looking nonetheless.

MAKES 12 SERVINGS

Cheesecake
1   Graham Cracker Pie Crust II, page 149
1-1/2 pints cottage cheese
3/4 cup sugar
1/4 cup sifted all-purpose flour
1/4 teaspoon salt
6   eggs, separated
1   cup unflavored yogurt
    Grated rind and freshly squeezed and strained juice of 1 lemon

Cherry Sauce
1/4 cup sugar (more if using sour cherries)
1   tablespoon cornstarch
1/3 cup water
3   cups pitted dark sweet or sour cherries
2   tablespoons kirsch or other cherry-flavored brandy or to taste

TO MAKE THE CHEESECAKE Prepare the graham cracker pie crust as directed in the recipe and press it evenly onto the bottom and sides of a greased 9 × 3-1/2-inch spring-form pan.

Force the cottage cheese through a fine sieve over a large mixing bowl. Add 6 tablespoons of the sugar, flour, salt, egg yolks, yogurt, lemon rind, and lemon juice. Whip until well blended and smooth. Alternatively, place the ingredients in the container of an electric blender. Cover and blend until smooth. Beat the egg whites until stiff, gradually adding the remaining 6 tablespoons sugar. Fold into the cheese mixture. Turn into the crust-lined pan. Bake in a preheated 325°F oven about 1 hour and 30 minutes or until the center of the cake is firm. Remove the cake from the oven and allow it to cool at room temperature. Cover and chill. To serve, remove the sides of the pan, place the cake on a plate, and pass the cherry sauce.

TO MAKE THE SAUCE In an enameled or stainless steel saucepan combine the sugar, cornstarch, and water. Add the cherries and cook, stirring, until thickened and clear. Remove from the heat and stir in the kirsch or cherry-flavored brandy. Cool, then turn into a serving bowl. Cover and chill.

CRANBERRY CHEESECAKE VARIATION Omit the cherry sauce. In a saucepan combine 1-1/2 cups cranberries, 1/4 cup freshly squeezed and strained orange juice, and 3/4 cup sugar. Cover and cook over moderate heat about 6 minutes or until the cranberry skins burst. Blend 1-1/2 teaspoons cornstarch and 1 tablespoon water and add to the cranberries. Cook, stirring, 2 minutes or until the mixture thickens. Remove from the heat and stir in 1/2 teaspoon grated lemon rind and 1 tablespoon cranberry liqueur, if desired. Chill, then spread it over the cheesecake just before serving.

NUT CHEESECAKE VARIATION Omit the cherry sauce. Garnish the top of the cheesecake with toasted whole blanched almonds or walnut halves.

CHOCOLATE CHEESE SQUARES

MAKES 24 SQUARES

1	cup unsifted all-purpose flour
1/2	cup sugar
3	tablespoons cocoa
1	teaspoon double-acting baking powder
1/4	teaspoon salt
1/4	pound butter
1	egg, separated
1	teaspoon vanilla extract
1/2	cup finely chopped walnuts
8	ounces cream cheese, at room temperature
1/3	cup sugar
1/2	cup unflavored yogurt
1	tablespoon all-purpose flour
1/4	teaspoon salt
2	teaspoons grated orange rind
1/2	teaspoon vanilla extract
1	egg
	Shaved sweet chocolate

Line the bottom and 2 opposite sides of a 9 × 9-inch baking pan with a strip of aluminum foil that overlaps the sides. Grease the foil and the exposed pan sides.

In a mixing bowl combine the 1 cup flour, 1/2 cup sugar, cocoa, baking powder, and salt. Cut in the butter until the mixture resembles coarse meal. Add the egg yolk to the flour mixture (reserve the egg white). Add the 1 teaspoon vanilla extract and walnuts and mix well. Turn into the baking pan and press firmly over the pan bottom. Bake in a preheated 325°F oven 15 minutes.

Meanwhile, in a large mixing bowl combine the cream cheese, 1/3 cup sugar, yogurt, 1 tablespoon flour, salt, orange rind, 1/2 teaspoon vanilla extract, egg, and the reserved egg white. Beat until well blended. Remove the pan from the oven and pour in the cheese mixture. Bake about 25 minutes or until set. Remove from the oven and cool the cake in the pan 1 hour. Garnish the top with the shaved chocolate. Cover and chill thoroughly.

To serve, lift out the cake by grasping the overlapping aluminum foil and cut into squares.

CREAM CHEESE AND YOGURT PIE WITH STRAWBERRIES

MAKES 6 SERVINGS

1   Graham Cracker Pie Crust I, page 149
8   ounces cream cheese, at room temperature
1/2 teaspoon vanilla extract
2   tablespoons honey
1   cup unflavored yogurt
1   pint strawberries, hulled and cut lengthwise in thick slices
3   tablespoons sugar or to taste

Prepare the graham cracker pie crust. Bake and cool.

In a small bowl cream the cheese until soft and smooth. Beat in the vanilla extract and honey. Gradually beat in the yogurt until well blended. Spread the mixture in the baked, cooled pie crust. Cover and refrigerate at least 6 hours.

Meanwhile, place the strawberries in a small serving bowl. Sprinkle with the sugar. Let stand about 30 minutes, stirring occasionally. Cover and refrigerate.

Serve the pie chilled, accompanied with the strawberries to be spooned over each serving.

VARIATION   Omit the strawberries and sugar. In a bowl combine 1/2 cup each firmly packed pitted dates, finely chopped, and slivered blanched almonds, coarsely chopped. Mix well. Sprinkle over the pie just before serving.

LEMON CHEESE PIE

MAKES 8 SERVINGS

1   Graham Cracker Pie Crust II, page 149
1/4 cup freshly squeezed and strained lemon juice
9   ounces cream cheese, at room temperature
2   eggs, beaten
3/4 cup plus 4 teaspoons sugar
1   tablespoon grated lemon rind
1   cup unflavored yogurt, at room temperature

Prepare the graham cracker pie crust as directed in the recipe and press it evenly on to the bottom and sides of an 8-inch pie plate. Combine the lemon juice and cream cheese in a bowl. Mix well. Add the beaten eggs and 3/4 cup of the sugar and beat until well blended and fluffy. Turn into the unbaked pie crust. Bake in a preheated 350°F oven about 20 minutes. Remove from the oven and cool 5 minutes. In a bowl mix together the lemon rind, yogurt, and the remaining 4 teaspoons sugar. Spread the mixture evenly over the pie. Return to the oven and bake 10 minutes. Cool to room temperature, then cover and chill at least 6 hours before serving.

LIME CHEESE PIE

MAKES 8 SERVINGS

  1 Graham Cracker Pie Crust I, page 149
1/2 pint large curd cottage cheese
  1 envelope (1 tablespoon) unflavored
     gelatin
3/4 cup sugar
1/2 cup milk
  3 eggs, beaten
  1 cup unflavored yogurt
1/2 cup freshly squeezed and strained
     lime juice
  1 tablespoon grated lime rind
     Few drops green food coloring (optional)

Prepare the graham cracker pie crust. Bake and cool.

Put the cottage cheese in the container of an electric blender. Cover and whirl until smooth. Or place it in a bowl and beat with an electric mixer until smooth. Set aside. In a heavy saucepan combine the gelatin and sugar. Stir in the milk. Cook over low heat about 10 minutes, stirring constantly. Blend the milk mixture into the beaten eggs, then stir back into the saucepan. Cook 1 minute, stirring. Remove from the heat. Add the cottage cheese, yogurt, lime juice, lime rind, and food coloring, if desired. Mix thoroughly. Pour into the baked and cooled pie crust. Cover and chill several hours or overnight before serving.

GREEK SESAME COOKIES

MAKES ABOUT 6 DOZEN COOKIES

1/2 pound butter
1-1/4 cups sugar
1/2 cup unflavored yogurt
  2 teaspoons double-acting baking powder
1/2 teaspoon baking soda
1/2 teaspoon ground cinnamon
  3 cups unsifted all-purpose flour
     (approximately)
  1 egg
  1 tablespoon cold water
     Sesame seeds

In a large bowl cream the butter until fluffy. Gradually beat in the sugar until thoroughly blended. Add the yogurt, baking powder, baking soda, and cinnamon and mix well. Stir in the flour, a little at a time, to make a soft dough. With lightly floured hands, break off small portions of the dough one at a time and roll out into ropes about 5 inches long and 3/8 inch thick. Press together the ends of each rope to form a ring. Beat together the egg and water. Brush each cookie with the egg mixture, then dip it in a dish of sesame seeds, covering it on all sides.

Arrange the cookies on 2 lightly buttered baking sheets. Bake in a preheated 350°F oven 15 to 20 minutes or until golden brown. Remove the cookies from the baking sheets and cool on wire racks. Store in an airtight container.

MIDDLE EASTERN DATE COOKIES

MAKES ABOUT 8 DOZEN COOKIES

Filling

1	16-ounce package pitted dates
1	cup ground walnuts or blanched almonds
2	tablespoons sugar
1	teaspoon ground cinnamon
2	tablespoons orange flower water*

Pastry

1/2	pound butter, melted
1/4	cup sugar
2	eggs, beaten
1/2	cup unflavored yogurt
1/2	teaspoon vanilla extract
3	cups unsifted all-purpose flour (approximately)
2	teaspoons double-acting baking powder
1/2	teaspoon baking soda
1	egg
1	tablespoon cold water

TO PREPARE THE FILLING   Grind the dates and combine them with the nuts, sugar, cinnamon, and orange flower water. Mix well. Roll about 1 teaspoonful at a time into tiny finger shapes. Set aside.

TO MAKE THE PASTRY   Combine the butter and sugar in a large mixing bowl and stir well. Add the eggs, yogurt, and vanilla extract and mix thoroughly. Sift the flour with the baking powder and baking soda. Add to the butter mixture, a little at a time, beating constantly until well blended and a soft dough is formed. Roll out the dough 1/8 inch thick on a lightly floured surface. Cut into circles with a 3-inch cookie cutter.

Place one "finger" of the date filling on each circle near one edge and roll up, forming cylinder-shaped cookies. Press the edges together, smoothing with your fingers. Beat together the egg and water. Brush each cookie with the egg mixture. Arrange the cookies on 2 lightly buttered baking sheets. Bake in a preheated 350°F oven about 20 minutes or until golden brown. Remove the cookies from the baking sheets and cool on wire racks. Store in airtight containers.

VARIATION   Omit the orange flower water. Use 2 teaspoons ground cinnamon and 1/4 teaspoon each ground cloves and nutmeg (nutmeg preferably freshly ground).

*Available at Middle Eastern groceries and some gourmet shops.

Desserts

FRESH FRUITS WITH YOGURT, BELGIAN STYLE

SERVES 6

2 cups soft Yogurt Cheese, page 148 (omit the salt), chilled
1 cup hulled strawberries, raspberries, or blueberries
1 cup cherries, stemmed and pitted
1 cup sliced peaches or nectarines, sprinkled with fresh lemon juice to prevent darkening
Honey
Ground cinnamon (optional)

Turn the yogurt cheese into an attractive glass bowl placed in a larger bowl filled with crushed ice. This will keep the yogurt well chilled. Surround with dishes of the berries, cherries, and peaches or nectarines. Serve accompanied with a small pitcher of honey and, if you wish, the cinnamon. Allow guests to help themselves. Each person spoons some yogurt cheese into a bowl, adds the fruit of his choice, drizzles with honey, and tops the whole with a dusting of cinnamon, if desired.

INDIAN YOGURT DESSERT

You may accompany this with a platter of melon wedges or green grapes.

SERVES 4

1 recipe Yogurt Cheese, page 148 (omit the salt)
Sugar or honey to taste
Seed from 1 cardamom pod, ground
1/4 teaspoon ground cinnamon
1/4 teaspoon ground nutmeg (preferably freshly ground)
1 teaspoon rose water* (optional)
1/4 cup chopped unsalted pistachio nuts
Whole unsalted pistachio nuts

Combine all the ingredients except the whole pistachio nuts in a bowl and mix thoroughly. Mound in the center of a serving platter, or, using an ice cream scoop, shape the mixture into balls and arrange on the platter. Cover and chill 2 hours. Serve garnished with the whole pistachio nuts.

*Available at Middle Eastern groceries and some gourmet shops.

MASCARPONE WITH APRICOTS

Mascarpone is a soft, creamy Italian cheese that is often blended with liqueur and accompanied with fruit. Cream cheese makes a good substitute.

SERVES 8 TO 12

16 ounces *mascarpone* or cream cheese, at room temperature
1/2 cup confectioners' sugar
1/2 cup soft Yogurt Cheese, page 148 (omit the salt)
1/4 cup Cointreau or other orange-flavored liqueur
Apricot halves

Combine the cream cheese, confectioners' sugar, yogurt cheese, and Cointreau in a large bowl. Beat until well blended and smooth. Mound on a serving platter in the shape of a cone. Cover and chill. Serve surrounded with the apricot halves. To eat, spoon a little into an apricot half.

VARIATION   Substitute peeled peach or nectarine halves for the apricot halves and, if desired, peach liqueur or light rum for the Cointreau.

PURÉED BERRY DESSERT

A luscious creation based on an English recipe.

SERVES 4

1 pint ripe raspberries, gooseberries, or blackberries
1/2 cup sugar or to taste
1 recipe Yogurt Crème Chantilly, page 98

Remove any stems from the berries and discard those that are badly bruised. Wash the fruit quickly in a sieve, drain, and place in a heavy saucepan. Cook over low heat 30 minutes, stirring and crushing the fruit with a fork to extract the juices. Add the sugar and stir until dissolved. Purée the berries in an electric blender and strain. Or force the fruit through a fine sieve set over a bowl. Cover and chill thoroughly.

Just before serving, using a rubber spatula, fold the puréed fruit into the crème Chantilly, being careful not to overmix (the finished dessert should have a marbled look rather than a blended one). Serve immediately in chilled parfait or sherbet glasses.

PEARS IN RED WINE

This is a classic dessert in France, Italy, and Spain.

SERVES 4

- 1 small orange
- 2 tablespoons Grand Marnier
- 4 firm, ripe pears
- 2 teaspoons freshly squeezed and strained lemon juice
- 1-1/2 cups red Bordeaux wine
- 1 2-inch piece cinnamon stick
- 2 whole cloves
- 3/4 cup sugar
- 1 piece lemon rind, 1 inch long
- 1/4 cup red currant jelly
- 1 recipe Yogurt Crème Chantilly, page 98

Peel the orange carefully, removing only the outside orange part of the rind. Reserve the fruit for another use. Cut the rind into thin slices and cook in boiling water 10 minutes. Drain and place the orange rind in a small bowl. Cover with the Grand Marnier and set aside to steep.

Peel the pears without removing the stems. Drop them immediately in water to cover, to which you have added 1-1/2 teaspoons of the lemon juice. This will prevent the pears from darkening. Set aside.

In an enameled or stainless steel saucepan combine the wine, cinnamon stick, cloves, sugar, and lemon rind. Bring to a boil, stirring constantly to dissolve the sugar. Add the drained pears, reduce the heat, and simmer, partially covered, about 25 minutes or until tender but still intact. With a slotted spoon transfer each pear to an individual dessert dish. Raise the heat and reduce the cooking liquid until it forms a very light syrup. Beat in the currant jelly until thoroughly dissolved. Stir in the remaining 1/2 teaspoon lemon juice. Spoon the syrup over the pears. Sprinkle them with the orange rind and Grand Marnier mixture. Cover and chill. Serve with the yogurt crème Chantilly.

VARIATION Omit the orange rind and Grand Marnier. Sprinkle the pears with toasted slivered blanched almonds and serve with unflavored yogurt dusted with cinnamon.

DRIED FRUIT COMPOTE WITH YOGURT

SERVES 6

- 4-1/2 cups water
- 3/4 cup sugar, or 1/2 cup mild honey
- 1 cup dried apricots
- 3/4 cup dried pitted prunes
- 3/4 cup dried peaches or pears, cut into bite-sized pieces
- 1/2 cup seedless raisins
- 1/4 cup blanched almonds, halved lengthwise
- 1/4 cup pine nuts
- 1 2-inch piece cinnamon stick
- 4 whole allspice
- 2 tablespoons toasted walnuts, chopped (see note)
  Unflavored yogurt or Sweet Yogurt Sauce, page 95

In a heavy saucepan combine the water and sugar or honey. Bring to a boil over moderate heat, stirring constantly to dissolve the sugar. Reduce the heat and simmer, uncovered, 5 minutes.

Add the dried fruits, nuts, cinnamon stick, and allspice. Cover and simmer about 15 minutes or until the fruits are tender but not mushy. Remove from the heat and cool to lukewarm. Remove the spices. Spoon into individual glass compotes or into a serving bowl. Cover and chill. Sprinkle with the chopped walnuts and serve with the yogurt or sweet yogurt sauce.

NOTE To toast the walnuts, spread them on a baking sheet and place in a 325°F oven 15 minutes or until golden brown, turning frequently. Watch closely to prevent burning.

PRUNE WHIP WITH PORT WINE

SERVES 6

8	ounces dried pitted prunes
	Water
2/3	cup sugar
1	strip lemon rind
1/2	cup port wine
1	recipe Yogurt Crème Chantilly, page 98
	Toasted slivered blanched almonds

Soak the prunes in water to cover several hours. Drain. Place them in a heavy saucepan and add the sugar, lemon rind, and 1 cup water. Bring to a boil over high heat, stirring to dissolve the sugar. Reduce the heat to low, cover, and simmer until the prunes are tender, adding more water if necessary. Drain, leaving the prunes in the saucepan. Add the port and cook 10 minutes. Force the prunes through a sieve, or purée in an electric blender. Add a little more port if needed to make the prunes moist. Taste and add more sugar if desired. Combine half the yogurt crème Chantilly with the prunes until thoroughly mixed. Use the remaining yogurt crème Chantilly as a garnish. Sprinkle with the toasted almonds.

APRICOT WHIP VARIATION Substitute dried apricots for the prunes.

MOLDED YOGURT CREAM

Light, delicate, and uncomplicated—an ideal dessert after a hearty dinner.

SERVES 4 TO 6

1	cup heavy cream
1/2	cup sugar
1-1/2	teaspoons unflavored gelatin
3	tablespoons cold water
1	cup unflavored yogurt
2	tablespoons Grand Marnier or strawberry liqueur
2	cups hulled strawberries or raspberries, crushed and sweetened

Combine the cream and sugar in a small saucepan. Cook over low heat until the sugar is dissolved, stirring constantly. Remove from the heat. Soften the gelatin in the cold water and stir it into the cream mixture until it is dissolved. Let cool, then beat in the yogurt with a wire whisk or a rotary beater until the mixture is well blended and smooth. Stir in the Grand Marnier or strawberry liqueur. Pour into a lightly oiled 2-cup mold or individual molds. Cover and chill until firm. Unmold (see unmolding instructions for Caribbean Mango Cream, following) and serve with the strawberries or raspberries.

CARIBBEAN MANGO CREAM

SERVES 6

3	very ripe mangoes, or enough to make 2 cups mango purée
1/3	cup cold water
1	envelope (1 tablespoon) unflavored gelatin
1/2	cup sugar or to taste
1	tablespoon freshly squeezed and strained lime juice
1/2	cup unflavored yogurt, beaten
1/2	cup heavy cream
	Mango slices
	Hulled strawberries (optional)
1	recipe Yogurt Crème Chantilly, page 98
	Toasted shredded coconut

Peel the mangoes. Cut the flesh away from the pits and chop coarsely. Purée the mango flesh in a food mill or rub it through a coarse strainer set over a bowl to make 2 cups purée. Stir in the sugar and lime juice and set aside.

Pour the cold water into a small heatproof measuring cup. Sprinkle with the gelatin and let it soften about 3 minutes. Heat the mixture over low heat or hot water until the gelatin dissolves. Stir into the mango mixture, then stir in the yogurt until well blended.

In a chilled bowl with chilled beaters, whip the cream until it is stiff enough to hold its shape softly. Set the mango mixture over ice and stir until it begins to thicken. Gradually fold in the whipped cream gently but thoroughly. Pour into a rinsed and chilled 5-cup metal ring mold. Cover with aluminum foil and chill 4 hours or until set.

To unmold, have ready a chilled dessert platter large enough to allow for the garnish. Run the pointed tip of a knife around the edges of the mold to release. Dip the mold up to the rim into a basin of hot water for just a few seconds. Place the dessert platter upside down over the mold. Hold the platter and mold together and invert. Shake gently to release the mango cream. If it does not release, redip the mold quickly into hot water and, if necessary, shake again to release. Carefully lift off the mold and refrigerate the mango cream.

Shortly before serving, fill the center of the molded cream with the mango slices. Surround with the strawberries, if desired. Serve with the yogurt crème Chantilly and sprinkled with the toasted coconut.

GERMAN LEMON CREAM

SERVES 6

1/4 cup cold water
2 teaspoons unflavored gelatin
3 egg yolks
1/2 cup plus 3 tablespoons sugar
1/3 cup freshly squeezed and strained lemon juice
2 teaspoons finely grated lemon rind
1/2 cup unflavored yogurt, beaten until smooth
3/4 cup heavy cream
3 egg whites
1/2 recipe Yogurt Crème Chantilly, page 98 (optional)
Shaved sweet chocolate, or
1 pint blueberries, sweetened to taste

Pour the cold water into a small heatproof measuring cup. Sprinkle with the gelatin and let it soften about 3 minutes. Stir the mixture over low heat or hot water until the gelatin dissolves.

Beat the egg yolks with 1/2 cup of the sugar until pale yellow and thick. Stir in the dissolved gelatin, lemon juice, lemon rind, and yogurt.

In a chilled bowl with chilled beaters, whip the cream until it is stiff enough to hold its shape softly. Using a rubber spatula, fold the whipped cream gently but thoroughly into the lemon mixture.

Beat the egg whites with clean beaters until frothy. Sprinkle with the remaining 3 tablespoons sugar and continue to beat until the egg whites stand in soft, stiff peaks. Carefully fold them into the lemon mixture until thoroughly blended.

Spoon the lemon cream into individual dessert dishes. Cover and chill. Serve topped with the yogurt crème Chantilly, if desired, and garnished with the shaved chocolate or blueberries.

PEKING DUST

This elegant chestnut dessert is named after the swirling, buff-colored dust that envelops China's ancient capital at each summer's end.

SERVES 6 TO 8

2 pounds chestnuts
1-1/2 cups milk
1/2 cup sugar
2 teaspoons vanilla extract, or
3/4 teaspoon ground ginger
1 recipe Yogurt Crème Chantilly, page 98
Preserved kumquats or glacéed pineapple or orange slices
Glazed almonds or walnuts

With a sharp knife cut a cross on the flat side of each chestnut. Place the chestnuts in a saucepan. Cover with cold water and bring to a boil. Boil 15 minutes. Remove from the heat. With a slotted spoon, lift out the chestnuts, a few at a time, and shell and skin them quickly while they are still warm. Scald the milk and sugar. Add the chestnuts and vanilla extract to the milk and sugar and boil over low heat about 30 minutes or until the chestnuts are very soft (if using ginger, stir later into the puréed chestnuts). Drain thoroughly, then purée in a food mill. Cool and chill 1 hour. Spoon the chestnut purée into a ricer and hold the ricer over a serving platter. Squeeze the ricer, allowing the purée to fall in a cone-shaped mound. Garnish the top with the yogurt crème Chantilly and decorate with the preserved kumquats and glazed almonds or walnuts.

VARIATION For the French counterpart to this dish known as *Mont-Blanc*, flavor the puréed chestnuts with 2 tablespoons Cognac. Grate sweet chocolate over the crème Chantilly topping and decorate the base with *marrons glacés* (preserved glazed chestnuts) or candied violets. The yogurt crème Chantilly may be flavored with 1 tablespoon crème de cacao or to taste.

COFFEE MOUSSE

SERVES 4 TO 6

- 1 envelope (1 tablespoon) unflavored gelatin
- 1/4 cup cold water
- 2 eggs, separated
- 1/2 cup sugar
- 1/4 teaspoon salt
- 1/2 cup milk
- 1/2 teaspoon vanilla extract
- 1/2 cup very strong black coffee
- 1 recipe Yogurt Crème Chantilly, page 98
  Ladyfingers

Soften the gelatin in the water. Beat the egg yolks in the top part of a double boiler. Add 1/4 cup of the sugar and the salt. Gradually stir in the milk. Cook over hot water until thickened, stirring constantly. Add the gelatin and stir until it is completely dissolved. Stir in the vanilla extract and coffee and chill until slightly thickened. Beat the egg whites until stiff. Gradually beat in the remaining sugar. Fold into the gelatin mixture, then fold in the yogurt crème Chantilly. Line dessert glasses with the ladyfingers. Spoon the gelatin mixture into the glasses. Cover and chill until firm.

APPLE CUSTARD

The melted brown sugar topping of this appealing dessert is characteristic of crème brûlée.

SERVES 4 TO 6

- 1 tablespoon butter
- 2 medium Golden Delicious apples, peeled, cored, and cut into 1/4-inch-thick slices
- 1/4 teaspoon ground cinnamon or cardamom
- 3 eggs
- 1/3 cup sugar
- 1 cup unflavored yogurt
- 1 cup milk
- 1/2 teaspoon vanilla extract
- 1/2 cup lump-free light brown sugar, firmly packed

In a large, heavy skillet melt the butter over moderate heat. Add the apples and turn in the butter to coat. Sprinkle with the cinnamon or cardamom, cover, and cook about 5 minutes or until tender. Transfer the apples to a shallow 8-inch-square baking dish.

In a mixing bowl beat the eggs and sugar with a fork or whisk until blended. Beat in the yogurt. Stir in the milk and vanilla extract until well blended and smooth. Pour over the apples in the baking dish. Place the baking dish in a larger baking pan. Carefully fill the larger pan with boiling water to a depth of about 3/4 inch around the dish, taking care not to spill any water into the custard. Bake, uncovered, in a preheated 325°F oven about 45 minutes or until a knife inserted about 1-1/2 inches from the center comes out clean. Remove the custard from the water bath and refrigerate several hours until thoroughly chilled.

Place the custard dish inside the larger baking pan and surround it with ice. Sprinkle the surface of the custard evenly with the brown sugar. Place the custard under a broiler so that the top is about 3 inches from the heat. Broil just long enough to allow the sugar to melt, watching closely to prevent it from scorching. Serve at once.

FROZEN YOGURT

A major reason for the tremendous surge in popularity of yogurt in recent years has been the appearance on the market of frozen yogurt, which in the relatively short time it has been widely available has achieved a success that is nothing less than phenomenal. Smooth and creamy in texture and with a unique tangy flavor, it provides a zesty alternative to ice cream, with only about half the calories. Commercial frozen yogurt can be purchased either dispensed from machines or prepackaged in the ice cream section of the freezer case in supermarkets. You can, however, make superb frozen yogurt in your kitchen at considerably lower cost using an electric or hand-crank ice cream freezer. Other frozen yogurt desserts can be made at home without an ice cream freezer. Once you have made your own frozen yogurt it will be difficult to settle for the storebought variety.

Notwithstanding the fact that it has been called "ice cream without guilt," frozen yogurt is much higher in calories than unflavored yogurt and consequently is not something to be consumed in large amounts by dieters. Also, though it shares the high nutritional value of unflavored yogurt, the bacteria in it have, of course, been killed by the freezing process, which means that technically it is not yogurt but a soured milk dessert.

FROZEN RASPBERRY YOGURT

MAKES 1 QUART

- 1 cup ripe raspberries or unsweetened frozen, thawed raspberries
- 1/2 cup plus 1 tablespoon sugar
- 1 teaspoon freshly squeezed and strained lemon juice
- 1 teaspoon vanilla extract
- 1 small egg, separated
  Pinch of salt
  Pinch of cream of tartar
- 2 cups unflavored yogurt

In a large enameled or stainless steel saucepan combine the raspberries and 1/2 cup of the sugar. Bring to a boil over high heat, stirring constantly. Reduce the heat to medium and cook about 2 minutes or until the fruit softens, stirring and crushing it with a fork. Remove from the heat and strain through a sieve to remove the seeds. Stir in the lemon juice and vanilla extract.

In a small mixing bowl beat the egg yolk lightly. Stir in 2 tablespoons of the hot raspberry mixture. Add the egg yolk mixture to the raspberry mixture, stirring constantly. Allow to cool to room temperature.

In a large mixing bowl beat the egg white, salt, and cream of tartar until soft peaks form. Beat in the remaining 1 tablespoon sugar until stiff peaks form.

In a large bowl beat the yogurt with a wire whisk until smooth. Fold the raspberry mixture into the yogurt until thoroughly blended. Carefully fold this mixture into the beaten egg white. Freeze in a 1-quart or larger hand-crank or electric ice cream freezer, following the manufacturer's directions.

FROZEN BLACKBERRY OR BLUEBERRY YOGURT VARIATION Substitute 1 cup fresh (or unsweetened frozen, thawed) blackberries or blueberries for the raspberries.

Substitute 1 cup thinly sliced ripe bananas (about 3 bananas), coarsely mashed, for the raspberries, combining them in the saucepan with 6 tablespoons sugar and 2 tablespoons honey rather than the 1/2 cup sugar. Also, increase the amount of lemon juice to 2 teaspoons and that of the vanilla extract to 1-1/2 teaspoons.

FROZEN CHOCOLATE YOGURT

MAKES 1-1/2 QUARTS

2	cups milk
4	egg yolks
3/4	cup sugar
4	ounces semisweet chocolate, melted
1-1/2	teaspoons vanilla extract
2	cups unflavored yogurt

In a medium enameled or stainless steel saucepan bring the milk almost to a boil. Remove from the heat and set aside. Combine the egg yolks and sugar in a bowl. Beat them with a wire whisk or rotary or electric beater until pale yellow and thickened. Gradually beat in the hot milk. Pour the mixture back into the saucepan and cook over moderately low heat, stirring constantly with a wooden spoon until it thickens to a custard that lightly coats the spoon. Do not allow the mixture to boil or it will curdle. Stir in the melted chocolate and vanilla extract. Strain the custard through a fine sieve into a large mixing bowl and allow it to cool to room temperature. In a bowl beat the yogurt with a wire whisk until smooth. Add to the cooled custard and mix thoroughly. Freeze in a 2-quart or larger hand-crank or electric ice cream freezer, following the manufacturer's directions.

FROZEN COFFEE YOGURT

MAKES 1-1/2 QUARTS

  2   cups milk
1-1/2 cups sugar
  2   eggs, beaten
  1   cup cold, very strong black coffee
 1/4   teaspoon salt
1-1/2 cups unflavored yogurt
  1   teaspoon vanilla extract
  2   tablespoons Kahlúa or other coffee-flavored liqueur or Grand Marnier

In an enameled or stainless steel saucepan heat the milk over low heat. Do not allow it to boil. Remove from the heat. Add the sugar and stir until it dissolves. Gradually pour the milk mixture over the beaten eggs, beating constantly until well blended. Transfer to the top of a double boiler and cook, stirring, over simmering water until thick and smooth. Cool to room temperature. Add the coffee, salt, yogurt, vanilla extract, and liqueur. Mix thoroughly. Refrigerate 2 hours or until well chilled. Freeze in a 2-quart or larger hand-crank or electric ice cream freezer, following the manufacturer's directions.

VANILLA YOGURT ICE CREAM

MAKES 1 QUART

  1   egg
  6   tablespoons sugar
 1/4   cup light corn syrup
 3/4   cup heavy cream
 3/4   cup unflavored yogurt
1-1/2 teaspoons vanilla extract
 1/4   teaspoon salt

Place all the ingredients in a medium-sized bowl and mix thoroughly. Refrigerate 2 hours or until well chilled. Freeze in a 1-quart or larger hand-crank or electric ice cream freezer, following the manufacturer's directions.

ORANGE YOGURT
ICE CREAM

MAKES I QUART

I	cup heavy cream
3/4	cup sugar
I-I/4	cups unflavored yogurt
6	tablespoons freshly squeezed and strained orange juice
I/4	cup Grand Marnier
I	tablespoon orange flower water*

In an enameled or stainless steel saucepan heat the heavy cream over low heat. Do not allow it to boil. Remove from the heat. Add the sugar and stir until it dissolves. Cool to room temperature. Add the remaining ingredients and mix thoroughly. Refrigerate 2 hours or until well chilled. Freeze in a I-quart or larger hand-crank or electric ice cream freezer, following the manufacturer's directions.

*Available at Middle Eastern groceries and some gourmet shops.

LEMON YOGURT
ICE CREAM

MAKES I QUART

I-I/2	cups heavy cream
I	cup sugar
I	cup unflavored yogurt
I/4	cup freshly squeezed and strained lemon juice
I-I/2	teaspoons very finely grated lemon rind
I/8	teaspoon yellow food coloring (optional)

In an enameled or stainless steel saucepan heat the heavy cream over low heat. Do not allow it to boil. Remove from the heat. Add the sugar and stir until it dissolves. Cool to room temperature. Add the remaining ingredients and mix thoroughly. Refrigerate 2 hours or until well chilled. Freeze in a I-quart or larger hand-crank or electric ice cream freezer, following the manufacturer's directions. Delicious as is or with a spoonful of kirsch poured over each serving.

CHERRY YOGURT ICE CREAM

MAKES 1 QUART

1/2 cup Bing cherry preserves
1-1/2 cups unflavored yogurt
1/2 cup heavy cream
1/2 cup sugar
1/8 teaspoon almond extract

In a small bowl combine the cherry preserves and yogurt. Mix well and set aside. In an enameled or stainless steel saucepan heat the heavy cream over low heat. Do not allow it to boil. Remove from the heat. Add the sugar and stir until it dissolves. Cool to room temperature. Add the yogurt and cherry mixture and the almond extract and blend thoroughly. Refrigerate 2 hours or until well chilled. Freeze in a 1-quart or larger hand-crank or electric ice cream freezer, following the manufacturer's directions.

PISTACHIO YOGURT ICE CREAM

MAKES 1-1/2 QUARTS

3/4 cup shelled unsalted pistachio nuts
1/8 teaspoon rose water* (optional)
1/2 cup sugar
1 tablespoon cornstarch
1/2 cup half-and-half
1/2 cup milk
2 eggs
1/4 teaspoon salt
1 tablespoon orange flower water* or to taste
3/4 cup heavy cream
3/4 cup unflavored yogurt
3 or 4 drops green food coloring (optional)

Pour boiling water over the nuts. Let stand about 1 minute, then drain. Pour cold water over them. Drain again. Rub off the skins. Pound the nuts in a mortar with the rose water, if desired. (Alternatively, you may blend them in an electric blender or chop them very finely.) Set aside.

In the top of a double boiler mix together the sugar and cornstarch. Add the half-and-half and milk and bring to a boil over direct heat, stirring constantly. Remove from the heat. In a mixing bowl beat the eggs slightly. Add the salt and mix well. Gradually beat in the hot mixture until well blended. Return to the top of the double boiler and cook, stirring, over simmering water until the mixture thickens. Remove from the heat and cool to room temperature. Add the orange flower water, heavy cream, yogurt, and green food coloring, if desired. Mix thoroughly. Refrigerate 2 hours or until well chilled. Freeze in a 2-quart or larger hand-crank or electric ice cream freezer, following the manufacturer's directions.

VARIATION Substitute 1 teaspoon vanilla extract and 1/2 teaspoon almond extract for the orange flower water.

*Available at Middle Eastern groceries and some gourmet shops.

FROZEN BANANA DAIQUIRI YOGURT

This and the following two recipes do not require the use of an ice cream freezer.

MAKES ABOUT 3-1/2 CUPS

1	cup coarsely mashed ripe bananas (about 3 bananas)
1/2	cup light corn syrup
1/4	cup sugar
1/4	to 1/2 teaspoon grated lime rind
1	tablespoon freshly squeezed and strained lime juice
2	tablespoons amber rum
2	cups unflavored yogurt

Place the bananas, corn syrup, sugar, lime rind, lime juice, and rum in the container of an electric blender. Blend at medium speed until the mixture is liquified. Add the yogurt and blend at medium speed until thoroughly mixed. Pour into a freezer tray or a 9 × 5 × 3-inch loaf pan. Cover with aluminum foil and freeze 3 to 4 hours or until firm. Return to the blender container and blend at medium speed about 1 minute or until liquified. Return to the freezer tray or loaf pan, cover, and freeze until firm.

FROZEN STRAWBERRY YOGURT VARIATION
Substitute 1 pint hulled strawberries for the bananas and freshly squeezed and strained lemon juice for the lime juice. Omit the lime rind and rum.

STRAWBERRY YOGURT SHERBET

MAKES ABOUT I QUART

2	cups unflavored yogurt
2	cups chopped hulled ripe strawberries
1/2	to 1 cup sugar, or to taste

Spread the yogurt in a freezer tray, cover with foil, and freeze to a soft mush. Purée the strawberries and sugar in the container of an electric blender, or combine them in a bowl and crush to a purée. Remove the yogurt from the freezer and beat into the strawberry purée. Spread in the freezer tray, cover, and freeze until the mixture attains the consistency of sherbet.

VARIATIONS   The strawberries may be steeped in strawberry liqueur or kirsch before puréeing. Two cups chopped peeled peaches may be substituted for the strawberries. If you wish, steep them in peach liqueur before puréeing. Other fruit such as apricots, plums, raspberries, or 1 cup each raspberries and strawberries may also be used.

PAPAYA YOGURT SHERBET

- 1   large, ripe papaya, or enough to make
  1-1/2 cups papaya purée
- 1   cup sugar
- 1/2 cup freshly squeezed and strained orange
  juice
- 1   tablespoon freshly squeezed and strained
  lemon juice
- 1-1/2 cups unflavored yogurt

Peel the papaya. Cut it in half lengthwise and scoop out the seeds, then chop the flesh coarsely. Purée the papaya in an electric blender or food mill, or rub though a coarse strainer set over a bowl to make 1-1/2 cups papaya purée. Dissolve the sugar in the orange juice and add to the papaya purée along with the lemon juice and yogurt. Mix until thoroughly blended. Pour into a freezer tray, cover, and freeze until the mixture attains the consistency of sherbet.

BOMBE METCHNIKOFF

A bombe made with frozen yogurt? The idea occurred to me when I found myself with a freezerful of the homemade product while testing recipes for this chapter. Frozen bacilli notwithstanding, I have named my version of this aristocratic dessert in honor of the professor, who, I think, might have been tempted to try it. This and the variations below are but a few combinations of colors and flavors that can be used to create bombes from either homemade or commercial frozen yogurts, ice creams, or sherbets. A freezer that maintains a temperature of 0°F is best. Bombes are usually made in fancy conical molds, but a melon-shaped mold, pudding mold, or simply a metal bowl will do.

SERVES 6

- 1   pint Vanilla Yogurt Ice Cream, page 133,
  or Pistachio Yogurt Ice Cream, page 135
- 1   pint Frozen Coffee Yogurt, page 133, or
  Frozen Chocolate Yogurt, page 132
- 1/2 recipe Chestnut Yogurt Crème Chantilly,
  page 99
  Whipped cream
  Marrons glacés (preserved chestnuts),
  steeped in brandy, curaçao, or rum
  Candied violets
  Chocolate curls

Place a 4- or 5-cup melon- or other dome-shaped metal mold or bowl in the freezer. Soften the vanilla or pistachio yogurt ice cream slightly and, using the back of a large spoon, press it inside the chilled mold in an even layer to line it completely. Freeze until firm. Soften the frozen coffee or chocolate yogurt slightly and press it evenly over the layer of ice cream. Freeze until firm. Fill the center of the mold with the chestnut yogurt crème Chantilly. Smooth the top and cover with aluminum foil. Freeze at least 4 hours or until firm.

　　To unmold, remove the mold from the freezer and let it stand at room temperature 5 minutes. Invert it onto a serving plate. Hold a hot, damp kitchen towel over the mold and shake to release the bombe. Return the bombe to the freezer until the surface is firm. Just before serving, working quickly, decorate the bombe with rosettes of whipped cream, the *marrons glacés*, candied violets, and chocolate curls. Slice in wedges and serve on doilied dessert plates.

BOMBE CHINOISE VARIATION   Substitute 1/2 recipe Kumquat Yogurt Crème Chantilly, page 99, for the chestnut yogurt crème Chantilly. Decorate the bombe with rosettes of whipped cream, preserved kumquats, and chocolate curls.

BOMBE CARDINAL VARIATION   Substitute 1 pint Frozen Raspberry Yogurt, page 131, for the frozen coffee or chocolate yogurt and 1/2 recipe Berry Yogurt Crème Chantilly, page 99, for the chestnut yogurt crème Chantilly. Decorate the bombe with rosettes of whipped cream and large strawberries steeped in strawberry or raspberry liqueur, kirsch, or Grand Marnier.

BOMBE ARMÉNIENNE VARIATION
Substitute 1 pint apricot yogurt sherbet (see variations for Strawberry Yogurt Sherbet, page 136) for the frozen coffee or chocolate yogurt and 1/2 recipe Apricot Yogurt Crème Chantilly, page 99, for the chestnut yogurt crème Chantilly. Decorate the bombe with rosettes of whipped cream, glazed apricots, and glazed whole almonds.

Beverages

Although many of the following beverages can be made by hand, an electric blender gives much better results.

ICED YOGURT DRINK

Abdug to the Persians, ayran to the Turks, and tahn to the Armenians, this traditional beverage is consumed extensively all over the Middle East and Caucasus.

SERVES 2

- 1 cup unflavored yogurt
- 3/4 to 1-1/4 cups ice cold water
  Salt to taste
  Fresh mint leaves (optional)

Place the yogurt, water, and salt in the container of an electric blender. Cover and whirl until frothy. Or combine the ingredients in a mixing bowl and beat with a wire whisk or rotary beater until thoroughly blended and smooth. Serve chilled over ice cubes, garnished with the mint leaves, if desired.

LASSI

A popular beverage from India.

SERVES 2

- 1 cup unflavored yogurt
- 1 cup ice water
- 1/2 cup crushed ice
- 1/8 teaspoon ground cumin or to taste
  Salt and ground white pepper (preferably freshly ground) or ground cayenne pepper to taste

Place all the ingredients in the container of an electric blender. Cover and whirl until frothy. Or combine the ingredients in a mixing bowl and beat them with a wire whisk or rotary beater until thoroughly blended and smooth. Pour through a strainer into chilled glasses.

SWEET LASSI VARIATION Omit the cumin and salt and pepper. Add 1/8 teaspoon rose water and 1 tablespoon superfine sugar or to taste to the remaining ingredients before blending.

BANANA-ORANGE DELIGHT

SERVES 2 OR 3

- 1 banana, peeled and thickly sliced
- 1-1/2 cups freshly squeezed and strained orange juice
- 1 cup unflavored yogurt
- 1/8 teaspoon ground cinnamon (optional)
  Superfine sugar to taste

Place all the ingredients in the container of an electric blender. Cover and whirl until well blended and smooth. Serve chilled.

BLUEBERRY CREAM

SERVES 3

- 1 cup milk
- 1 cup unflavored yogurt
- 1 cup blueberries
- 1 tablespoon honey or to taste
- 1/2 teaspoon vanilla extract

Place all the ingredients in the container of an electric blender. Cover and whirl until well blended and smooth. Serve chilled.

STRAWBERRY COOLER

SERVES 4

- 1 cup unflavored yogurt
- 2 cups strawberries, hulled
- 1 cup ice water or milk
- 1/4 cup superfine sugar or to taste

Place all the ingredients in the container of an electric blender. Cover and whirl until well blended and smooth. Or in a mixing bowl crush the berries to a purée. Gradually beat in the yogurt until well blended and smooth. Add the water or milk and sugar and stir until the sugar is dissolved. Serve chilled.

PINEAPPLE-STRAWBERRY DREAM

SERVES 4

- 2 cups diced fresh pineapple
- 1/2 cup hulled strawberries or raspberries
- 1 cup milk
- 1 cup unflavored yogurt
- 3 tablespoons superfine sugar or to taste
- 1 ounce kirsch or strawberry liqueur or to taste (optional)
- 1 cup crushed ice

Place all the ingredients in the container of an electric blender. Cover and whirl until smooth and frothy. Serve in chilled glasses.

PINEAPPLE-BANANA SHAKE

SERVES 2

1   cup unflavored yogurt
4   ice cubes, crushed
1   cup diced fresh pineapple
1/2   banana, peeled and thickly sliced

Place all the ingredients in the container of an electric blender. Cover and whirl until smooth. Serve in chilled glasses.

CANTALOUPE SHAKE

Here is a richly textured, Cointreau-spiked temptation.

SERVES 4 TO 6

1   ripe medium cantaloupe, peeled, seeded, and coarsely chopped
1/4   cup milk
1/2   cup unflavored yogurt
2   teaspoons freshly squeezed and strained lime juice
2   tablespoons superfine sugar or to taste
2   to 3 tablespoons Cointreau
1   pint vanilla ice cream

Place the cantaloupe, milk, yogurt, lime juice, sugar, and Cointreau in the container of an electric blender. Cover and whirl until well blended. Add the ice cream and blend until smooth. Pour into chilled glasses and serve immediately.

PEACH OR APRICOT SHAKE

Fragrantly delicious, with a hauntingly sweet flavor, the very essence of the fruit.

SERVES 4 TO 6

- 4 cups peach or apricot pulp
- 1 cup milk
- 1 cup unflavored yogurt
- 1/4 cup honey or to taste
- 1 cup crushed ice

Place all the ingredients in the container of an electric blender. Cover and whirl until smooth. Serve very cold in chilled stemmed glasses.

ICED FRUIT SHAKE

SERVES 2 OR 3

- 1/2 cup crushed ice
- 1/2 cup unflavored yogurt
- 3 tablespoons honey
- 3 tablespoons sugar or to taste
- 3/4 cup hulled sliced strawberries
- 1/2 cup cut-up ripe cantaloupe
- 1/4 cup cut-up ripe papaya
  Fresh mint leaves (optional)

Place all the ingredients in the container of an electric blender. Cover and whirl until smooth. Serve in chilled glasses, garnished, if you like, with the mint leaves.

FRULLATA DI FRUTTA
(Italian Iced Fruit Shake)

This extravaganza can be made with a variety of fruits. Yogurt replaces some of the milk used in the traditional recipe.

SERVES 4

1	unpeeled apple (preferably McIntosh), cored
1	banana, peeled and thickly sliced
1	peach, peeled and pitted
3/4	cup cantaloupe pulp
14	strawberries, hulled
1/2	unpeeled, thin-skinned orange, seeded, and chopped
2	thin slices lemon (use the rind but remove the white part)
1	cup milk
3/4	cup unflavored yogurt
10	ice cubes, crushed
1/4	cup superfine sugar or to taste

Place the apple, banana, peach, cantaloupe, strawberries, orange, lemon, milk, and yogurt in the container of an electric blender. Cover and whirl until the fruit is blended. Add the crushed ice cubes and sugar and blend until smooth. Serve at once in chilled glasses.

VARIATION   Two cups orange or lemon ice or sherbet may be substituted for the crushed ice cubes.

RASPBERRY YOGURT NOG

Here is a splendid alternative to eggnog. However, since raw eggs may contain salmonella bacteria, do not make this recipe unless you are absolutely certain that your egg supply is uncontaminated.

SERVES 8 TO 10

2	cups unflavored yogurt
1	pint raspberry sherbet
3	eggs
1/2	cup amber rum

Combine the yogurt, raspberry sherbet, eggs, and rum in the container of an electric blender. Cover and whirl until well blended and smooth. Serve at once in chilled stemmed glasses.

PAPAYA FRAPPÉ

A glorious Caribbean-inspired concoction, sweet yet with an underlying tang.

SERVES 3

1	medium ripe papaya
1/3	to 1/2 cup milk
1/2	cup unflavored yogurt
3	tablespoons freshly squeezed and strained lime juice
1/2	teaspoon finely grated lime rind
1/4	cup superfine sugar
1/2	teaspoon vanilla extract
3/4	cup finely crushed ice
	Thin lime slices for garnish

Peel the papaya, cut it in half lengthwise, and scoop out the seeds. Chop the papaya flesh coarsely. Place the papaya, milk, yogurt, lime juice, lime rind, sugar, vanilla extract, and crushed ice in the container of an electric blender. Cover and whirl until well blended and smooth. Pour into chilled tumblers. Serve at once, garnished with the lime slices.

LEBANESE ICED COFFEE

Turkish coffee is ideal for this exotic drink.

SERVES 4

1-1/2	cups hot, very strong black coffee, sweetened to taste
3/4	teaspoon orange flower water*
1/2	recipe Yogurt Crème Chantilly, page 98 (omit the vanilla extract)
1/4	teaspoon ground cinnamon
	Ground nutmeg (preferably freshly ground)

Pour the coffee into a deep bowl. Add the orange flower water and cool. Gradually beat in 3/4 cup of the yogurt crème Chantilly until well blended. Stir in the cinnamon. Cover and chill. Just before serving, beat again and pour into 4 chilled stemmed glasses. Garnish each with a dollop of the remaining yogurt crème Chantilly and a dusting of nutmeg.

*Available at Middle Eastern groceries and some gourmet shops.

CAFÉ CHANTILLY

Fill demitasse cups about 3/4 full with hot, strong black coffee. Add 1 teaspoon or more banana liqueur, curaçao, Cointreau, Tia Maria, or crème de cacao to each cup. Top with a dollop of Yogurt Crème Chantilly, page 98.

CAFÉ AU RHUM

Rum adds a seductive note to this rich-tasting creation.

SERVES 4

- 1 cup milk
- 1 cup unflavored yogurt
- 2-1/4 teaspoons instant coffee
- 2 tablespoons rum or to taste
- 1/3 cup coffee or chocolate ice cream

Place all the ingredients in the container of an electric blender. Cover and whirl until smooth. Serve in chilled glasses.

CAFÉ AU GRAND MARNIER

Suave and elegant.

SERVES 4

- 1 cup milk
- 1/2 cup unflavored yogurt
- 1/2 cup cold, very strong black coffee
- 2 tablespoons Grand Marnier or to taste
- 2 tablespoons superfine sugar

Place all the ingredients in the container of an electric blender. Cover and whirl until smooth. Serve in chilled glasses.

VARIATION   Curaçao, Tia Maria, or crème de cacao may be substituted for the Grand Marnier.

COFFEE-CHOCOLATE PUNCH

SERVES ABOUT 12

- 2 ounces unsweetened chocolate
- 1/4 cup sugar
- 1 cup hot, strong black coffee
- 1 cup milk
- 1/2 cup Kahlúa or other coffee-flavored liqueur
- 1 2-inch piece cinnamon stick
- 1 cup unflavored yogurt
- 1 pint coffee ice cream or Frozen Coffee Yogurt, page 133
  Ground cinnamon
  Shaved sweet chocolate

In the top of a double boiler melt the chocolate over low heat. Stir in the sugar. Remove from the heat and gradually stir in the coffee, milk, coffee liqueur, and cinnamon stick. Cool to room temperature, then beat in the yogurt until thoroughly blended and smooth. Cover and chill the punch.

About 20 minutes before serving, place the ice cream or frozen yogurt in a large bowl and break into pieces with a spoon. Let stand until softened, then beat with a whisk or with an electric mixer at low speed until creamy. Remove the cinnamon stick and gradually beat in the punch until frothy. Transfer to a chilled punch bowl. Sprinkle lightly with the cinnamon, garnish with the shaved chocolate, and serve.

Basics

DRAINED YOGURT

The yogurt I grew up with, which was richly flavored, very thick, and creamy, is the kind preferred for cooking. If you are using a thin yogurt, it is best to drain it to remove excess liquid. The longer it drains, the firmer it will become. Yields will vary depending on the initial thickness of the yogurt. After draining for 1 to 2 hours, the yogurt can be used in salads; after 4 to 6 hours, it will be suitable for dips, sauces, soups, and beverages. After 24 to 48 hours, it will attain a consistency resembling that of cream cheese (see Yogurt Cheese, following). It is important to use the freshest, best-tasting additive-free yogurt you can find, because draining will intensify its flavor.

Drained yogurt can often be substituted for whipped cream, clotted cream, *crème fraîche*, sour cream, *mascarpone*, and cream cheese.

Set a fine stainless steel strainer over a deep bowl; the bottom of the strainer should be suspended at least 2 inches above the bottom of the bowl. Spoon additive-free, unflavored yogurt into the strainer. Cover and let the yogurt drain in the refrigerator 1 to 48 hours, depending on the consistency desired. Pour off the whey as it accumulates so that the yogurt can drain freely. Stored in an airtight container, the drained yogurt will keep in the refrigerator for up to 5 days.

YOGURT CHEESE

Despite its name, this is not really cheese but simply yogurt drained of its whey until it becomes thick. The longer it drains, the firmer the cheese will become.

Yogurt cheese is an excellent low-calorie alternative to cream cheese. In the Middle East it is served as an appetizer or breakfast dish, drizzled with olive oil and accompanied with pita bread or *lavash*. It is delicious eaten with fresh herbs such as mint and dill, black olives, and tomatoes, cucumbers, and other raw vegetables. Yogurt cheese also goes well with melon, grapes, and other fruit in season. Try it as a spread for tea bread, sweetened with honey or spiked with orange-flavored liqueur.

MAKES 1-1/4 TO 1-3/4 CUPS

- 1 quart unflavored yogurt, made without gelatin or other thickeners
- 1 teaspoon salt or to taste (optional)

In a large bowl combine the yogurt with the salt, if desired. Follow the recipe for Drained Yogurt, preceding, allowing the yogurt to drain about 24 hours for a soft cheese or up to 48 hours for a firmer one. Stored in an airtight container, the yogurt cheese will keep in the refrigerator for up to 5 days.

YOGURT CHEESE BALLS

Follow the recipe for Yogurt Cheese, preceding, using 1-1/2 teaspoons salt and allowing the yogurt to drain until it is quite dry. With lightly oiled palms, roll into 1- to 1-1/2-inch balls. Place the balls 1 inch apart on a tray large enough to hold them in one layer. Chill several hours or until very firm. Pack the cheese balls in a sterilized glass jar and cover with extra-virgin olive oil. Seal the jar and store in the refrigerator up to 2 weeks. Remove the jar from the refrigerator at least 1 hour before serving.

To serve, place as many cheese balls as needed in a serving dish and spoon a thin coating of olive oil over them. Sprinkle lightly with paprika, if desired. Accompany with pita bread, *lavash*, or sesame crackers.

GRAHAM CRACKER PIE CRUST I

MAKES I 9-INCH PIE CRUST

20	graham crackers
3	tablespoons sugar
1/4	teaspoon ground nutmeg (preferably freshly ground) or cinnamon
4	tablespoons butter, softened and cut into 1/2-inch bits

Pulverize the graham crackers in a blender, or wrap them in waxed paper and crush them finely with a rolling pin. Combine the graham cracker crumbs, sugar, and nutmeg in a bowl and mix well. Add the butter bits, and with your fingers rub the crumb mixture and butter until they are thoroughly combined. Press the mixture evenly onto the bottom and sides of a 9-inch pie plate. Bake in a preheated 375°F oven about 8 minutes or until golden brown and firm. Cool on a wire rack before filling.

GRAHAM CRACKER PIE CRUST II

MAKES I PIE CRUST

20	graham crackers
1/4	cup sugar
1/4	cup blanched almonds, finely chopped (optional)
4	tablespoons butter, melted
1/8	teaspoon salt

Pulverize the graham crackers in a blender, or wrap them in waxed paper and crush them finely with a rolling pin. Combine the graham cracker crumbs, sugar, almonds, butter, and salt in a bowl and mix well. Press the mixture evenly onto the bottom and sides of a greased pie plate or springform pan. Chill.

PARTIALLY BAKED
PIE PASTRY

MAKES I PARTIALLY BAKED 9-INCH
PIE CRUST

1-1/2 cups sifted all-purpose flour
1/2   teaspoon salt
4   tablespoons butter
1/4   cup vegetable shortening
3   tablespoons cold water (approximately)

Sift the flour and salt into a mixing bowl. Cut in the butter and shortening with a pastry blender, 2 knives, or your fingers, working quickly until the mixture resembles very coarse cornmeal. Sprinkle with the water, a little at a time, mixing well with a fork after each addition until a soft dough is formed. Gather the dough into a ball. Roll out on a lightly floured board into a circle about 1/8 inch thick and 1-1/2 inches larger than a 9-inch pie plate. Line the pie plate with the dough, pressing lightly against the bottom and sides of the plate. Trim the edges of the dough slightly larger than the outside rim of the plate.

Prick the pastry at 1/4-inch intervals with a fork. Line with buttered foil and fill with dried beans, spreading them up to the rim all around. This will keep the pastry from swelling during baking. Bake in a preheated 450°F oven 7 minutes. Remove from the oven, remove the foil and beans, and prick the pastry again with a fork. Return to the oven and bake about 5 minutes or until the pastry has barely started to color. Remove from the oven and cool.

COCONUT MILK

MAKES ABOUT 1/2 CUP

Combine 1/2 cup diced coconut meat with 1/2 cup hot, but not boiling, water in the container of an electric blender. Cover and blend until the coconut is very finely grated, almost puréed, then squeeze it through a double thickness of dampened cheesecloth to extract all the liquid. Alternatively, soak 1/2 cup freshly grated coconut meat in 1/2 cup hot, but not boiling, water 30 minutes, then squeeze through cheesecloth as above.

COCONUT CREAM   Substitute warm half-and-half for the hot water.

CLARIFIED BUTTER

MAKES ABOUT 1-1/2 POUNDS

In a heavy saucepan melt 2 pounds butter over
low heat, taking care not to allow it to burn.
Skim off the foam with a spoon as it rises to the
top. Remove from the heat and set aside about
3 minutes, then slowly and carefully pour the
clear liquid into a container, discarding the
creamy residue at the bottom of the pan. Cover
well and refrigerate.

INDEX

ABOUT THE AUTHOR

SONIA UVEZIAN is the author of highly acclaimed cookbooks, many of which have been Book-of-the-Month Club selections and published internationally. A leading authority on Middle Eastern and Caucasian cooking and a recipient of the R.T. French Tastemaker Award, Ms. Uvezian has contributed articles and recipes to various publications, including *Gourmet*, *Bon Appétit*, and *Vogue*. She and her husband divide their time between the United States and Europe.